Developing Hospitality Properties and Facilities

Developing Hospitality Properties and Facilities

Second edition

Edited by
Josef Ransley and Hadyn Ingram

Routledge
Taylor & Francis Group

LONDON AND NEW YORK

First published by Butterworth-Heinemann

First published 2000
Second edition 2004

This edition published 2011 by Routledge
2 Park Square, Milton Park, Abingdon, Oxfordshire OX14 4RN
711 third Avenue, New York, NY 10017, USA

First issued in hardback 2015

Routledge is an imprint of Taylor & Francis Group, an informa business

British Library Cataloguing in Publication Data
A catalogue record for this book is available from the British Library

Library of Congress Cataloguing in Publication Data
A catalogue record for this book is available from the Library of Congress

ISBN 13: 978-1-138-17085-8 (hbk)
ISBN 13: 978-0-7506-5982-6 (pbk)

Contents

Figures

Illustrations

Tables

Contributors

Editors

Josef Ransley, Hotel and Leisure Consultancy
Josef Ransley has been involved in the design and development of international hotels and leisure projects since 1973. He is currently Managing Director of Hotel and Leisure Consultancy and was formerly Chairman of the Ransley Group. Josef is a visiting lecturer at the University of Surrey and ESSEC Cornell University in Paris, where he teaches courses in Property Management and Hotel Development and Construction. He has written or contributed to a number of books and articles and is a regular speaker at industry conferences.

Hadyn Ingram, Professor, Revans Corporate University
Hadyn Ingram trained in hospitality management and worked in hotels in London and Yorkshire. He held lecturing posts at the Universities of Bournemouth and Surrey, and has written widely on hospitality topics. He is currently Professor, Revans Corporate University and Chairman of CP Consulting, specializing in accredited workplace learning and executive coaching. He keeps in touch with his operational roots through ownership of a hotel in the cathedral city of Salisbury.

Chapter contributors

David Bridge, Executive Vice President, Hotel Asset Management, Jones Lang Lasalle Hotels

David Bridge trained as a chartered accountant and has worked in the hotel industry since 1980. Since that time, he has been involved in financial control, implementing reporting systems, opening a hotel, managing hotels in receivership, leading negotiations for the sale and purchase of hotels and hotel chains in France, Germany, Spain, Belgium and the UK as well as ancillary issues such as operating agreement renegotiations, planning issues, financing and corporate structures. David is in charge of pan-European asset management for Jones Lang Lasalle Hotels. His current tasks include management contract and leasing advice and negotiation, hotel financing, due diligence, financial and operational supervision of clients' assets as well as development supervision.

Sue Davis, Divisional Director, Scott Brownrigg

Sue Davis is a Divisional Director of Masterplanning and Architectural practice Scott Brownrigg and heads the specialist hospitality interior design division Ransley Group. Sue's appointment followed the merger between Ransley Group and Scott Brownrigg in 2003. With over 14 years' experience in the hospitality industry, Sue has an in-depth knowledge and understanding of the highly specialized hotel and leisure sector, and has worked with many of the major international operators, as well as private investors/developers, on both new build and refurbishment projects throughout Europe. Sue has a special interest in encouraging the designers of tomorrow, and in addition to guest lectures at Lausanne and IMHI, regularly lectures at Surrey University.

Arthur de Haast, Jones Lang Lasalle Hotels

Arthur de Haast is Global CEO of Jones Lang LaSalle Hotels, responsible for an international team of more than 100 professionals worldwide. Arthur has extensive experience within the global hotel market having been involved in, or having led, a wide range of both advisory and transactional assignments. He has also been involved in expanding the group's services to encompass innovative financial structures such as the Airport Hotels Partnership, a $350m limited partnership created to enable BAA Lynton, the property division of the British Airports Authority plc (owner of most of the UK's major airports, including Heathrow) to dispose of the majority of their hotel property assets.

David Pantin, Managing Director, Rocco Forte Hotels
David Pantin was educated in South Africa and commenced his career as a management trainee with Trusthouse Forte in 1977 and, prior to the take-over of the company by Granada, he held the positions of Managing Director of London's Café Royal, and Regional Vice President of the company's Caribbean hotels. David subsequently held the positions of Senior Vice President with Hutchison Whampoa and Vice President of Operations for Hilton UK. He has been Managing Director of Rocco Forte Hotels for the last 5 years, holds an MSc degree in Hospitality Management, and is married with two children.

Kevin Pearce, Design Manager, Mowlem plc
Kevin Pearce has been involved in managing design and build projects for over 20 years. Having started his working life as a surveyor, he joined Tern in 1981 and quickly moved into design and client management. It was in this role that, with Josef Ransley, he successfully completed two 'turn-key' hotel projects in Cardiff and Merry Hill for Copthorne Hotels. Having developed Quality and Environmental Management Systems at Group level, he has spent the last six years on the road with Amey as Bid Manager and Project Executive on large government PFI and PPP projects. He is now back home in Wales with Mowlem.

Dick Penner, Professor, Cornell University
Richard H. Penner is professor at the Cornell University School of Hotel Administration where he teaches courses in hotel development, planning, and interior design. He regularly conducts professional seminars in hotel design around the world. In addition, Penner is the author of Conference Center Planning and Design (1991) and a co-author of Hotel Design, Planning, and Development (2001). He has received teaching honours at Cornell and the Platinum Circle award from Hospitality Design magazine.

Simon Rawlinson, Partner, Davis Langdon and Everest
Simon Rawlinson is a partner in the Cost Research Department of chartered quantity surveyors, David Langdon and Everest (DLE). He is a regular contributor to construction industry journals. DLE is a Western Hemisphere partner of the worldwide quantity surveying practice, David Langdon and Seah International. DLE's core services are cost consultancy, cost planning and cost management of construction projects in all market sectors.

Jan deRoos, Professor, Cornell University
Professor Jan A. deRoos is the HVS International Professor of Hotel Finance and Real Estate at the Cornell University School of Hotel Administration. On the faculty of the Hotel School since 1988, he has devoted his career to research and teaching in the area of hospitality real estate, with a focus on hotel valuation and investment decision making. Prior to joining Cornell University, Professor deRoos worked extensively in the hospitality industry. His current research interests concentrate on hotel leases as an alternative to management contracts and the value of goodwill in hotel property.

Chris Rouse, Senior Director, CB Richard Ellis Hotels
Chris Rouse is responsible for the growth of CB Richard Ellis Hotels' professional services, including portfolio assessment, asset management, hotel development and management contract negotiations. His previous experience in the UK, continental Europe and Asia includes Regional Director with Jones Lang Wootton, Asia and Development Director with the following groups: Compania Hotelera del Mediterraneo, Spain; Forte plc, BAA Hotels and Copthorne Hotels, all in the UK and the Mandarin Oriental Hotel Group, Hong Kong. Chris graduated in Law and is a Fellow of HCIMA and an Associate of the British Association of Hospitality Accountants. Chris is also a founder member of the International Hospitality Strategy Forum and is Honorary Treasurer and Deputy Chairman of Central London YMCA.

Paul Slattery, Director, Otus & Co

Paul Slattery is currently director of Otus & Co, which provides strategic advice on the hospitality, travel and transport industries. Paul worked for Dresdner Kleinwort Wasserstein for 15 years until 2002. He was head of hospitality research until 1998, then he joined Corporate Finance. Paul has worked for several international hospitality companies and was also an academic at Huddersfield University in England. He has an undergraduate degree in Hotel and Catering Management and an MSc by research. Paul writes for academic and industry publications, he is the visiting Professor at Oxford Brookes University and Chairman of The International Hotel Investment Council.

Trevor Ward, Director, TRI Hospitality Consulting

Trevor Ward is an experienced international hotel consultant, who has worked on hotel and leisure projects in more than 70 countries in his 20-year career. The projects on which he has worked range from 5 star to budget, extensive mixed-use developments to small hotels. Much of his work has been in developing countries in Africa, Central and Eastern Europe, Central Asia and South America. He is a Director of TRI Hospitality Consulting in London, and Managing Director of their office in Nigeria, where he now spends most of his time, working from there throughout sub-Saharan Africa.

Foreword

by David M C Michels

Since I wrote the foreword for the first edition of this book, in 1999, much has happened radically to change the world and the hospitality industry. It is even more risky nowadays to invent, initiate, plan, cost and deliver the product, and it requires greater professionalism than ever to find that indefinable ingredient: 'Will the customers really like what I'm spending this money on?'

Such uncertainty requires informed opinion and this is provided in this second edition, with chapters from some impressive international contributors. My interest in the subject continues and I recommend this to you as an even better book than the first.

David M C Michels
Chief Executive
Hilton International

Introduction

Josef Ransley and Hadyn Ingram

The first edition of this book, published in 2000, provided an introduction to developing hospitality properties. The editors produced it as a guide for students, practitioners and specialists in the industry to help understand the complex nature of developing hospitality properties. Since that date, the imperative in a changing market to periodically refurbish and refocus the concept and product has become more complex, but even more important. The nature of the process of development was encapsulated in Figure I.1.

Published at the start of a new millennium, the book acknowledged the radical changes that had occurred in the latter half of the twentieth century. These changes helped move the hospitality industry from being a provider of accommodation and related services to offering consumer products in a highly sophisticated, competitive and developed marketplace. Today, the development process entails a lengthy process of conceptualization, planning and construction before it becomes operational and starts to generate income. Further, this requires ever larger capital investment, risk assessment and a wider range of management skills.

Buildings of a highly serviced nature, such as hotels, have historically been of a single use type – difficult and expensive to alter. As the building or property forms the essential physical component of the hospitality product, altering the facilities or product profile is a major and costly undertaking. The property configuration is critical to achieving a number of key aims, including attracting customers, ease of operations and providing an acceptable return on investment. Drawing a parallel with the motor industry, in a developing market place the producer/supplier can dictate the characteristics of the product. In an emerging market, Henry Ford is reputed to have said that he offered, 'cars in any colour as long as it's black'. In a more developed market, the focus shifts from the provider to the consumer, as evidenced by a wide range of

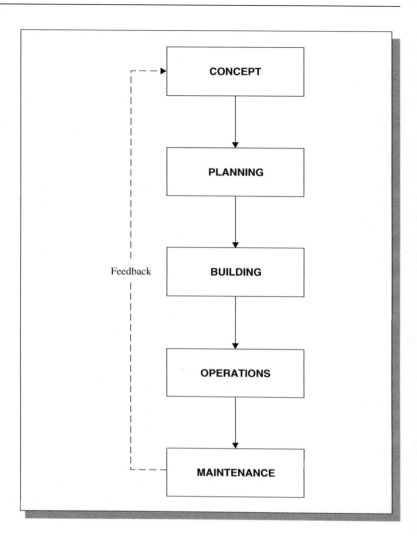

Figure I.1
The development process
Source: Ransley and Ingram
(2000: 3)

current car products. Modern motor vehicles are made available to the consumer to suit every type of taste, preference and pricing level.

The hospitality industry is moving through a similar evolutionary process, in which the supply-led market is changing to a demand-led market, although many different opinions exist as to which stage is the current one. Countries too, are in differing stages of development, reflecting factors such as regional economies, local and international markets and culture. As the hospitality industry becomes more globalized, this is an additional complication or challenge. In the current climate of choice, the notion of guests waking up in a branded hotel room and wondering where they are from the décor, is less accepted. The business and leisure traveller of the twenty-first century, like the modern motorist,

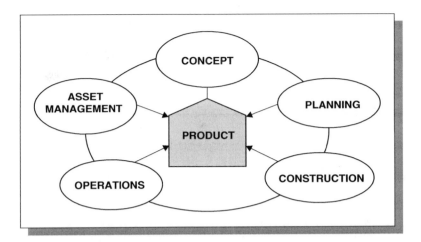

Figure I.2
Revised model of
the development
process

confidently expects the basic physical product to be acceptable, thus making their criteria for selecting a particular purchase more complex and discerning than those of previous generations. A more sophisticated market, in turn, requires a more augmented and responsive product. Heightened competition requires differentiation and market segmentation. These factors and others require the physical product, service and operations to be more efficient, all of which present a greater challenge for those concerned with hospitality development.

This second edition, therefore, attempts to reflect these changes and greater complexity. The focus moves on from introducing the fundamental elements of developing hospitality properties and facilities, to an exploration of some of the current and future challenges. In an age of change, it is important that anyone concerned with, or interested in, hospitality development should consider these issues if they are to understand and manage the development process effectively. As in the first edition, the development process has been conceptualized into a diagram which shows its sequential component parts. This diagram, shown in Figure I.2, has been refined to emphasize the cyclical nature of the development process, as well as the importance of regular reviewing of such major assets. This also reflects the important role that asset management has established in the industry over the last few years, for both owner and operator.

Figure I.2 shows the five stages in the development process:

1 Concept. The first task in the development process is to envision, in conceptual terms, how the finished product might look and what market it might serve. This usually entails communication between the developer and a designer to draw up plans and concept drawings. For larger organizations, this might be part of an overall development and brand management strategy, and will take in issues of asset management.

2 Planning. The concept must be planned and costed so that it can be completed within a suitable budget and to an agreed standard. The project will usually include a feasibility study and planning for finance and legal issues.

3 Construction. The construction stage takes place when building, renovation or adaptation takes place. This process may involve the services of an architect, quantity surveyor and builder.

4 Operations. After construction, comes the installation of the equipment and furniture that is necessary for the property to operate as a hospitality unit. At this point, it is necessary to consider operational planning and relationships, as well as functional issues of planning accommodation and to provide suitable service levels for the target market.

5 Asset management. The final stage of the process is concerned with managing the asset. This involves unit operations, including the maintenance and repairs that are necessary to comply with the law and keep the property in good order. Asset management is also concerned with regular reviewing of the trading performance of the unit and any opportunities for maximizing the asset value of the property. This can involve refurbishment or repositioning of the product to suit, for example, a change in the market. As the industry is internationally based, and development occurs in a wide range of global locations, factors such as geography, climate and culture affect the process.

Once complete and operational, the trading and efficiency of the product needs to be periodically reviewed to ensure that the unit is attaining its planned performance, and whether this can be enhanced to capitalize on changes or perceived trends. These may include changes to the environment, market conditions, organizational needs, corporate strategy or property value. The latter may entail refurbishment or repositioning of the product, and so the cycle will begin again.

As before, this edition addresses some questions about the process, including:

- How does the process of developing a hospitality property work?

- Who should be consulted at the different stages of the project?

- What are the challenges which need to be resolved?

- What must happen for the project to succeed?

Each chapter has been written by an expert with specialist knowledge and experience of the issues, current practice and trends in their field. In this second edition, this expertise has been augmented by contributors from around the world, thus reflecting more accurately the internationality of hospitality developments. The editors offer grateful thanks to these contributors for taking time to articulate this knowledge so that many can share it.

It is inevitable that the style and approach of the contributors will vary, and this reflects the breadth, diversity and richness of the subject. As editors, we have tried to ensure that the chapters are comprehensible and that any technical terms are defined in the text or glossary. Although the book is aimed at the hospitality industry at large, many of the examples and case studies used are drawn from hotel developments, perhaps because this represents the main area of development activity.

Our grateful thanks go to those specialists who have contributed their valuable time to writing chapters and those such as Anthony J. Horst, Robert Caston, Geoff Parkinson, Michael Brooker, Graham McCourt, Trevor Skan, Martin Armitstead and Paal Borrenssen (deceased October 2003), notable among many for contributing the benefit of their experience to certain sections of the book.

Similarly, our thanks go to Liz Wilton for her invaluable administrative help and Jesse Ransley for her proofreading and general contributions to the form and structure of the text.

Josef Ransley
Hadyn Ingram
October 2003

Concept

Concepts

Josef Ransley

In the model proposed in the introduction, the conceptual stage is the first in the cycle, because this is where the vision for the property begins to be articulated on its long journey to become reality. This chapter will cover the following:

- Definitions
- Historical perspective
- The conceptual process
- Practical considerations
- Examples
- Conclusion.

Definitions

Any development process usually starts with a concept, normally conceived by an individual or resultant of a collective group's analysis of a challenge or recognition of an opportunity. So what constitutes a concept? The Concise Oxford Dictionary of Current English (1996:274) defines the word concept as:

1 General notion

2 An abstract idea.

The origins come from the Latin, and, more particularly the French word 'concevoir', meaning to formulate in the mind or imagine a plan or scheme.

While dictionary definitions are always a good starting point and, in the context of this chapter subject, the Latinate origins are interesting, but for our purposes a hospitality concept could be defined as:

> An idea with definition and identity that defines an image

Such a concept must have attributes of a commercial nature as illustrated in Figure 1.1.

As illustrated in Figure 1.1, in hospitality a 'concept' normally consists of a service delivered in a purposely-designed property,

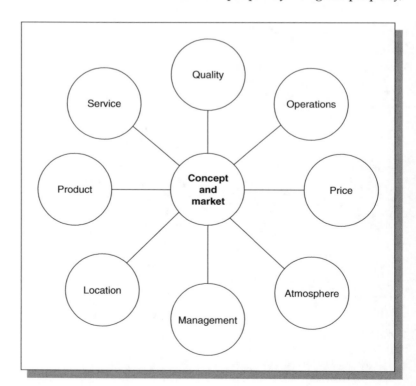

Figure 1.1
The hospitality concept
Source: (Lundberg and
Walker, 1993)

4

whose quality, atmosphere, service style and content, supported by a specified operation and management in a specific location determine price and define the product.

Historical perspective

From the days of travel by coach and horses, followed by the age of steam trains, to the advent of the car, the aeroplane and now, perhaps, the spacecraft, the hospitality industry has historically been driven by evolution in modes of travel. Coach travel was synonymous with the coaching inn; trains gave rise to the great railway hotels in Europe, the Americas and elsewhere in the world where the great cities were joined by steel rails. Travel then was still a luxury, but Henry Ford changed that forever, with the introduction of the mass-produced car. Volume production at affordable prices led to volume accommodation at comparative pricing in hotels. Market segmentation focused on quality of accommodation and pricing. By the 1950s Holiday Inn had opened their first motel and, in the UK, the Automobile Association (AA) introduced its quality star rating system.

Travel by most people, however, was primarily still undertaken within national boundaries. In the 1960s, the growth of the airline industry led to the development of the package holiday with its consequential boom in resort developments in the Caribbean and Mediterranean. Similarly, the post Second World War rebuilding programmes, largely funded by the Marshall plan, led to an

Illustration 1.1
Midland Hotel, Manchester: a railway hotel (Courtesy The Paramount Hotel Group)

increase in international business travel. The airlines became active in hotel ownership and operations, developing their own international chains in competition with the expanding US chains such as Holiday Inn, Hilton and Sheraton. In Europe, Lufthansa owned Penta Hotels, KLM funded Golden Tulip, and US carriers expanded Intercontinental. Each country saw growth of its local national chains, Trusthouse Forte and Grand Metropolitan Hotels in the UK, Accor in France, Scandic in Scandinavia. Meanwhile, the USA in the 1960s boasted 23 000 hotels, 40 000 motels and 170 hotel chains.

It was to the USA that the world looked for the development of new concepts and operational management systems, not least because of their economic prosperity and widespread internal travel. The development of US hotels outside of the motherland was funded, not by those companies, but by local investors, while the hotel companies provided the operational expertise, the distribution systems and most importantly, the product. Owners just signed a management contract and effectively handed over the asset for periods of up to 25 years, and looked for a return from the hotel property's turnover. To increase their expansion in the mid-scale hotel sector, Holiday Inn used the franchise agreement. Essentially, this provided the owner/operator with the right to use the brand name if they complied with the company's standards and systems, in return for an entry fee and fee per reservation delivered by the Holiday Inn distribution network.

These hotel products were established concepts originally developed in the USA and standardized to facilitate ease in expansion and operations internationally. Initially conceived to service home market customers when travelling on business or leisure, the hotel facilities provided were similar to those built at the beginning of the twentieth century. These included bedrooms with en-suite facilities, conference and banqueting rooms, bars, restaurants and the ubiquitous coffee shop. Designed to be self-sufficient, the back of house facilities included a bakery, butchery, laundry, extensive storage areas and a range of kitchens with their associated preparation and chilled storage areas. With computerization in its infancy, administrative processes, while standardized, lacked the centralization of today and, consequently, administration, management staff and their facilities were much more extensive than today.

Although the format of standardization was primarily a management tool to control and ease the process of development, it also offered great reassurance to the guest because it ensured a recognized and consistent standard of service and facilities. These were designed to be similar, or of an aspirational standard, to those experienced at the guest's home. These standards evolved into one of the early benefits of brand value for the home market customer, identified by the immortal quote from an unnamed hotel guest:

> I'm not sure whether I'm in Paris or Berlin, but I am staying in a Holiday Inn!

Unarguably, for travellers from North America, such product standardization in the 1970s provided added value, as the local alternative products were shrouded in myth. These stereotypical hotels were often based on tales of their fathers' experiences in Europe and elsewhere during the Second World War, ranging from those strange French toilets and contaminated drinking water to the exotic, but strange and inedible, food on offer. The same standardization approach applied to the large-scale development of package holiday resort hotels and, while many of these properties were developed and managed by local entrepreneurs, the product content and systems used were cloned from the US chains. Many such properties still trade in the older resort destinations in the Mediterranean and other resort areas around the world.

With the increase in wealth in the developed countries and the expansion in internationally based regional offices and manufacturing plants, the hospitality industry enjoyed a boom in development throughout the 1980s. This resulted in an increase in the number of operating companies both on a national and international basis. With increased competition, especially in the home markets, greater brand name recognition and more effective distribution systems, the industry began to move away from the established quality star rating system and began to explore the potential of market segmentation. Crowne Plaza by Holiday Inn and Courtyard by Marriott were early examples of this phenomenon. Simultaneously, product types were developed to provide airport, all-suite, conference, health spas, marina, golf and ski hotels, with resort developments moving into timeshare and the creation of destination venues such as theme parks and other family-based activity parks. Not surprisingly, most of these concepts were initially developed in the USA. This was driven by its greater wealth and fiercer competition, the demand for continuing growth and return on investment proved the ideal laboratory for commercial innovation. The budget or limited service product unit was a classic example. Adapted to suit local conditions internationally, primarily in size, area and number of bedrooms per unit, the budget sector witnessed rapid growth and separately provided a new entry level for people who had previously not used hotels other than for vacationing.

The Gulf War at the start of the 1990s resulted in a dramatic decline of travel worldwide and, combined with an economic recession for much of the world, the hospitality industry suffered dramatically with low financial performance. Many companies were left unable to service debt and ownership of many units fell into the hands of the banks and other financial institutions. Emerging from this challenging period, the industry witnessed a move to consolidation, and the value of brands became a recognized benefit. Similarly, lenders and investors demanded greater transparency and involvement in the supervision of the operation of the businesses. Asset and yield management established themselves as disciplines through which the owner could manage the manager and, as methods of maximizing the value of individual units with non-performing properties or part of properties being converted to alternative use if these provided greater returns. Similarly, yield management (adapted from the airline industry) focused on maximizing revenue rather than status. The prevalent attitude of brands, however, was that they required international coverage to be meaningful. This need for rapid geographical expansion and resources to match led more companies to seek capital on the stock markets, with the consequential requirement for short-term returns fuelling the standardization of product and depersonalization of service in the industry. Technology eased the demand on staffing numbers and skill levels, outsourcing, processed ready meals, computerization and other automated systems all impacted on reducing capital and operational costs. Management skills levels focused on managing processes rather than innovation or leadership and the industry focused on 'punter processing' (servicing customers) in order to compete for capital with manufacturers.

Consolidation to attain globalization became the key objective of the late 1990s. More energy was focused on strategic planning, market analysis and financial forecasting than any other aspect of the business. Development became a process of replication and product development an issue of cost reduction and, not surprisingly, the limited service sector boomed and the full service sector struggled. While the number of product lines in the car industry and other consumer products exploded, the hotel sector's product line offer stayed relatively static. The restaurant sector, at the same time, witnessed an explosion in product lines. This was spurred on by the recognition that the average consumer's wealth, confidence, knowledge, international experience and greater leisure time had instilled a desire and ability for greater discretionary spending. Equally relevant, spend on leisure activity was considered essential for the average household and such spend was selected from a wide product range mixing clothing, sporting activity, health and beauty products, dining experiences with short accommodation breaks. Restaurant development boomed and the branded hotel sector faced a paradox, geared to product roll-out programmes, it was suddenly assailed by a consumer demanding differentiation. Not surprisingly, new players in the market exploited the opportunity to develop a range of niche products such as town house, designer or so-called 'lifestyle hotels'.

These units inevitably were of a smaller scale, specific service standard and very individual in their product and management style. Since they were adaptable to conversion of existing properties whether offices, houses, warehouses or other types of buildings, they were able to place themselves in prime city locations. In some of the early examples such as Malmaison in the UK, the desire for differentiation led to guests staying in secondary locations, yet happy to pay prime location rates.

Consequently, as the twentieth century drew to a close, the industry faced a series of dilemmas. These included issues of how to:

- Differentiate its full service brands between each other and those of the competition
- Standardize product and still reflect local culture and environment
- Obtain funding for global expansion
- Establish a management structure for a worldwide multi-product, service and operating group
- Maintain short-term returns on capital intensive and long-term development projects requiring individual management
- Raise staff skill and retention levels while maintaining affordable staffing costs
- Maintain or extend planned product life cycles
- Deal with rising market fragmentation in terms of age, culture and consumer lifestyle aspirations
- Address the increase in competitive distribution systems available through the Internet
- Keep control of room stock pricing
- Grow the overall market in competition with other consumer discretionary products
- Reduce exposure to a more volatile travel environment.

Other external factors that have, and will continue to impact on the industry's development include:

- Environmental considerations and consumer expectations
- Increased consumer protection legislation and liability claims
- Increased recognition of minority group requirements and legislation aimed at reducing discrimination against, for example, disabled persons
- Increased employment legislation.

These challenges and others were the embryonic topics of debate as the world moved into the twenty-first century, and no sooner had the millennium celebrations finished, than the world was changed by the tragic events of 11 September 2001 and the resultant wars in Afghanistan and Iraq. These events and other crises in the financial sectors, the SARS scare and a general worldwide unease resulted in a general economic slowdown.

The year 2004 is, perhaps, an opportune time for the editors to be publishing a revision of this book. This is because, other than fire-fighting in a difficult economy, it provides the industry with the opportunity to reflect on its evolution and consider the content and method of its development of product, property and facilities in the early part of a new century that, inevitably, will see great changes occurring on the planet.

The conceptual process

As has been shown from the above historical perspective, the hospitality industry has reached a stage in its evolution where it requires adaptation and the application of greater flexibility to its existing and new products. This will entail the development of new concepts with inherent ways or means to change content, service or image in an economical way. Service methods can be readily altered as they are primarily based in personnel skills, investment in people will need to increase and retention of staff will require a new approach to human resource management. The more difficult element will be the ability to create flexibility in the physical property. However, two aspects can influence this:

1 *Construction systems are becoming more systemized and manufacture-based*: The provision of flexible internal space is no longer revolutionary as airport terminals and such buildings as the Pompidou Centre in Paris and the Lloyds building in London demonstrate. On a smaller scale the biannual drive down International Drive in Miami dramatically illustrates how a serviced building shell can have its restaurant product completely altered on an economical basis. The challenge therefore is perhaps not so great as the need to alter the established process of management thinking. The new century may be more about innovation in management than the management of systems, an approach that is taking hold in some of the more enlightened management schools. While many will argue that investors are too 'hard-nosed' for such thinking, it should be remembered that investment is simply about balancing risk and return ratios, something that all those working in the financial world are only to aware of but may be a little reticent to share in a public forum.

2 *Bricks and brains*: From an investment point of view, the industry has already seen a divergence of operations and property; the

Illustration 1.2
Lloyd's Building, London: flexible
internal space in a building
(Photograph courtesy of Lloyds
of London)

infamous 'bricks and brains' headline. This, however, suggests that, if the 'brains' or operation does not deliver suitable returns, those managing the asset have no hesitation in changing the nature of the operation, as the inherent value in property still tends to revolve around location. Value increases in all types of property when they are located where the most people want them to be. Therefore today's office is tomorrow's hotel or vice versa. Provide a versatile serviced and flexible building shell, and building use can be adapted to maximize inherent value, thereby investment risk is inherently lower. From a 'bricks' or property investor's perspective, the increased capital cost to attain such flexibility delivers longer-term returns and control of, or exposure to, non-performing 'brains' or operations.

Before this idea or 'concept' can be progressed, it must pass the test of the financial concept viability cycle. While financial viability can be tested in many ways, the acid test is to fulfil the basic requirement of one simple equation:

$$(Selling\ Price \times Volume) - Cost = Profit$$

Chapter 5 looks at some of the systems that are commonly used for hotel development in the industry. However, if the industry moves into a period of innovation, it needs to develop more economical and less time-consuming methods of testing new ideas and concepts. Ideas, like potential sites, are plentiful, less available are the resources to test each and everyone, hence the need to have initial hurdle tests to select those ideas and concepts that warrant further investigation and development. This is where the development of a concept brief or project brief is vital. The concept brief defines the concept in relatively detailed written form, combining the context of a new hotel concept with the operational philosophy and area standards. These two documents, if in a proper format, should provide sufficient information to estimate the concept's operational and property development costs from benchmark costs widely available in the industry. While market studies are designed to establish specific demand, pooled industry analysis of different hotel locations' performance and pricing, regionally, nationally and internationally is widely available. Such sources provide sufficient data to establish (within defined risk factors) a quick viability test to determine which concepts or projects are in principle of potential value to warrant further research, development and investment of resources available. Similarly, simplistic guidelines established in the hotel sector over a number of years, such as, £1 ADRR = £1000 capital cost and land value not to exceed 10–15% of the total development costs, continue to be valid rules of thumb.

The five elements that form the cycle shown in Figure 1.2 may seem self-explanatory at first glance, but what is a 'project brief'? At this stage of the concept development stage it can be a relatively simple document that sets out the idea or concept. However, as it entails physical property being developed, it is essential that it incorporates an 'area schedule' to determine, in principle, the total area to be developed. Such a schedule can be developed relatively easily for any property concept using the format illustrated in Figure 1.3.

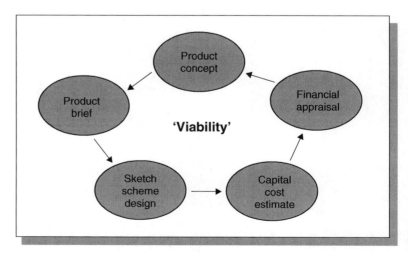

Figure 1.2
The hospitality viability cycle

150 Key Bedroom Hotel

A.* 1 Module is 26.28 m² (net internal 7.2 m × 3.65 m)

B.

	No. of Module	Size	Keys	Modules
'Standard' Bedrooms	(1×)	26.28 m²	106	106
'Superior' Bedrooms	(1×)	26.28 m²	30	30
'Junior' Suites	(1½)	39.42 m²	4	6
'Suite' sq + lnge + tw	(3)	26.28 m²	4	12
Executive Lounge	(3)	78.84 m²	–	3
Disabled Bedrooms	6	26.28 m²	6	6
TOTAL			150	163

C. Floor Level Service Pantry

- Trolley storage
- Guest supplies store
- Furniture Store
- Open area with sinks and counter tops
- Linen chute

} 26.28 m² per accommodation floor level (adequate for 30–60 bedrooms per level)

D. Bedroom Corridor Width
(1400 mm nett increased to 1900 mm width with recess at bedroom entrance)

E. Public Areas and Facilities

	Nett m²
Lobby, Foyer and Lounge area, Public Telephone	180 m²
Reception, Information, Cashiers, Porter Counter	20 m²
Porters Baggage Store	10 m²
Cleaners' Closet	1.5 m²
Shop with Store	16 m²

Centralized Public WCs:

- Female — 20 m²
- Male — 20 m²
- Disabled — 4.0 m²

F. Business Services Facility
plus Conference and Banqueting Manager and Secretary — 20 m²

G. Daylight Required

Front Office/Reservations Area and CCTV Control	25 m²
Computer Equipment Room	12 m²
Stationery Store	3 m²
Front Office Manager	10 m²
Admin. Staff WC Washbasin & Lobby (M + F)	10 m²
Telephone Operator Switchboard Room	7 m²
Coffee/Tea making facility with cupboard and shelving recess	3 m²

H.

Financial Controller	14 m²	
Accounts Office Area	20 m²	} 39 m²
Architects' Storeroom	5 m²	

Note: All m² listed are net internal m² requirements

(*Continued*)

	Nett m^2	
General Manager	14 m^2	⎫
Sales Manager, F&B Manager, Secretary	25 m^2	⎬ 69 m^2
Secretary & Typists Area	18 m^2	⎪
Personnel Manager's Office	12 m^2	⎭

I.

Main Bar & Lounge Area W/Bar and Store (75 seats)	145 m^2
Main Restaurant (85 seater) with Buffet display unit	160 m^2
Informal Cafe Restaurant (40 seats)	80 m^2
Restaurant Store	6 m^2

J. Function Rooms Area

• Main Function Room (2 into 1) (20 m × 10 m)	200 m^2
• 3 Syndicate Rooms (8 m × 5 m each)	120 m^2
• 3 Purpose set-up Boardrooms with storage and cloaks, inter-connecting (8 m × 5 m)	120 m^2
• Separate Entrance Lobby Area	18 m^2
• Cloakroom Facility	8 m^2
• Operating Equipment Store	8 m^2
• Furniture Store	20 m^2
• Service – Hold Pantry	5 m^2
• Pre-Function Area with Dispense Bar	80 m^2

K. Pool Fitness Centre Facility · 450 m^2

Pool – water surface (15 m × 7 m)	153 m^2
Changing Rooms – Male & Female	72 m^2
Solarium Room (2×)	12 m^2
Fitness Equipment Area	64 m^2
Sauna Room 'UNISEX'	8 m^2
Turkish Bath with high impulse shower area	t.b.a.
Pool Area Shower(s)	34 m^2
Spa Bath/Whirlpool	8 m^2
Plant/Pump Area (circulation inclusive)	30 m^2
Reception counter, refreshment and seating area	46 m^2
Attendants/Manager Office and Store Room	12 m^2
One each of M & F Toilet via Reception	7 m^2

L. Main Kitchen Area · 150 m^2

Comprising: cold prep. area + hot prep. area.
Dish, glassware and potwash areas

Chef's Office (raised)	6 m^2
Chef's Day Store	4 m^2
Room Service	11 m^2
Staff Dining Room with equipment	38 m^2
Crockery/cutlery, etc. … Store	8 m^2
Cold Room I II III + Freezer Room	19 m^2
B.o.H. Corridor width: 1.75 m	t.b.a.

M.

Dry Store	15 m^2
General Store	16 m^2
Beer Cellar	16 m^2
Beverage & Wine (chilled)	14 m^2
Tobacco, Wine, Spirits	14 m^2

N.

Empty Bottle Store	10 m²
Refuse Store	12 m²
Receiving/Delivery Platform (covered)	18 m²
Cost Controller and Receivers Office	15 m²

O. Housekeeping Department (including circulation) 80 m²
- Linen/Uniform issue/storage
- Guest Supplies Store   3 m²
- Housekeeper's Equipment Store   6 m²
- Housekeeper's Office   7 m²
- Sorting Area   12 m²
- Trolley Storage Area
- Detergent Store   6 m²

With Laundry

    Additional for Equipment   22 m²

P. Staff Changing Facilities
- Male (lockers, showers, urinals, wbasin, wc's)   26 m²
- Female (lockers, showers, wc's, wbasin, Bunny)   30 m²

Q.

Maintenance Manager Office	8 m²
Workshop Maintenance Dept. (1.4 m × 2.85 m) × 2	20 m²
Spare Parts/Tools Room	8 m²

R.

Telecommunication, Emergency supply equipment, Battery Room (chilled A/C)   10 m²

S.

Telephone Hardware, U.P.S. Equipment Room, chilled A/C   10 m²

T. Plant Room Area (excluding Pool Plant)

If Bedrooms are not cooled i.e. Radiators and Pressurized Corridors A/C   3.5–4% of total gross surface square meterage

Public Facilities and Admin. Areas A/C comfort cooling

Food Prep. Areas A/C with spot cooling

If Bedrooms are comfort cooled or chilled A/C with all Public Areas/Facilities and Admin. Areas A/C comfort cooling and Food Preparation Areas A/C with spot cooling   4.5–6% of total gross surface square meterage

U.

The following areas are not specific as they depend on completion of concept designs, particularly height and joint planning with Consultants:

Internal
- Circulation generally
- Lifts
- Lift Lobbies – guest, staff/service
- M & E Services, including:
  - Water storage and heating
  - All ventilation and air conditioning

(Continued)

-   – Fuel storage if applicable
-   – Electrical substation – high voltage
-   – Control and switchrooms
-   – Emergency generators
-   – Lifts' motor rooms

External
- Circulation generally
- Taxi ranks
- Coach and car-parking
- Covered access to entrances/porte cochères
- Flag poles and signs

Nett Gross surface area per room average to target	53 m²	7 950 m²	56 m²	8 400 m²

This comprises all levels inclusive of:

- Plant Rooms and access to escape staircases
- Emergency staircases
- Corridor stairways
- Stairway lobbies
- B.o.H. corridors
- All internal circulation areas
- Any facilities located within
- Underground car-park levels
- External wall thicknesses

Notes
- All square meterages specified are *NETT* requirements.
- Areas of service ducts, flues, chutes and lift shafts are not included in usable areas.
- If cost effective, plant should be located in the roof void/space areas.
- Gross surface square meterages excludes:
    - – Underground car parking spaces and related circulation
    - – External terraces, walkways, etc.
- Loading dock delivery yard area should include space for skip and compactor

Figure 1.3
A typical hotel area schedule (150 Key Bedroom Hotel)

As can be seen from the example in Figure 1.3, each operational and public area seen as required for delivering the relevant service and product is scheduled and an appropriate space allocated. The total building area can then be estimated in a simple manner by multiplying the area with the benchmark building cost per square foot/metre for the relevant location. Building costs for relevant building types can be accessed from benchmark data published by such companies as Davis Langston Everest – International Cost Consultants. For the hotel sector they publish *Quality Time & Cost*, which is updated annually and gives benchmark-building costs for each hotel market segment type. There is lack of a uniform system of definitions for such elements as Furniture, Fixtures and Equipment (FF&E) in the hotel industry. The effect is that caution must be used in elemental figures for comparative purposes. The total costs per square metre or square foot are satisfactory for an initial capital cost estimate. It should be noted that such data are based on various assumptions related to the site's condition and other aspects, many of which need to be considered. It is therefore advisable to obtain local professional advice. Most experienced industry sector cost consultants should be able to prepare a preliminary cost plan based on a schedule of areas and basic knowledge of the site constraints and other conditions, without the building having to be designed in detail. The criteria that will normally affect cost levels include:

● Site area – storey height

● Unit size – staffing

● Location – labour costs

● Construction time – volume

● Building services – quality standards.

Similarly, potential earnings in any given location will be influenced by:

● Demand and supply

● Brand and pricing policies

● Competitive supply

● Brand and product suitability

● Size and facility mix.

A simple and useful way to evaluate hospitality concepts can be undertaken by defining a project brief with schedule of areas, resultant capital costs and running a financial feasibility model. This is shown in the alternative catering concepts in Illustration 1.3. Remember that Concept 2 utilizes a traditional format while Concept 1 introduces 'flexibility' in terms of location so the traditional financial model will require adjusting for Concept 2. For the financial model the applicable land and building costs in your own locality can be used. It must, however be remembered that the exercise is simply to test the concept in general terms. Accordingly, there is no necessity to go into detail, as the purpose is to determine the most suitable investment option, for further investigating more detailed design, operational systems development and financial analysis.

Practical considerations

A good military commander, before embarking on a new campaign, will want to ensure that the strategy, based on the information

(i)

Illustration 1.3
Two alternative catering
concepts

(ii)

available, is sound, the resources are in place and the troops are ready. After the most careful planning, all that can be expected is the unexpected! Development, whether that of a new concept or refurbishment of an existing property, presents the same dilemma to the manager. One can plan and assess risk in depth, only to

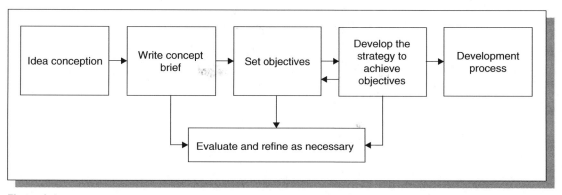

Figure 1.4
The conceptual process

find as the process evolves that the unexpected arises to present a challenge. Experience teaches some to plan for the things that most often go wrong and we can briefly look at a few examples, however, it should be remembered that by acknowledging that the unexpected will arise some contingency planning should always be provided for, predominantly in terms of costs and time.

Paperwork

Development is exciting, demanding and usually involves large expenditure. Funding normally comes from third parties and when things go dramatically wrong it inevitably ends in legal action. At that point the paper trail through the brief, meeting notes, agreements, dayfile notes, correspondence, and so on, is of most weight in the process of adjudication, as the law prefers the written word to the spoken. Surprisingly, those involved in the process more and more fail to keep proper records; the professional indemnity insurers in the UK are currently settling claims at a value of £1 m per day. If things do go wrong, records are essential to attain quick settlement. More importantly, a good paper trail, reviewed regularly, can prevent many human errors.

Professionals

Many people remark that standards appear to be dropping. Perhaps they are, but it is more relevant to observe the world is getting a little more complex each day, and everything has to move much faster. It is unrealistic to expect an architect to know the developer's business, or necessarily to rely on his or her management skills. In recent years the architect has been trained primarily as a designer, a creative person. Construction and construction law are now much more complex than fifty years ago. Hence, the architect's knowledge of both is, not unreasonably, less in these areas. So far as planning the hotel is concerned, the developer should also not expect the architect to understand operational requirements in detail. This is the operator's skill, but it needs to be communicated. While projects generally have the architect as the lead consultant, this is not project management. It is generally recognized that creative people are neither the best managers, nor the most commercially minded. Selecting the professional team should, therefore, be undertaken with a proper understanding of the skills required, and those parties should be managed in a formal way.

Communication

The most common reason for project failure, especially in an international industry, is through a lack of communication. Too little or too much information at the wrong time is a classic error, as is the perception that communication in 'my' language will be idiomatically understood by foreigners. Culture and context can lead to misunderstanding. For example, on a project in Cuba the hotel development manager asked a local engineer if the electrical supply was reliable. Having received an affirmative reply, he omitted the provision of standby generators. When the electrical supply consistently failed he challenged the local engineer, to be told, ' but sir, the power supply consistently fails once a week, you can rely on that'. It is advisable to always check that what was needed to be communicated has been understood correctly. A little extra time in this regard can save a lot of problems later.

Whose money: yours or mine?

The value of both is the same (although I might not feel this personally), but there is no difference in its purchase value. How often this simple rule is forgotten in the development, an arena where so many seem to believe that their money will buy more for less and hence project overruns. The only thing that makes your dollar go further than the other guy is greater efficiency.

Chinese whispers

This dinner party game involves the person at the head of the table whispering a short phrase to the person on the left, to pass along until it reverts back to the originator. The results can be hilarious and/or confusing. In most developments the chain of communication can extend to hundreds or thousands of people, therefore the means of communication are critical to success. The Chinese whispers syndrome is a clear illustration of one of the potential pitfalls.

Assumptions

Another pitfall is to remember that it is wise never to rely on assumptions. The development and construction industry can provide numerous examples of cost overruns as a result of assumptions. One classic example is the common assumption that to convert a beautiful and historical building into a hotel is cheaper than building new. After all, the building shell already exists, so common sense suggests it has to be cheaper. Unfortunately such buildings were designed for a different use and do not adapt easily to provide an efficient operational hotel, as many bankrupt developments of this nature can demonstrate.

Examples

The classic example of how an idea can evolve into a hospitality product is Mickey Mouse, a cartoon character originated by Walt Disney, and featured in countless media and films. As Walt Disney's success grew in the film industry, so did the range of his cartoon characters to which were added a range of successful films based on classic children's stories. Committed to family entertainment from the early days, Walt Disney envisaged building a theme park based on his now famous characters and films. His vision was to build a theme park to amuse and dazzle children and their parents. That vision was realized in 1955 with the opening of Disneyland in California. His brother Roy later fulfilled Walt's plan for a similar but grander version on the east coast in 1971, with the opening of Walt Disney World in Florida. The Disney theme parks, now including one in Paris, France, are the largest example of hospitality development in the world. These products originated from an idea, were converted into a concept and then, through the determination of two brothers, developed using the same principles and processes of development that are utilized today. Numerous other examples exist, although on a smaller scale, when an individual idea or concept has been developed into a successful enterprise. Similarly, there are examples of a gap in the market being identified, and an appropriate concept or product being developed to satisfy that need. One example, the limited service (or budget) hotel product, was developed to provide a no-frills core accommodation hotel room product to deliver a low price hospitality option into the marketplace. This concept immediately proved successful not least, because it provided an affordable hotel option that served to introduce a new customer base into the industry. Indeed, the concept has proved to be so successful and profitable due to its low cost requirement in capital and running costs that this sector has now started to segment into a range of different hospitality products of different physical quality standards. In catering, the original fast food concepts such as McDonald's have given rise to a new industry sector covering a wide range of diverse food offers including hamburgers, chicken and pizzas. Recently, the soft drinks industry has witnessed an explosion in the development of new ranges of coffee, health drinks and other specialized outlets in the western world, while Internet cafés have flourished in even the most remote areas in the world.

Conclusion

This chapter has endeavoured to identify how an idea can evolve into a concept and then be converted into a viable commercial enterprise. The process of changing an idea or concept into a physical entity in hospitality involves following established steps in the cycle of development. The first step consists of putting the idea into a written brief that facilitates a process of communication. The skill applied to originating the brief and communicating its content to a number of contributors or participants normally directly impacts on the financial viability of the project. In turn, managing the process of design, procurement, construction and, finally, operations is dependent on focusing on and maintaining the clear objectives defined in the brief and communicating them efficiently throughout the process. This is not to say the process is straightforward. Like the waters of a mountain stream trying to reach the sea, the river often changes its course, but never loses sight of how to reach its objective. Development can be comparable in that it is a fluid process that needs to attain the most efficient route to achieve its objective if it is to provide the required return on investment.

References

Lundberg, D.E. and Walker, J.R. (1993) *The Restaurant from Concept to Operation*, Wiley, New York.

Rutes, W.A., Penner, R.H. and Adams, L. (2001) *Hotel Design, Planning and Development*, Architectural Press, New York.

The Concise Oxford Dictionary of Current English (1996). Thomson, D. (editor), ninth edn, BCA, London.

Review questions

1 What are the main differences between the historical hospitality industry and that of today?

2 Suggest some of the current challenges for concept development.

3 Outline some practical considerations for developing concepts.

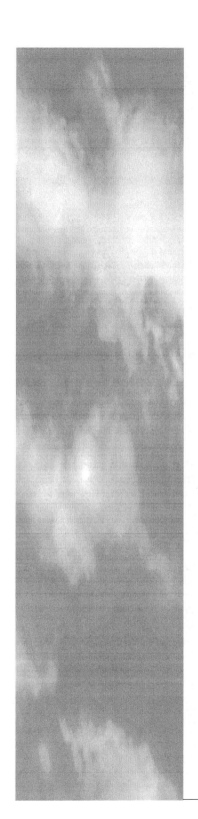

Feasibility

Trevor Ward

Before developing any property, this fundamental question must be answered:

Is the project feasible?

The word 'feasible' refers to whether the project is practicable, possible or conveniently done (*Concise Oxford Dictionary 1996:* 492).

This chapter explores some of the issues of feasibility in hospitality development, using the following structure:

- The objectives of a feasibility study

- Feasibility methodologies:
  - Site appraisal
  - Market research
  - Information review
  - Financial analysis: volume, price and revenue, costs, income projections
  - Reporting
  - Conclusions.

Context

Hotels and other hospitality facilities are hybrids, a combination of property and business. The developer of a hotel, for example, will build that hotel for the carrying out of a specific type of business, and the design of that building must be exactly in tune with that intention. An office developer, on the other hand, will pay little regard to the nature of the business to be carried on within his new office block, whether it is banking, insurance or even the headquarters of a hotel company.

The design of a hotel, even a simple bedroom block, can be very complicated – how is the front door to be orientated, what views can be afforded from the bedrooms, where do the light switches need to be placed, how are the deliveries to be brought to the building without interfering with guest ingress? These and a million other decisions need to be taken before the first pile is sunk into the ground. While some of these considerations need to be taken into account when designing an office block, they are of less importance.

Further, the business of a hotel is also complicated – a large property can have literally thousands of transactions taking place each day, of differing values, many in cash, and an equal number of 'people movements' which need to be controlled by management. A leisure centre can be equally complex, again with thousands of individual transactions, and a large variety of types of activity being undertaken at any one time.

This complexity means that the planning process for hospitality facilities needs to be that much more detailed, and needs to be guided by a market and financial feasibility study from the outset. This chapter examines the nature of a feasibility study, and gives a guide on how to carry one out.

The objectives of a feasibility study

It is fairly obvious that one of the objectives of a feasibility study is to determine whether a project proposal is feasible! But you will rarely if ever see a negative feasibility study – a report which concludes that 'this project does not work'. Except in exceptional circumstances[1], a report which says that is of no practical use. A feasibility study is not undertaken in isolation, but is prepared by a specialized consultant in conjunction with the

---

[1] TRI was once requested by a developer to prepare a report which demonstrated that hotel use on a particular site he owned was *not* a viable proposition. He had bought a run-down hotel, on a prime piece of seafront real estate, and wanted to convert it into residential apartments, for which demand was high. Our study was required to submit to the planning authorities in support of a change of use application, to prove that hotel use was non-viable based on low levels of demand and the high cost of refurbishment. Our client was successful in achieving change of use.

Illustration 2.1
Orbiting Space Resort
(Photography courtesy of
Wimberley, Allison,
Tong & Goo)

architect, the client, the source(s) of funding, the management company and any other parties involved with the project. If during the preparation of the feasibility study it looks like the project proposal is likely to be not workable, then the consultant will work with the client and the other members of the team to derive a project that *does* work.

So therefore it can be deduced that a feasibility study is more than a report which says 'yes, this is feasible'. The objectives of a feasibility study can be summarized as follows:

• To provide information to the project promoter regarding the environment in which the project will be operating. The promoter needs to understand where the proposed project fits into the market as a whole, in terms of supply and demand, government policies towards the hospitality sector, and factors external and internal to the sector that will affect operations and therefore profitability and viability. The various risks to which the project will be exposed – political, commercial, environmental, construction-related etc. – will be identified and quantified, for the promoter to assess and more importantly understand. In some cases, the client will ask the consultant to assist in the definition of the concept for the project – what should I build that will take best advantage of the characteristics of the site and of the market opportunities? This may be within fairly tight parameters, such as the type of hotel that should be built, or a much wider brief, which then becomes a best-use study, to identify the use of the site which will generate the best return to the developer. It is often the case, particularly where the promoter of a project is the investor (and perhaps also the operator) for the Board of Directors to require

25

an independent verification of the internal sponsor's recommendations prior to authorizing expenditure of further funds on the planning and development of the project.

- To provide a brief to the architect as to what the market requires from the project. The market research that is undertaken for the study will look at the current supply of facilities of relevance and competitive with the project, and will discover the strengths and weaknesses of the existing facilities. The design of the project should seek to exploit the weaknesses of the existing supply, for example by having larger bedrooms in the case of a hotel, or the latest types of treatment in the case of a health and leisure centre. The research will also investigate demand characteristics – both for the existing facilities and for the proposed facility. This will include examining the market's opinions of the existing supply, and how users' needs might be changing, and therefore factors which the new project can exploit.

- To provide the information that a potential lender or investor in the project will require, in order to make an investment decision. This investor may well, of course, be the project promoter, but there are few hospitality facilities of any size which do not require third party funding. The lender or investor will need to be informed about the risks inherent in the project, which will impact upon the equity returns or upon the ability to service debt. These will be the same risks as those which the promoter will be assessing, but the promoter will likely be taking a much more optimistic view of how well the project will do. A third party funder, especially a debt provider, will always look at the downside risk – the likelihood of political events negatively impacting on the projected income, indeed the potential impacts of unseen events such as terrorism and natural disasters. Put simply, third party investors and lenders want to know how quickly they will get their money back. The lender wants to know that the project can generate sufficient profits (and cash) to pay both interest and principal when it is due, and that if the projections of profit are not met, there is sufficient leeway to prevent default on these payments. The lender also wants to know that the various risks which the project will be subject to are removed or at least minimized. The investor will also want to know that there will be profit to distribute as dividends, and will look at how long it will take for the total of those dividends to equal the sum originally invested.

- To present the case to the planning authorities in support of planning applications. An analysis of the market may be required where change of use of a building or site is required, for example.

- To assist in negotiations with management companies. In the hotel sector, operators are often approached by promoters of new hotels seeking their services. The hotel companies are approached by many promoters in this way, and the existence of a professionally prepared study shows that the promoter is serious, and is funding the necessary studies to move the project forward. In addition, the projections of revenue and profit in the feasibility study can form a basis for negotiation of fees payable to the management company, and can be used to benchmark their performance once the hotel is operational.

Feasibility methodologies

At TRI Hospitality Consulting, the methodology for carrying out a market and financial feasibility study has five main components:

1 Site appraisal

2 Market research

3 Information review

4 Financial analysis

5 Reporting.

The following pages describe each of these components. To illustrate the process, the example of a new-build hotel is used, but this is just one type of hospitality facility, and one type of project. A feasibility study is an appraisal of supply and demand, the factors affecting supply and demand, particularly factors likely to have an impact in the future, and an assessment as to how the project proposal can exploit the opportunities in the market which are foreseen. Where a project proposal has yet to be formulated, the study will determine and define what concept will best exploit the market opportunities.

It can therefore be deduced that the methodologies inherent in a feasibility study can be used for a variety of investment proposals:

- A new build facility

- An acquisition

- An extension to an existing facility

- A refurbishment proposal

- A renovation programme, to reposition a facility.

One difference that the first type has compared to the others is that the latter will normally benefit from historic operating data regarding the existing facility, which makes future projections easier (although this is not always the case for acquisitions).

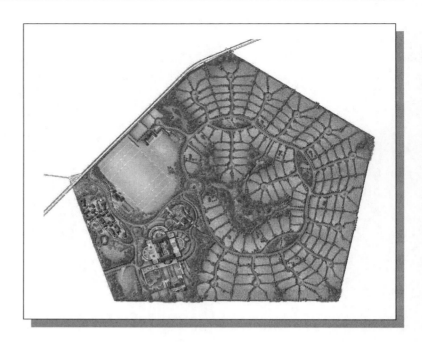

Illustration 2.2
Site master plan (Courtesy of
Scott Brownrigg)

1 Site appraisal

It is widely held that 'location, location and location' are the three most important factors for the success of hospitality facilities. While this author does not fully subscribe to this view (on the basis that a location can be changed by the development of a hotel or other facility, and that locations change over time), there is no doubt that location is very important, and needs to be right. A restaurant in a prime location should do better than one less-favourably located (so long as the food, the service, the ambience, are all equally good!), and a poorly-located restaurant may not do well. But, if the food, the service, the ambience are superb, then the location becomes less important. The phrase 'location, location and location' is just too simplistic.

Notwithstanding these comments, the location proposed for the project needs to be suitable for the use proposed. There are many factors that will affect 'suitability', as shown in Table 2.1.

A site appraisal therefore needs to consider many factors, and each site is unique. The appraisal will conclude with a summary of the site's strengths and weaknesses, and therefore its competitive positioning in relation to other facilities. Where weaknesses are identified, they need to be closely examined and ways to mitigate or remove them proposed. This may be through design – if a neighbouring use is less attractive than is considered desirable, then the new hotel can be oriented to exclude that view from guest bedrooms and public areas. Staff accommodation and other back-of-house facilities can be placed on that side of the site.

Factor	Considerations
Size	The site needs to be sufficiently large to accommodate the size of project proposed. This is not only the area of the site, but needs also to take into account planning regulations such as set-back (the area between the boundary and the building), site utilization ratio (the proportion which can be built upon), building density (the ratio of building area to the site area) and similar issues
Positioning	What neighbouring uses are there (or are likely to occur in the future) and what is their impact likely to be on the proposed hospitality facility? The more upmarket a proposed hotel or restaurant, the more important it is that the neighbours are 'appropriate'. Budget hotels are often to be found in industrial estates, deluxe hotels are more often to be found in office and residential areas, or on rural estates
Access	Patrons have to be able to get to the hotel or other facility, and for most ease of access by road, or in some cases rail, is essential to success. For certain facilities, however, such as some exclusive resorts, or country pubs, their very inaccessibility and therefore isolation becomes part of the product
Visibility	This is a similar point to access. A facility which looks to attract passing trade (i.e. patrons who have not pre-booked) must be seen by those patrons, while more exclusive establishments choose obscurity on purpose. In London, for example, there are numerous small hotels and private clubs which have no identification on their exterior
Relationship to demand generators	A restaurant which is seeking to attract custom from shoppers needs to be conveniently located for that market. Likewise a hotel serving business visitors to a city needs to be convenient for those visitors to get to their place of business. This may need to be balanced by the need to be accessible, and to be located convenient to other facilities
Relationship to other facilities	This is most important for hotels, where a guest is spending a greater amount of time, and therefore has greater needs, than a guest visiting a restaurant or health club for a specific activity. Therefore a business visitor may want to be close to restaurants and shops, and a tourist will want to be near to tourist attractions, or at least to modes of transport which will provide access to them
Relationship to competitors	Popular/family restaurants, which rely primarily on passing traffic, will benefit from being in close proximity to similar establishments, and therefore from 'browsers' who choose where they eat from the look of the place and the menu offer

Table 2.1
Factors to consider in site appraisal for hospitality facilities

An example of a strengths and weakness summary is shown in Table 2.2.

It is not uncommon for the list of weaknesses to be small compared to the list of strengths. While the feasibility study must be objective, and therefore must tell it like it is, warts and all, the study is a selling document (to attract investors and others to participate in the project) as well as an appraisal and therefore needs

Proposed hotel development, Hightown: site analysis	
Site strengths	**Site weaknesses**
Positive response from corporate users with regard to the location of the site	The immediate area, while up-coming, is not fully established as a key commercial, touristic or hotel district
Proximity to the major communication networks	Traffic volume on the adjacent road is heavy during the day and early evening
Excellent access to High Street and surrounding local attractions	
An excellent location, within close proximity to the city centre	
Within short distance from major business and embassy areas	
Ancillary facilities and demand generators in close proximity	
Attractive setting, due to its peaceful atmosphere and distance from the city's main arterial routes	

Table 2.2
Strengths and weakness summary

to promote the positive factors. In addition, few promoters are going to choose a site for development which has major negatives relative to its development potential.

In the above example, the perceived weakness of the area not yet being fully established may be why the promoter has chosen that site; he sees an opportunity to take advantage of the growth of the area, and has bought land which is likely to appreciate in value as the area improves. The effect of traffic noise on the proposed development can be mitigated by double or triple glazing the windows, an added but necessary cost.

2 Market research

This will start before the site appraisal, and will continue afterwards. The objective of the market research is to identify and gather sufficient information to enable the consultant to reach conclusions regarding the project proposal as to its appropriateness for the market, its likely acceptance, demand characteristics and the facilities demanded by the market, competition, and so on.

Table 2.3 lists the types of information sought, the reasons for obtaining that information, and examples of typical sources.

The research techniques used will include personal observation and measurement, telephone and face-to-face interviews, questionnaires (postal or e-mailed), Web-based searches, other database interrogation, press searches, and various literature

Information	Use	Source
General economic data	To determine the health of the national/regional/local economy, particularly growth, which will affect demand for hospitality facilities	Published data, newspapers, Internet, government periodicals and economic development agencies, banks
Population and demographic data	An indication of economic activity, sources of demand, income, labour supply	Published data, newspapers, Internet, government periodicals and economic development agencies
Transportation	To determine the ability of guests and supplies to access the proposed facilities	Observation, airport and airline officials, government transport and economic development departments, maps
Existing supply of competitive facilities	To assess the size of the market for the proposed facilities, its maturity, geographic clustering, and to identify market niches	Telephone and other directories, newspapers and trade press, observation, Internet, government tourism and leisure departments
Future supply of competitive facilities	To assess the growth of supply	Management of existing facilities, planning authorities, developers, architects, economic development departments, observation
Demand profiles and characteristics	To judge the strength of demand for existing facilities and likely growth in that demand	Management of existing facilities, travel agents, tour operators, booking agencies, corporations, government tourism departments, airlines, personal observation
Labour laws	To identify factors which will affect the costs of operation and/or the success of the operation	Management of existing facilities, government economic development agencies, lawyers, trade press
Regulations affecting operations (licensing etc.)	To identify factors which will affect the costs of and/or the success of the operation	Management of existing facilities, government economic development agencies, lawyers, trade press

Table 2.3
Types, uses and sources of information

reviews (directories, government publications etc.). On-line information sources on the hospitality industry are numerous, particularly in the hotel sector, where one can find market reviews, operating statistics, information on projects, details of current supply, and more. However, these sources need to be double-checked, and the Web should never be used to the exclusion of other information providers.

3 Information review

Reviewing information is not a discrete activity, but will be ongoing during the first two stages. A great deal of information can be found and, while it is good practice to collect everything available during the information gathering process, time needs to be devoted to sorting, assimilating and orienting this information in order to reach conclusions. It is common for more than one person to be involved in this stage, on the principle that two heads are better than one. The client and other members of the professional team (architect, project manager, cost consultant) may also be involved.

4 Financial analysis

Financial projections for a proposed new hospitality facility will normally comprise estimated statements of profit and loss, and of cash flow, based on which an investment analysis is prepared. Other chapters of this book deal in detail with the methodology of calculating and appraising investment of returns. This section therefore concentrates on the methodology of projecting estimates of income and expenditure, which form one part of the investment analysis (the others being capital expenditure and the financing plan). A projection of profit and loss will have three main platforms – volume, price and cost. Using a proposed hotel development as an example, the methodologies of calculating these three components are discussed below.

Volume

This means the number of rooms sold by the hotel, the number of covers served in the restaurant, the utilization of the hotel's business centre, the number of members in the leisure club, and so on. (It can be noted that a hotel is a conglomeration of a number of hospitality outlets, and therefore the principles described apply to appraisals of stand-alone restaurants, health clubs and other projects.) For a hotel, the selling of bedrooms is normally where the majority of the profit is generated (the exceptions being hotels, normally small ones, where the restaurant and bar are the main activity). Thus the appraisal will start with an analysis of how many roomnights can be sold.

The assumption in this case is that a developer wants to build a 100-room 4 star hotel in Hightown, where there are already five hotels of that quality, which would be directly competitive. The information collected is shown in Tables 2.4 and 2.5.

It was also discovered that the occupancies last year (shown in Table 2.4) were higher than the year before, and that this rising trend has continued to the time of the research.

The weighted average market occupancy is calculated to be 73.4%. This is also the 'fair share' occupancy, which is defined

Hotel	A	B	C	D	E	Total
Number of rooms	100	120	80	140	120	560
Room occupancy last year (%)	75	75	80	70	70	73.4

Source: TRI field research

Table 2.4
Existing hotels in Hightown

Hotel	A	B	C	D	E	Total
Number of rooms sold last year	27 375	32 850	23 360	35 770	30 660	150 015
Daily rooms sold	75	90	64	98	84	411
Penetration factor	102.2	102.2	109.0	0.954	0.954	100.0

Source: TRI hospitality consulting research

Table 2.5
Existing hotels in Hightown: market analysis

below. From this information, Table 2.5 shows how this can be analysed.

The analysis shown in Table 2.5 suggests the following:

- Some hotels (A, B and C) are performing better than the market average – their occupancies are higher than the average (73.4%), which means they are achieving better than their fair share of the market, and this is also expressed in the penetration factor. Hotel C is achieving 9% better than its fair share of the market; had it achieved 73.4%, the daily number of rooms sold would have been only 59. The consultant now needs to consider why these hotels outperformed the market average. Is it because of their physical condition, or is it something less tangible, such as their marketing activity, or the standards of service. Is it price? Are they much cheaper than their competitors? Is it their location? Is it related to their branding?

- Other hotels (D and E) are underperforming the market. Why?

- The total daily roomnight demand that is being accommodated in these hotels is 411, or an average of 82 per hotel. The consultant needs to dig deeper into the annual occupancy figures to determine whether there is other demand which, on certain nights or at certain times of the year is being turned away by these hotels, and is displaced elsewhere. Hotel managers, booking agents and other sources may be able to reveal how many nights the hotels are fully booked, and the volume of demand that is being turned away, and where it is being displaced to. This research may reveal that the true market size, including this displaced demand, is greater than 150 015 roomnights.

The next step is to project how this market is expected to grow (or decline) in the future. This is a judgement call, to be based on the research undertaken, and the information gathered. Historic performance will always be a guide to future performance, but by no means the only factor on which to make a judgement. Here are some of the factors to consider:

- What are transport links like to Hightown, and what is happening in the future? Are any major new roads being built, which might make Hightown easier to get to (and easier to leave!). What's happening at the airport, are there any new flights scheduled for the future? Is the ferry service at the harbour doing well, and likely to increase its frequency of sailings? What is the rail service like? In other words, is Hightown going to continue to be accessible to potential hotel guests?

- As well as transportation links, hotels depend on there being a reason for guests to visit the hotel and its locale. What is the health of the local economy? Is there an inward trend of investment and businesses to Hightown? What is the local or regional authority doing to attract inward investment, and how successful are they? How are the local tourist attractions doing, the theatres, the nightclubs, and so on? Is Hightown a regional or national retail centre? What is the local and national tourism board doing about promoting Hightown? How is the town's convention centre doing, and what are they doing to promote greater utilization, particularly during periods of low demand? Are the airlines using the airport increasing their need for accommodation for flight crew?

- How do the existing hotels market themselves, and create demand for their facilities through their marketing activities? Is it based on their specific product offering, for example their leisure facilities, or a terrific spa product, or perhaps their excellent conference facilities, or is it based on the attractions in and around Hightown?

In summary, this analysis is considering the ease of access for guests, and their motivation for travelling to Hightown. Each market sector – business, conference, aircrew, leisure etc. – will be affected by different factors. For example, a resort hotel will attract its market from a much wider area than one catering primarily to aircrew. The distance, and the ease of access, will therefore be very different considerations. While a hotel catering to aircrew needs to be minutes away from the airport, a resort hotel will consider both the distance from the airport, measured in hours, and also the flight times from various source markets. A hotel seeking to attract the regional conference market needs to be highly accessible by car from major urban conurbations.

Let's assume that, based on historic and current performance, and an assessment of all the above factors that the demand for 4 star hotel accommodation in Hightown will increase by 5% a year. The research has also determined that, in addition to the 150 015 roomnights that the five existing hotels accommodate, another 5% of that amount is displaced into lower category hotels when it cannot get into the 4 star hotels. Table 2.6 shows the total market size for the next five years, and the fair share occupancies for the five existing hotels in Hightown:

Clearly, Hightown's hotel market is strong, and there is a desperate need for more hotel accommodation in the town if these projected increases in demand are to be realized. There can be no guarantee that they will be – forecasting the future is often called gambling! But the projections are based on assumptions, which in turn are based on information, research, knowledge and expert judgement, so are more likely to be accurate than mere 'guesstimates'. This is a fundamental point relating to the projections contained within a feasibility study – they are based on the assumptions and information available to the consultant at the time of their preparation. Unforeseen events can and will affect the eventual outcome, and this is where the risk inherent in any capital investment lies.

What happens to these projections if we add our own project to the forward projections? For now, we will assume that it has already been decided that the hotel will have 150 rooms, but the model can also be used to determine the optimum size (within a range) of the hotel, by projecting occupancies for different numbers of rooms, taking into account seasonality and particularly periods of peak demand, the size of the site, and the size of project (by value) with which the developer is comfortable.

	Last year	This year	Year +1	Year +2	Year +3	Year +4	Year +5
Roomnight demand	157 516[1]	165 392	173 661	182 344	191 462	201 035	211 087
Fair share occupancy (%)	77.1[1]	80.9	85.0	89.2	93.7	98.4	103.3

[1] *Note*: This includes the estimated 5% demand, and therefore the fair share occupancy is higher than the 73.4% market achieved average calculated before. This new figure is the *unconstrained* fair share occupancy, which would have been achieved had the hotels not had to turn business away on nights of peak demand, and assuming no increase in the supply of hotels

Source: TRI hospitality consulting estimates

Table 2.6
Future demand projections for Hightown

	Last year	This year	Year +1	Year +2	Year +3	Year +4	Year +5
Roomnight demand	157 516	165 392	173 661	182 344	191 462	201 035	211 087
Daily rooms available	560	560	560	710[1]	710	710	710
Fair share occupancy (%)	77.1	80.9	85.0	70.4	73.9	77.6	81.5

[1] *Note*: It is assumed that the new hotel can be open at the beginning of Year +2

Source: TRI hospitality consulting estimates

Table 2.7
Future demand projections at Hightown, including this project (150 rooms)

	Last year	This year	Year +1	Year +2	Year +3	Year +4	Year +5
Roomnight demand	157 516	165 392	173 661	182 344	191 462	201 035	211 087
Daily rooms available	560	560	560	810[1]	810	810	810
Fair share occupancy (%)	77.1	80.9	85.0	61.7	64.8	68.0	71.4

[1] *Note*: It is assumed that both new hotels open at the beginning of Year +2

Source: TRI hospitality consulting estimates

Table 2.8
Future demand projections at Hightown, including this project (150 rooms) and one other project (100 rooms)

When the project is added to the projections for Hightown's future hotel demand, the result is shown in Table 2.7.

Given the strength of demand in Hightown, it is likely that other developers will also be looking at building new hotels there. Table 2.8 shows the effect of adding another hotel of 100 rooms to the market, opening in the same year as our project (Year +2).

The next assessment is the extent to which the proposed new hotel will penetrate the market, i.e. whether it will achieve its fair share of demand, or whether it will achieve more or less than that amount. This will be based on a number of considerations, such as the location, the proposed branding and marketing, the proposed pricing strategies, the facilities to be offered, the market orientation of the property, which might, for example, determine that the hotel will not accommodate aircrew (and therefore the fair share of that particular market sector will be zero), the quality of the hotel compared to its competitors, and so on.

It is normal for a new hotel to take a while to build its market position – although a new hotel can benefit from the novelty factor, it will also suffer from the fact that markets such as conference organizers will not book accommodation until they have seen that the hotel is finished, and have approved the quality of the facilities on offer for their event. Demand from that source will therefore be lower in the first year or two of operation. The market penetration assessment is therefore most likely to be undertaken on a market-by-market basis – as indeed will be the whole demand model used above. The analysis presented is simplistic, in order to demonstrate the methodology; in practice, information on the demand volumes by market sector will be obtained from the existing hotels, demand growth will be considered and projected separately by market sector, as will the new hotel's market penetration.

Based on the following factors, the consultant makes a judgement of the new hotel's market penetration:

- The hotel has a highly desirable location

- It will offer more up-to-date conference facilities than those offered by the competition

- It will be a new hotel, and therefore of better quality than most of the competitive hotels

- It will not have a feature spa, which two of the other hotels have

- It will adopt an aggressive pricing strategy, discounting where necessary to gain a greater share of demand

- The market penetration factors are assumed to be 0.98 in Year +2 (i.e. 2% less than fair share), 1.02 in Year +3 and 1.05 in Year +4. At this point in time, and for the purposes of these projections, the occupancy of the hotel is determined to have stabilized, or to have reached equilibrium – clearly it is not logical to assume continuing increases in occupancy, because other new hotels are likely to enter the market as occupancies increase, because the project will reach capacity occupancy at around 75 to 80%, due to seasonality of demand, and because the further one tries to project into the future, the more difficult it becomes to provide justification for the assumptions used. Table 2.9 shows the projections of occupancy for this project.

As noted, the description of how these occupancy projections have been arrived at is relatively simplistic. More accuracy would have been obtained by analysing existing and future demand by market sector, and by a greater analysis of the strengths and weaknesses of this project compared to other hotels, and in each

	Year +2	Year +3	Year +4
Roomnight demand	182 344	191 462	201 035
Daily rooms available	810	810	810
Fair share occupancy (%)	61.7	64.8	68.0
This project market penetration	0.98	1.02	1.05
This project room occupancy (%)	60.4	66.1	71.4

Source: TRI hospitality consulting estimates

Table 2.9
Proposed new hotel, Hightown: occupancy projections

market sector. Conversely, a much simpler calculation could have been made. The market as a whole last year achieved 73.4%. This project will achieve that occupancy in its second year of operation, and say 70% in its first year and 75% in its third year. There is nothing wrong with that in itself, except for the wealth of detail about the dynamics of the market that it does not specifically take into account, and therefore the projection cannot be tested for changes in the assumptions made (what, for example, would be the effect on the occupancy projection for this project if growth were only 3% per annum?). But it is fine as a starting point, for something which is for an initial consideration of the project, and which is not intended to be scrutinized by third parties such as lenders. The above has been concerned solely with the volume of demand for the rooms division of the hotel. Here are some factors to consider when assessing demand for the other facilities of the proposed new hotel:

- **Restaurants**: A hotel situated in an area with other restaurants and bars will achieve a lower utilization from hotel guests of its in-house facilities than one which is isolated (e.g. a country house hotel). Residential conference delegates will normally be on a package which includes three meals each day, so therefore their utilization will be 100% per meal. A leisure-oriented hotel, for example in a ski resort where the guests are out all day, will have a low lunchtime utilization from that market. Non-resident guests (known as 'chance') will be affected by other considerations. How attractive to the office market at lunchtime, and to local residents at dinner time, is the restaurant? Does the local population have a high or low propensity to eat out, and to use hotel restaurants (this can be influenced by income as well as cultural factors)? What is the demand in the local area for banqueting facilities? Wedding demand is normally a good source of utilization, particularly at weekends during the spring and summer.

- **Bars**: Similar considerations will apply. A resort hotel might find that guests on package holidays from one country will use the bars more than those from another country.

- **Room hire**: This will be generated by conferences, banquets and other events.

- **Telephone**: Usage of telephone networks in hotels has been declining due to the use of mobile phones. A business and conference hotel is likely to have higher usage of telephones than a leisure hotel.

- **Laundry**: Usage will depend on the type of guest, and their length of stay. Guests using the hotel for one night before departing from the local airport are unlikely to use laundry facilities, while a business visitor staying for one night will use it more.

- **Health club and leisure facilities**: Utilization will be generated by residents of the hotel, and also by non-residents, on a daily or membership basis. Observation of other clubs in the area will indicate the demand for hotel club facilities.

- **Rentals**: This will be earned from shops, showcases, airline desks and the like. The demand for such space in the hotel will depend to a large extent on the types of resident guests, and the local offer of shopping facilities.

Price and revenue

Combining projections of volume with assumptions regarding price, one can project revenues for the proposed hotel. As with the section on volume, we will concentrate here on the pricing of rooms, with indicators as to factors affecting the prices for other facilities.

As noted previously, the projections of occupancy (roomnights sold) cannot be made without some reference to the price to be charged for the rooms. The intended quality of the hotel will be a reference point, as will the recommended pricing strategy which becomes one of the assumptions underlying the market penetration factors. The research will reveal the published prices (tariff) of the existing hotels, and will also ascertain the prices actually charged – most often very different. Thus the amount of discounting being applied to each market sector can be calculated, and the pricing strategies of the competition determined. The practices vary – there are hotels which 'never' discount, although in practice that means that they offer corporate rates, and other special rates, which are not regarded as being 'discounts'. There are those hotels which discount to almost every guest, and therefore their published tariff is an aspiration, and part of their marketing message. And there are those hotels, such as resort properties, which contract all their rooms to tour operators and travel agents at negotiated rates, and do not even have a published tariff.

To project prices and therefore revenues for our proposed hotel in Hightown, there are a number of methods which can be adopted:

- Investigate the average room rates achieved by the existing competitive hotels, and assume an achieved average rate relative to those benchmarks. That rate, multiplied by the number of roomnights sold, equals rooms revenue

- Assume sector rates, again by reference to the competitive set, and from interviews with demand generators, and calculate rooms revenue by each market sector

- Adopt a more complex model, making assumptions regarding the published tariff by room type, the discounts to be offered to each market sector, the proportion of each market paying rack rate, and the utilization of each room type. From this devolves the total rooms revenue, and the average rate is calculated by dividing that figure by the total number of roomnights sold.

Again, it depends on the amount of justification required for the projections of average room rate as to which methodology is adopted. For other hotel facilities, the price levels to be incorporated in the financial model will be determined by reference to the existing hotels, other competing facilities in the area (for example stand-alone restaurants), and where applicable the corporate policy of the owner/manager of the hotel, who might, for example, have a standard menu used in all hotels in that chain. Different pricing assumptions might be applied to different market sectors, for example for telephone or bar usage.

Costs

In the hotel industry, the costs of operating a hotel are categorized according to the rules of the Uniform System of Accounts, which divide them broadly into departmental expenses and undistributed (or central) costs. Departmental expenses will include payroll costs for each operating department (but not central services such as marketing or maintenance), consumables (the food used in the kitchen, the drinks served in the bar, and the cost to the hotel of providing a telephone line), and other expenses (cleaning materials used by the departments, stationery, linen, and the like). Central costs will include payroll (the general manager, the accountants, the engineers etc.), marketing expenses, energy (although this is sometimes allocated to the operating departments), repairs and other costs which relate more to the whole hotel than to any individual department.

As with any aspect of projecting profit and loss for a new hotel, there is more than one way of projecting operating costs. The simplest way is to use percentage relationships, benchmarking against the existing hotels, and against industry publications. This is fine so long as such data exist, which is not the case in many markets. Where comparable data are not available, best estimates must be made based on the initial research, using information on the cost of different inputs, the salaries paid, energy costs per kilowatt hour. Percentage relationships will still be used for certain items, such as marketing costs, which tend not to vary from one country to another, although the type of hotel needs to be taken into account – a resort hotel selling the majority of its rooms through tour operators will have far lower marketing costs than a city centre hotel relying on a number of different markets.

Income projections

Revenue less operating costs equals gross operating profit. Does that give any indication as to the feasibility of the project? No, not really. Feasibility will normally be defined as meeting a pre-defined measure of return on investment, along with other measures such as debt service coverage and equity payback. These, and the whole subject of investment appraisal, are covered in detail in Chapter 5.

If a feasibility study does not conclude whether a project is feasible or not, can it then be called a feasibility study? Well, that is the term used in the industry, for what is really an appraisal (but note that an appraisal in the USA is what in the UK and Europe we call a valuation!) of a development, or acquisition, or renovation opportunity which gives an independent and objective view of the project. It provides the author's informed opinion regarding the project, and sufficient information for the developer and others to make decisions as to whether the project should or should not proceed, and in what form.

5 Reporting

This final stage in the feasibility process provides a report with the study findings back to the client, usually in written format and presented at a meeting.

Conclusions

This chapter has sought to describe the nature of a feasibility study for a hospitality facility, and how to undertake such a study, using a hypothetical hotel development as an example. A feasibility study is an assessment of supply and demand, the factors affecting the market, and how the proposed facility can fit into and exploit the market for profit. It is suggested that experienced consultants are used to undertake feasibility studies, and that they use a logical and tested method, such as has been suggested: site appraisal, market research, information review, financial analysis and reporting. Feasibility studies are 25% information, 25% common sense, 25% experience and judgement, and 25% analysis. Maybe not in that order, or in those exact proportions, but without them all, the study will lack the robustness it needs to satisfy the client.

References

The Concise Oxford Dictionary of Current English (1996), Thomson, D. (editor), ninth edn, BCA, London.

Review questions

1 Outline the objectives of conducting a hotel feasibility study.

2 Comment on suitability factors for a new build, acquisition, extension, refurbishment and repositioning.

3 Give specific examples of sources of information for a feasibility study for a new build hotel and spa in upstate New York.

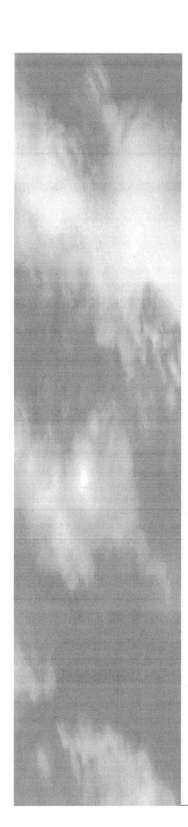

Design

Josef Ransley

Managers of hospitality properties are not only responsible for the unit's operations, but also for formulating a strategy that will develop the property to reflect both the needs of customers and the demands of the owners. Such a strategy is always forward-looking, as it seeks to improve product and service in the unit. Often, unit managers need to coordinate this development strategy, using the expertise of specialists from inside and outside the organization. This chapter considers the role of the designer and the importance of both the design briefing document and management of the design process, in the following headings:

- What is design?
- The role of the designer
- The components of design
- The purpose of design
- A model of the design process
- Factors affecting design
- Sensory design responses
- Aesthetics and style
- The project brief
- Evaluating the design proposals
- Project implementation
- Future challenges
- Conclusion.

What is design?

The word design comes from the French word meaning to draw, and can signify a 'drawing that shows how something is to be made' (Hawkins, 1988:218). Design has also come to be understood as a 'model, pilot, purpose or plot' (Oxford University Press, 1971:698). A third meaning for this word is the general form or arrangement, especially of a building. Thus design incorporates the planning, drawing and arrangements of properties, and the design process represents the operationalization of a project from ideas to drawings and reality.

The role of the designer

The role of the designer in the hospitality industry is to provide a commercial design service to individual managers or owners, or to multi-unit organizations. The commercial aims of the design process should be to maximize the capital investment and financial return of the owners, rather than to satisfy the designer's artistic sensibilities. Successful designs are those that find favour primarily with the end user; the hospitality customer, as customer acceptance and repeat purchase behaviour will result in a financial return on the development investment. It is important that the designer and hospitality client do not place their preferences above those of the customer.

The task of the designer is to establish a harmonious balance between the following factors:

- Image

- Style

- Operating efficiency

- Customer comfort.

Image and style are the means through which an organization communicates messages, such as brand identity or quality, while operating efficiency and customer comfort are more tangible operational considerations. A new or adapted hospitality design should be one that can be operated by the staff and management. Consideration should be given to practical operational issues such as the flow of people, materials or information. For example, the design of a customer interface area such as a bar or reception should include space behind the counter for the storage of documents and should be able to accommodate the number of staff required to serve customers at maximum capacity. The designer and the client need to work closely together to ensure that both aesthetics and practicalities are balanced.

The designer is responsible for the following elements:

- Space planning
- Form and colour
- Finishes and durability
- Lighting and audio-visual systems
- Technology
- Costs.

In essence, the design incorporates all these elements, and the designer acts as the interface between the building form, structure, building services and the operation, in order to turn a concept into reality.

The components of design

Design incorporates both interior and exterior elements. The exterior presentation of property involves signs, building form, window dressing, entrances, canopies, outdoor activities, terraces, patios and landscaping. It is the exterior presentation that gives the hospitality property a distinctive presence in its neighbourhood and offers the customer a first image to inform their perception of the product.

Interior design aims to make best use of the space available in the property, both for front and back of house activities. The internal configuration of facilities includes accommodation, food and beverage areas, reception areas, leisure amenities, storage and services (for example, heating, air-conditioning, gas, water, lighting, power, and communications). Consideration must be given to the circulation pattern of customers and staff, so that bottlenecks do not cause frustrations for staff and possibly lower the standard of service defects for guests. Moreover, there is a primary need to ensure that the interior design itself should not present hazards that may affect the safety of the building or its occupants, with regard to accidents or fire risk. This necessity extends to the interior construction of rooms and spaces, the linings, furnishings and surface finishes, all of which need to be designed with appearance, practicability, cost and safety in mind.

The design of a hospitality property is also a reflection of the operating standards of the unit and includes factors such as:

- Capacity of bedrooms, public areas and food and beverage facilities
- Layouts of table groupings
- Anticipated product and service turnover, and consequent flexibility of accommodation and seating

- Method of food and drink service, staffing and support arrangements.

The purpose of design

Effective hospitality designs are those that are planned around a number of key criteria:

- *Marketing*. Appealing to the target market by projecting the desired image and providing the required price and quality

- *Ambience*. Creating attractive internal environment and conditions that support a suitable social atmosphere and the service style

- *Operations*. Meeting the practical needs of serving guests efficiently and to the required standard

- *Maintenance*. Ensuring fabric and facilities can be maintained to suitable standards easily and replacements are available (for example rare foreign carpet, tiles, toilets)

- *Capital costs*. Matching the planned capital cost expenditure, which will have been based on the anticipated return on investment.

Once again, it is imperative that design should balance the needs of customers, owners and operators.

A model of the design process

The design process, shown in Figure 3.1, begins with a desire on the part of the property managers or owners to change the tangible product. Initially, there will be some discussion within the organization about what form this development should take and the approximate resources that might be allocated to fund it. At this stage, a designer is appointed to explore the idea with the organization and develop the idea for a new concept. Such a concept for

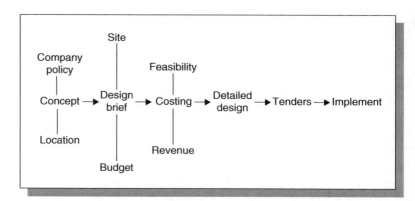

Figure 3.1
A model of the hospitality
design process

the internal development of a hospitality property will be constrained by its location and any company policy on product branding. For example, firms such as Whitbread, Holiday Inn and Accor have a number of branded hotels that must be designed within tight specifications, in order to maintain brand integrity.

The next stage is the development of a design brief. This is produced according to the characteristics of the site and within budget guidelines. Subsequently, the design can be costed and feasibility studies carried out concerning the effects of the proposals in terms of revenue, costs and profit. If these meet the needs of the organization, a detailed set of design specifications is produced and tenders invited from contractors to implement the design.

Factors affecting design

A hospitality design concept can be affected by a number of factors, particularly:

- *Company policy*. Product style, brand and future development strategy
- *Concept*. Objectives and market orientation
- *Location*. Type of premises, surroundings and constraints
- *Function*. Space usage, seating capacity and operational needs
- *Aesthetics*. Style, character and design features
- *Budget*. Investment criteria, payback, financing and resources
- *Business*. Strategy: planned life cycle and future changes
- *Logistics*. Critical dates, stages and contractors.

Equally, a number of factors may constrain the design process, such as location, market, budget and company policy. In this sense, few hospitality developments start with a 'blank sheet' and, therefore, design skills can overcome restrictions and plan changes that will meet the needs of all concerned. Design is not about creating from a blank canvas, but also creating solutions within the constraints of individual developments.

Sensory design responses

Design is both functional and sensory. It creates visual and emotion appeal through, for example, lighting, richness of colour, and the texture of furnishings. Mirrors, lighting and sound can transmit excitement and atmosphere in hospitality properties. More specifically, it is necessary to design a room size and its proportion in relation to the purpose and the number of people who may use it.

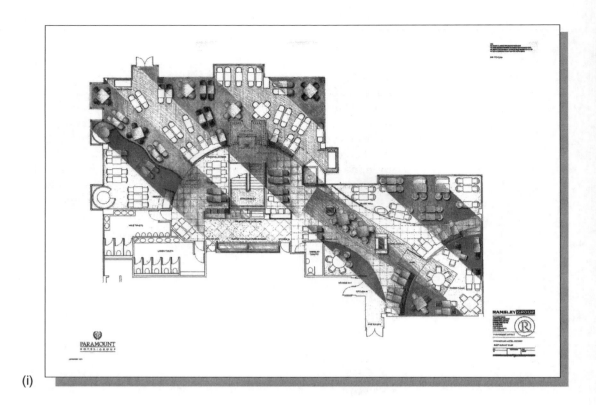

(i)

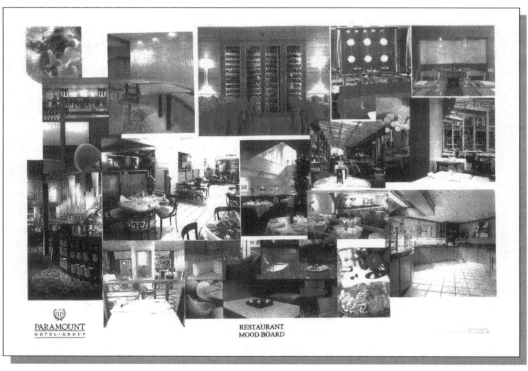

(ii)

Illustration 3.1
A design presentation: plan and mood board (Courtesy of Scott Brownrigg)

Public areas, for example, should give sensory clues as to the quality and prices of the services on offer and present a warm and inviting ambience. Warmth or coolness can be created using materials, textures and colours, while variations of light and shade can give the illusion of space and form. The extent and importance of these as design features will depend upon the target market. Customers in the luxury market will expect more sophisticated aesthetics, and may be more appreciative (and perhaps critical) of items such as antiques and paintings, added to create an atmosphere of sophisticated elegance.

Aesthetics and style

The atmosphere that can be created by design, feelings such as calmness, sociability and intimacy, augments a customer satisfaction with hospitality products and services. Mood can affect the way that an individual responds to an experience and mood can be affected by social and environmental conditions. Since hospitality products are often consumed in social conditions, customers might be more aware of others in a half-empty restaurant or bar, than in one which is crowded with people. Paradoxically, some hospitality units are all the more desirable for being crowded, and it is the job of the designer to help to create a balance between size and atmosphere. Paradoxically, it is often style that distinguishes a property from those of competitors through branding or product differentiation. Branding style conveys information about product and prices, often through the creation of a theme, such as those represented by McDonalds or Travelodge. Themes are able to express mood (novelty, escapism), historical period, and fashion or ethnic origin. Equally, there is also a trend towards cleaner, simpler, less fussy lines, which reflect a contemporary current lifestyle and are also easier to maintain.

The project brief

A project brief is the pivotal document that establishes the project's objective and parameters for all the parties concerned, including owners, managers/operators and design team. The project brief should address a number of key issues:

- *Objectives* of the development: why a change is needed and what is required

- *Budget*: spending limits and the required rate of return

- *Time*: desired start and finish date to maximize selling opportunities and minimize disruption

- *Quality*: standards and durability required from the development.

As with any other form of communication, the message from the client should be as clear, concise and briefly stated as possible. It will also be affected by the amount of detail about the constraints that are felt necessary by the developers, as well as the knowledge and ability of those charged with writing it. The length of the briefing document will also depend upon the extent to which the product has been articulated and needs to be replicated in other locations. For example, McDonalds, the multi-national fast food restaurant chain has created a world-famous brand based on an established process and formula. In creating a new outlet, it is imperative that the components of foodservice and space planning are repeated exactly so that brand identity and recognition are promoted. Alternatively, an independent restaurant developer who wishes to create a new and original dining experience to compete with established brands might write a comparatively unbounded brief that leaves the design team free to develop original and creative ideas.

The definition and communication of requirements is at the heart of a good brief. The success and value for money of a hospitality development project depends on writing a good brief. This is as crucial to the project as are foundations to a building. Good briefs are characterized by the following:

- *Logical structure.* As with any document, a clear structure will make it accessible, readable and understandable

- *Presentation.* Should always be attractively presented

- *Consistency.* The brief should express cohesive ideas

- *Progressive.* Define the stages of development and the approval needed at each stage.

A project brief must include both fundamental matters and the required attributes can be characterized as fundamentals and attributes.

Fundamentals

- *Objectives.* These should be sorted into priorities, for example costings, marketing, operational and maintenance issues

- *Resources.* Budgets and content, timescale, planned life cycle, operational elements and staffing levels

- *Context.* Scope, relevant legislation, technical facts, nature of site, building fabric and area specifications

- *Planning.* Services, space relationships, function, operational methods and seating capacities

- *Marketing.* Market segments, customer profile, spend per head and duration of stay, service standards, usage and entertainment.

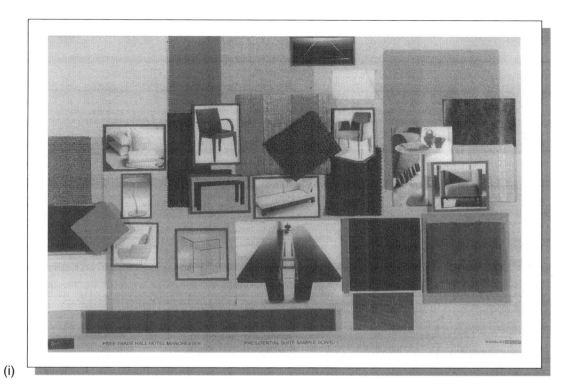

(i)

(ii)

Illustration 3.2
A design presentation: visual and sample board (Courtesy of Scott Brownrigg)

Attributes

- *Realism*. Realistic in terms of objectives, resources, context, planning and quality

- *Relevance*. Information related to the project only

- *Flexibility*. Specific enough for decisions to be taken and flexible enough to encourage the exploration of options

- *Operation*. Define the organization's standards, informed by the client's experiences of the durability of materials and running costs.

Evaluating the design proposals

Having briefed the designer, the next issue for the client is to evaluate the design proposals. Many people argue that the hospitality industry has avoided expenditure on research and development and has relied on the small entrepreneur to develop new concepts and innovation, only to be bought out and replicated by larger companies. In the future, this will lead to inevitable change as greater discernment by hospitality customers will require the sort of product development expenditure that is common in many developing industries, in which there is a focus on creativity for market leadership. Accordingly, the hospitality clients of the future should evaluate design proposals in a more professional and forward-thinking way.

Design evaluation should not be clouded by the personal preferences of the client, because the proposal should mirror the organization's objectives. If the proposal does not reflect these objectives, the client should give the designer an opportunity to redress this misalignment, or seek another designer. Some of the fundamentals of the brief are generally factual and relatively simple to evaluate, including objectives, resources, context and planning (because the client will have developed a clear idea of what is required). Marketing, however, is less tangible and gives the client a number of choices of market, price and product specification.

Many people confuse interior design in the hospitality industry with domestic interior decoration or the aesthetics of good design as defined by an elite minority. Commercial interior design can be regarded in the same way as packaging in the retailing industry, where products from breakfast cereals to toys are wrapped attractively to appeal to the buying public. In the same way, the hospitality product is 'packaged' in an environment and atmosphere that is designed to appeal to the customer base and not necessarily to the client, his wife or any other individual. Consequently, the appraisal of the marketing element of the briefing fundamentals is the most difficult element to evaluate in all cases. However, the design proposals should be always be integrated into the design brief.

Project implementation

The critical elements to achieving any successful building project are time, cost and quality. These factors are even more important in hospitality projects, which can be complex, especially in major refurbishments where the unit is to remain open and trading. A clear, concise and specific client briefing document defining, not only the parameters of cost, time and quality but also operational requirements, space standards and area relationships is therefore essential to the successful implementation of a development. The general perception in the design and construction industry is still that hospitality developments focus on quality in terms of space and decorative standards and are not sensitive to overall cost. The reality is that hospitality projects are probably more sensitive to capital cost expenditure for their viability than any other form of building.

Since the early 1990s capital valuations have been more influenced by multiples of profit than any other factor. The relationship between capital cost and return on investment driven by earnings and profit are therefore direct and measurable. In turn this means that hotels must be planned to be functional and operationally efficient with minimum maintenance and running costs, as well as being designed to provide guest comfort, and appeal to suit specific markets. This is equally applicable to budget and luxury hotels, resort or city hotels, branded or individual hotels.

There is a adage in golf development that 'new golf courses are developed by individuals with a passion who end up bankrupt before completion'. The project is then bought by an enthusiast who finishes it, but cannot get a return on the investment, and subsequently sells out to the mainstream operators at a realistic price, who can then make a handsome profit. This analogy is applicable to the Western European hotel market, which has matured financially in a dramatic way over the last ten years. Most major hotel-owning companies and financiers have shed any emotional tendencies and have developed sophisticated financial systems and controls to manage their assets. To that end the buyers are predominantly mainstream industry companies and valuations reflect this reality.

Capital costs for different hotel product and market profile properties need to be compatible to industry norms. Such capital cost norms will consequently define quality standards that have to be achieved within strict time schedules if costs are to be controlled. Similarly, hotel lettings need to be planned well in advance to suit refurbishment works.

Future challenges

With the advent of the separation of ownership and operation of a hospitality property there is a case for the design of a property to be considered on a more long-term basis. Differing property use values are not static and a location's use value may change. Many examples exist where offices have been converted into hotels when letting values for office space in their area have fallen. As the process of construction continues to change from skill based techniques to more pre-manufactured methods, designers will have the opportunity to design more flexibility into the built form. Initially, incorporating such flexibility will entail a higher capital cost. However, if such additional cost can be contained as a small percentage of the overall cost, the long-term benefit to the owner, being able to change the operational use of the building at a low cost, could enhance the overall returns on the building over its planned lifecycle. One of the constraints on raising finance for hotel development has historically been its single use option and very limited scope for change. In the past, this was the case for offices. Now they are designed with a view to providing flexibility. The essential requirement is the ability easily to change location access to power or information technology configurations and provision of lighting, air conditioning and internal space separation. If such adaptability were provided for water and waste services, while the same building techniques for the other building services were applied, a building form with multi-use options at a low cost for change would change the financial criteria for the property investor.

Illustration 3.3
'The discerning customer'
(Courtesy of Michael Winner,
Photograph, Terry O'Neill)

For the operator, the need to change the physical product is also proving more essential now, as the customer becomes more demanding in aspirations for experiencing newer products. For example, in the restaurant sector, there has been a reduction in the mainstream product lifecycle. The impact of this is that return on investment now has to be measured over a shorter period with a subsequent increase in risk. If this trend continues and extends into the hotel sector, where the initial investment is far greater, its impact on the mainstream market could prove to be even more dramatic, unless, of course the flexibility of the building form is enhanced.

Similar pressure exists in the developed countries as a consequence of the reducing land resource available for development in the main areas of demand. The lack of penetration of the limited service or budget hotels into city centre locations due to the high entry cost demonstrates this. As does the fact that many mid-market hotels are now renovated, and repositioned as a superior product despite the high cost of refurbishment. However, trading up the product is a finite option in most locations and does not satisfy the demand in the mid-market sector, which is the largest segment of the industry. Consolidation and acquisition of the product available by the major groups and brands with only minor refurbishment to satisfy brand standards may provide a short-term solution for under-performing product and brand representation. However, it does not increase available stock. As demand is forecast to increase, the issues will be resolved by way of more flexible building form or the nature of the product. The latter may be driven by the nature of property investment and development, which is moving more to the development of multi-use buildings, occasioned by a need to maximize the value of a property in particular locations. Such development trends pose challenges for developer, owner and operator alike. All of this will require the designer to respond to more complex issues in future.

As the ownership structure of the hospitality industry adapts in terms of ownership and its nature alters in terms of operations, so have design and construction industries changed. The aspects of change in the construction industry are covered in detail in Chapter 9. For the design industry, change appears to be about reverting back to its roots. In the early part of the last century, architects, for instance, were only responsible for design, the implementation and realization of the building being the skills provided by others. Traditionally the great Victorian architects concerned themselves with the aesthetics of the building design leaving the master builder to realize personal aspirations and those of the owners. As the volume and scope of building increased through industrialization, the architect's role was extended to maintain control and status. This role was extended to manage the delivery of the building as designed, by adding the management of the building process to service provision. Thus, the architect/designer gained authority over the process. Sensibly for them, because such authority was not linked with responsibility, at least not in a contractual way. This was achieved by diversifying the role into separate professions, namely quantity surveying, structural, mechanical and electrical engineering and later a host of other specialists including interior and landscape designers to name but two. This resulted in major projects having up to twenty different consultants all working under the direction and coordination of the architect. Not trained as managers it was not surprising that in the 1980s, architects having failed fully to satisfy clients' requirements lost managerial control, responsibility of which was taken over by the project manager. Similarly, construction companies moved into the provision of design and build construction management or 'turn key' as it is known in the USA. This came about because the companies attempted to address the issues by way of a management contract form and realized that management without authority could not produce the required results, While the benefits and weaknesses of the varying methods of construction, particularly those which deliver the best in terms of quality, time and cost, are still being debated, it is interesting to note that the architectural and design schools are expending more time on the teaching of the theories of design rather than the management of the process of construction. Similarly, as the methods of construction continue to change from skill to manufacture based systems the larger international construction companies who have the resources to invest in development, but require a secure work flow have moved into partnering. This involves the supplier and procurer entering into longer-term agreements to develop multiple units in varying locations. By simplifying the management structure of the design and construction process, such partnerships seem to be delivering more and more projects in various industry sectors including hospitality. Perhaps it will prove to be partnering or a similar process that will evolve to embody the change in design and construction in the twenty-first century.

The fact that the UK recorded its highest temperature ever (over 100°F) on 10 August 2003 may not be confirmation that the global climate is changing. However, it does have an impact on the UK hotel industry. While in the past air conditioning was an option, now it is a basic requirement in hotel facilities. Climate change and the environment will inevitably impact on the design and cost of hospitality property in many different ways, including the nature of the building shell, the management of the internal environment, the cost and availability of utilities and consequently the nature of operational services and facilities. Consumer demand for environmentally considered products is growing as is national legislation in certain parts of the world and some predict it will eventually impact on our ability to travel at will. Whatever transpires in this regard designers, builders, developers, owners and operators will undoubtedly be challenged to address the complex issues of the environment, flexibility, multi-use buildings and the separation of ownership and operations in a more competitive marketplace in the future.

Conclusion

In this chapter, it has been suggested that the role of the designer is to work with the hospitality client to develop a final product that meets the needs of the client and satisfies the consumer. A balance must be struck between factors such as image, style, operating efficiency and customer comfort, and between aesthetics and practicalities. The external design of hospitality properties must be practical and appealing, while internal design should make the best use of the space available. The designer is responsible for planning the space available and for filling it with suitable furnishings and fittings, so that the flow of people and materials is facilitated. Design is, however, affected by factors such as company policy, location, budgets and logistics, and a good designer needs to be aware of such considerations. The design of bedroom accommodation requires more attention to tangible factors than food and beverage facilities, where there is more of a requirement to create an environment in which to enjoy the dining experience. Design may be regarded as a sequential process from concept to implementation, and the design brief is a key document in which the project objectives and parameters are set out. The briefing document should be clear and concise. Its length will depend upon the extent to which the hospitality product needs to be branded. Design proposals should be evaluated objectively, with special care taken in how the new product should be marketed. Hospitality products, like any other product, must be carefully packaged so that they appeal to the consumer's senses and add to the experience. Any development project is affected by the critical factors of time, cost and quality, and hospitality projects are no exception. There may even be greater complexity if the unit is required to continue trading while the project is completed. In recent years, projects have increasingly be assessed by the return on investment, and it is the task of the hospitality design team to develop new schemes that may achieve this aim

As Rutes et al. (1985) remark:

> Perhaps the most basic difficulty for the neophyte hotel designer is learning that hotel operation must earn a profit out of its building... In a hotel you are both leasing to the public every night and catering to their every need. Therefore, rather than a monument or mere rental space, a hotel must provide a total living environment, with all the needed multicomplex functions and activities.

It is likely that this complex format will be further challenged in the immediate future by the separation of ownership and operations, environmental considerations and the greater need for the product to be flexible to adapt to the changing aspirations of the consumer.

References

Oxford University Press (1971) *The Compact Edition of Oxford English Dictionary*, Book Club Associates, OUP, Oxford, p. 698.

The Oxford Paperback Dictionary (1988), Hawkins, J.M. (compiler), Oxford University Press, Oxford, p. 218.

Rutes W.A., Penner, R.H. and Adams L. (2001) *Hotel Design, Planning, and Development*, W.W. Norton, New York.

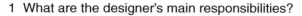

Review questions

1 What are the designer's main responsibilities?

2 Explain how sensory responses affect design.

3 Outline some of the factors which will affect future design trends.

PART 2

Planning

C H A P T E R   4

Development strategy

Paul Slattery

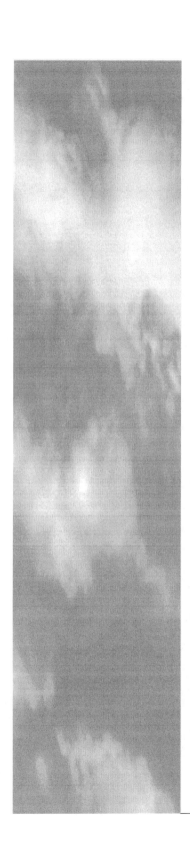

This chapter offers an explanation as to how hotel chains have grown and developed, especially in the last decade, and offers some projections from Otus on the European hotel industry in 2011. The development process in hotel chains is explored and some conclusions offered for the future.

The structure is in five sections as follows:

- Conceptual background

- Context

- The evolving structure of the hotel industry
  - Global overview
  - Economic structures
  - The structure of the hotel industry in Europe
  - Demand growth and share of new hotel rooms
  - Capital availability and hotel migration
  - The European hotel industry 2011

- The development process in hotel chains

- Conclusion.

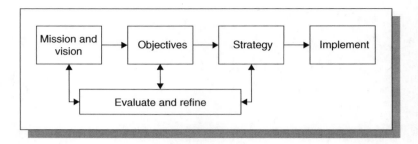

Figure 4.1
The planning process

Conceptual background

This first section reviews some of the underpinning concepts of planning and of development strategy. Every business plans for the future and hospitality organizations are no exception. If firms plan carefully and objectively, they can, at least to some extent, prepare for the possible impacts of key factors such as changes to target markets, sales, volumes and trends. Armitstead (2000) suggests that the planning process starts with articulating a mission and vision, before setting objectives, developing and implementing a strategy, as shown in Figure 4.1.

As seen in Figure 4.1, planning is often seen as a linear, but flexible process, in which mission, vision and strategy are regularly refined and re-evaluated according to unexpected changes in circumstances. Similarly, a good brand development strategy will consider internal and external factors including:

Internal

- Objectives of organization and its shareholders and stakeholders
- Current brands, products or services supplied by the organization
- Internal strengths and weaknesses
- Pricing policy and price sensitivity of market

External

- Competitive brands and their strategies
- Strategies for competitive advantage
- Customer base and characteristics
- External influences and trends, including political, environmental, economic or legislative.

Most chain hotel providers brand their products in order to distinguish them from others and to communicate and market the product

Illustration 4.1
Rezidor brand portfolio
(Courtesy of Rezidor Hotels &
Resorts).

to a selected target market. Armitstead (2000) points out that the benefits of branding are in attracting funding and drawing potential employees, as well as creating barriers to competition and making marketing easier.

Context

The conventional wisdom about hotel development is grounded in single venues. The process is designed to reduce risk for capital providers by giving assurance that once developed the venue will be able to attract sufficient demand with a cost structure that will produce the target returns.

At the time of writing this analysis (February 2003) the performance of hotels, particularly in major cities is as weak as it has been since the early 1990s when similar twin depressants prevailed – the first Gulf War and economic recession in multiple countries. Thereafter, hotel chains in the USA grew room stock by 50% adding almost one million rooms. During the same period in the UK, hotel chains grew by almost 60%. It is opportune, in the midst of the current market downturn, to consider the medium- to long-term

Country region	Total rooms (m)	Chain rooms (m)	Concentration (%)	Citizens per room	Citizens per chain room
USA	4.27	2.98	70	67	95
European Union	3.67	0.96	26	102	393
10 New EU states	0.39	0.06	15	187	1213
Rest of Europe	0.65	0.06	9	350	4030
Rest of world	6.02	0.60	10	887	8900
Total	15.00	4.65	31	400	1290

Source: Otus & Co., IHRII and WTO

Table 4.1
The structure of the global hotel industry 2002

prospects for the hotel industry in Europe and also to consider how far the development process is keeping up with the progress.

The evolving structure of the hotel industry

Global overview

The only barely credible estimate of the total hotel room stock in the world is provided by the World Tourism Organization 1, which estimates 15 million rooms. Otus & Co. calculate that 4.7 million rooms are affiliated to hotel chains in an uneven pattern as shown in Table 4.1.

Economic structures

The global imbalance in the structure of the hotel industry is a function of the imbalance in the structure of economies. Otus classifies economies into five types: experience, market service, citizenship service, industrial and subsistence. The classification is based on a range of measures including GDP (gross domestic product) per citizen from agriculture, GDP per citizen from industry and GDP per citizen from services; the percentage of GDP from agriculture, the percentage of GDP from manufacturing, and the percentage of GDP from services; the percentage of male employment in agriculture, manufacturing and services; the percentage of female employment in agriculture, manufacturing and services. The structures of the European economies at the end of 2001 are shown in Table 4.2.

In 2003, there are only three experience economies in the world: USA, Canada and UK, which rate highest in each of these measures while subsistence economies rate lowest.

In subsistence economies, the bulk of economic activity is in agricultural and extractive industries and only a minute proportion

	Experience economies	Market service economies	Citizenship service economies	Industrial economies	Subsistence economies
GDP/citizen agriculture ($)	586	582	512	362	185
GDP/citizen industry ($)	8 232	8 583	7 579	1 185	134
GD/citizen services ($)	19 587	19 894	10 788	1 832	214
Services as % of GDP/ citizen	69.0	68.5	57.1	54.2	40.2
% GDP agriculture	2	2	3	10	35
% GDP industry	29	30	40	37	25
% GDP services	69	68	57	53	40
% of GDP in services	69.0	68.0	57.0	53.0	40.0
% Males in agriculture	4	8	8	25	49
% Males in industry	31	36	37	30	23
% Males in services	56	56	48	40	27
% of male employment in services	61.5	56.0	51.6	42.1	27.3
% Females in agriculture	1	3	5	24	47
% Females in industry	12	19	16	18	16
% Females in services	80	75	69	51	35
% of female employment in services	86.0	77.3	76.7	54.8	35.7
European economies	UK	Denmark France Netherlands Norway Sweden Switzerland	Austria Belgium Finland Germany Ireland Italy Luxembourg Spain	Belarus Bulgaria Croatia Cyprus Czech Republic Estonia Greece Hungary Latvia Lithuania Macedonia Malta Poland Portugal Romania Russia Slovakia Slovenia	Albania Armenia Bosnia Georgia Moldova

Source: United Nations National Accounts

Table 4.2
European economic structures 2001

of the indigenous population are a market for hotels. This is the reason why the small hotel industry in developing countries relies on foreign visitors for its demand. In the industrial economies, consumer spending is higher than in subsistence economies and it is concentrated on consumer durables, which with other basic manufactured goods form key elements of the economic output. Leisure activities in industrial economies are more heavily focused in the home and consumer spending on hotels is relatively limited. Factory production, in which higher productivity is achieved through larger size and fewer workers, generates limited demand for hotels and that comes mainly from sales and marketing executives. When industrial economies reach a high degree of efficiency, the GDP is produced by fewer citizens and manufacturing is progressively transferred to lower cost economies. The emerging economic problems include rising unemployment and a workforce trained in redundant skills. In mature industrial economies a material proportion of the citizens own a range of white goods and brown goods, furnishings, apparel, cars and houses that were acquired during the phase of industrial expansion when the availability of consumer credit also grew. The availability of credit makes the replacement of goods relatively automatic, but a factor in the slowing growth of mature industrial economies is the diminishing marginal returns from the ownership of consumer goods. Once they have been acquired the rate of growth in demand declines to the level of replacement of redundant items.

The solution to the declining contribution of manufacturing to GDP, the rising unemployment and the redundant skills is found in the emergence and growth of the service sector. In the first instance, citizenship services, which are controlled predominantly by the state, expand. Services such as health grows from curative to preventative health, tertiary education expands and social services develop into areas such as senior citizen communities. On their own the growth of citizenship services is insufficient to reduce unemployment and simultaneously to grow GDP. They also provide little more business demand for hotels than the manufacturing industry. At this same stage of economic development market services are typically small, fragmented, but growing businesses.

It is only when an economy develops larger and more concentrated market services that it is able to reduce unemployment materially and to grow GDP, because the limits to the growth potential of market services are not yet known. Ownership of consumer goods such as cars produces gratification each time they are used. In contrast, when a market service such as a holiday, a hotel stay or a meal in a restaurant has been experienced all that remains to provide gratification is the memory. The only way to experience further gratification is to buy again. This inherent growth is reinforced by the conspicuous feature of service consumption and in the case of hospitality, travel and transport the association of consumption with enjoyment. Thus, the growth potential in market services is determined more by factors such as lifestyle and time availability than by diminishing marginal returns.

As the market service economy develops so do the critical relationships at work, which change from the worker/machine relations of the manufacturing and extractive industries to worker/worker and worker/customer relationships in service industries. Work becomes more mental than manual, more social and cleaner. Gender equality becomes the norm and the number of dual career families increases. The distinction between work and leisure becomes less dichotomized and leisure activities outside of the home become a prime growth market. The number of meals eaten outside of the home, the number and frequency of holidays taken, the frequency of visits to gaming venues, sports venues, cinemas and theatres all begin a stepped growth in the market service economy and produce changes in lifestyle.

Service firms are also different from manufacturing firms. They are far more diverse in their functions and they are far more geographically dispersed. As a result they provide the highest level of business travellers to hotels drawn from across the full range of executive functions.

The most developed stage of an economy is the experience economy in which market services become the prime contributor to GDP and to employment. Market service firms in industries such as financial services, communications and media grow to become among the largest and most consolidated in an economy. The hotel industry in experience economies is not only more concentrated, but also larger due to the higher frequency of both business and leisure demand. The industry has national representation throughout all market levels and all configurations of hotel facilities. It is not only the hotel industry that grows, but also all of hospitality, travel and transport, which collectively become a significant contributor to GDP. Spending on hospitality moves from being a periodic luxury to being a central feature of life style and standard of living. Apartments in New York and London with minimum or occasionally no kitchen facilities are in demand, since the occupants eat most of their meals in restaurants. Such a practice would be inconceivable at any other stage of economic development.

The structure of the hotel industry in Europe

The pattern of concentration in the hotel industry reflects the structure of the economies. Experience economies have the highest hotel concentration, while subsistence economies have the lowest. The contrast in the structure of the hotel industry in the economies in Europe can be seen in Table 4.3.

The UK scores higher in the structural measures than any other European economy, it is an experience economy and at 52% has the highest level of hotel concentration in the region. Denmark, France, Netherlands and Sweden come closest in structure to the UK economy. They are market service economies and collectively

Country	Year end (2002)			
	Total rooms	Chain rooms	Unaffil. rooms	Chain share %
Experience				
United Kingdom	379 890	196 320	183 570	52
Experience	379 890	196 320	183 570	52
Market services				
Denmark	39 350	10 950	28 400	28
France	592 330	214 380	377 960	36
Netherlands	77 070	22 300	54 770	29
Sweden	95 920	27 850	68 070	29
Market services	804 670	275 480	529 200	34
Citizenship service				
Austria	91 350	14 980	76 370	16
Belgium	61 330	16 360	44 960	27
Finland	54 600	21 320	33 280	39
Germany	609 000	145 360	463 640	24
Ireland	50 550	11 850	38 700	23
Italy	707 000	43 540	663 460	6
Luxemburg	7550	1720	5830	23
Spain	597 320	197 600	399 720	33
Citizenship service	2 178 700	452 730	1 725 960	21
Industrial				
Greece	204 000	15 030	188 970	7
Portugal	97 310	15 770	81 540	16
European industrial	301 310	30 800	270 510	10
Total EU	3 664 570	955 330	2 709 240	26
10 New member states	389 860	59 840	330 020	15
Rest of Europe	645 130	56 230	588 900	9
European total	4 699 560	1 071 400	3 628 160	23

Sources: WTO, IHRII, Otus & Co.

Table 4.3
European hotel supply 2002

have 34% hotel concentration. The economies of Austria, Belgium, Finland, Germany, Ireland, Italy, Luxemburg and Spain score lower on the structural measures. They are citizenship service economies and collectively have 21% hotel concentration. Greece and Portugal have the lowest structural scores in the European Union, are industrial economies and have only 10% hotel concentration. The proposed 10% new EU member states are mainly from Eastern Europe, are industrial economies, have a smaller hotel industry and a concentration of 15%. The other non-EU states, with the exceptions of Norway and Switzerland, which are market service economies, are industrial and subsistence economies

Illustration 4.2
Growing hospitality recognition

with the smallest hotel industry in Europe. The concentration of the non-EU states is only 9%.

The very low levels of hotel concentration in Greece and Italy is the result of the lack of interest by most chains in the seasonal beach holiday markets that dominate these countries and the low levels of domestic business demand for hotels. These economies are also characterized by a low ratio of citizens to total hotel rooms due to the preponderance of small, part-time, quasi-domestic and seasonal hotels that also are a feature of these countries.

The history of the pan-Atlantic hotel industry over the past 30 years has been dominated by the emergence and growth of hotel chains, yet the chains still have a long way to go to develop a national presence across all of the European countries. It has been easier for them to grow in their home country and only multi-brand chains such as Accor, Hilton, Marriott International and Six Continents have developed a mass presence in more than one country.

In Europe there are 370 hotel brands accounting for 1.1 million hotel rooms. Only one brand, Accor's Ibis has more than 50 000 rooms, giving it a little more than 1% market share, while there are 180 brands that together share less than 2% of the rooms and have an average of only 460 rooms per brand. There are too many brands with too few rooms so that most hotel brands in Europe are too small to develop an effective brand infrastructure. Only the largest multi-brand chains have the size to make a loyalty programme effective. The marketing and sales structure, the investment in distribution IT and yield management systems are limited by the cash flow generated by the hotels and media spend is out of the question for most of the brands. Consequently, the cost to the smaller brands to capture demand is too high and the returns generated are invariably too low to excite the capital markets.

The position is no better when it comes to brand length. There are only 17 brands with more than 100 hotels in Europe and none with more than 1000 hotels while there are 182 brands, each with less than 10 hotels. The short brands are unable to provide national or even regional coverage and are thus handicapped in their ability to compete in the wholesale markets. The problems for short chains are similar to those for unaffiliated hotels. The vicious circle is that, to compensate for the lack of brand infrastructure, unaffiliated hotels and those in short chains are too frequently over-specified for the market level at which they compete. The resulting higher investment invariably makes the target returns even harder to achieve.

Demand growth and share of new hotel rooms

The continental European economies are at a crucial stage because their structural developments are likely to shift the classifications of several of the economies over the next decade or so. The precise timing of such shifts cannot be pinpointed precisely, but Otus projects that the structural developments in the economies will produce a stepped growth in hotel demand across Europe by the end of 2011 and that this will be accompanied by a marked growth in hotel concentration.

Over the next decade it is expected that at least some of the market service economies in the EU: Denmark, France, Netherlands and Sweden will progress to become full-blown experience economies. This will boost their domestic growth in hotel demand and in hotel concentration. The view is that the citizenship service economies – Austria, Belgium, Finland, Germany, Ireland, Italy, Luxemburg and Spain – will progress and several will become market service economies. Further, the secular change in hotel demand in these countries over the medium to long term will be accompanied by significant growth in the size and concentration of their hotel industries. The anticipation is that the Greek and Portuguese economies will also develop, but that the reliance on foreign holidaymakers will remain paramount and they will continue to have relatively low levels of hotel concentration. The 10 states due to join the EU in 2004 will probably produce accelerating economic growth as a result over the period and their hotel industry will grow and concentrate from their currently low levels. The progress in the remaining industrial and subsistence economies will be positive, but the hotel industry will remain small and concentration will remain relatively low.

In parallel to the structural analysis of demand growth in the European economies, the World Travel and Tourism Council 2, which provides the most comprehensive and systematic medium- to long-term forecasts for world tourism growth, projects that by

2012 business travel in the EU will grow by 96% and leisure travel by 93% from current levels.

The first two issues about the medium- to long-term projection of hotel supply in Europe are how many new rooms will be developed and how many of the new rooms will be affiliated to chains. If the demand growth inherent in the structural developments in the European economies and in the WTTC projections is achieved then within the next 10 years around 675 000 new hotel rooms, a compound average growth rate (CAGR) of 1.5%, will need to be added to stock if there is to be any hope of supply keeping up with demand. Of this total Otus anticipates that more than 500 000 will be added in the current member states of the EU.

In the USA there is an anticipated slower rate of growth adding circa 475 000 new rooms, a CAGR of 1.2% over the period, even though it is already an experience economy and has already achieved much of the domestic growth in demand and in hotel concentration. The Otus estimate assumes that the USA will continue to bulldoze obsolete hotels and that in the medium to long term the main growth in demand in the USA hotel market will be derived from foreign visitors. The UK is closer to the USA in terms of its economic structure than it is currently to the continental economies; however, Otus project a CAGR in room supply of less than 1% due to the reluctance to demolish obsolete hotels. This reluctance is not only a significant factor in the slower growth in new room stock, but also a drag on the rate of further growth in hotel concentration, since most obsolete hotels are unaffiliated and of little or no interest to the chains.

The second issue in the medium- to long-term projection of hotel supply in Europe relates to the share of new rooms that will be affiliated to hotel chains. The two main drivers of the expansion of hotel brands across the whole market spectrum are demand and capital access. Fortunately, the industry is at a stage when the medium- to long-term growth of both is accelerating.

Illustration 4.3
Express by Holiday Inn
(Courtesy of Intercontinental
Hotels plc)

Holiday Inn Express, the mid-market limited feature brand, was introduced in 1993 and has developed 1300 hotels, that is, one hotel opened every 3 days for 10 years. All but around 100 of these hotels are in North America. The explanation has little to do with the paucity of demand for the brand in other parts of the world, but it has a lot to do with the availability of capital in North America for hotel investment and the ease with which franchisees and other hotel owners have access to it.

Travel Inn, an economy lodging brand in the UK, developed at a rate of a hotel every 10 days for several years during the 1990s. Whitbread, which owns the brand, funded most of the hotels while no more than a handful of the hotels are franchised and none are held on management contracts. Unlike the situation in North America the capital markets in the UK and the continent insufficiently understand and are insufficiently committed to the hotel business to provide more capital and Whitbread with its own resources has been unable to keep up its earlier pace of development of the brand.

For the past decade in the USA and UK circa 95% of capital invested in new rooms has been in hotels affiliated to chains. Currently in continental Europe no more than 45% of the capital invested in new hotel rooms per year finds its way to affiliated hotels and this has inflicted a higher risk on the capital provision to hotels in this region compared with the USA and the UK. As a result continental Europe has too many small new hotels built in the wrong places with idiosyncratic facilities owned and managed by amateurs.

The first initiative in the effort to solve this problem is for capital providers to reduce the investment in new unaffiliated hotel rooms. This is the single most important development that is necessary to improve the structure and performance of the hotel industry and to reduce the risk attached to hotel capital.

The time it will take for continental Europe to reach the current situation in the USA and the UK depends on the commitment of lenders and other capital providers to make the change, but the decision-making structure in continental banks is a constraint on the speed with which the change can be made. Our current working assumption is that, within 10 years, 67% of capital provided for new hotel rooms will be chain affiliated, up from 45% at present. On this basis circa 450 000 of the new rooms will be affiliated to chains over the period and that circa 220 000 new unaffiliated rooms also will have found capital. This implies only a 6% growth in unaffiliated rooms compared to a projected 40% growth in chain rooms.

Capital availability and hotel migration

The next issues in estimating the medium- to long-term growth in the European hotel industry are how much capital will be provided to acquire existing unaffiliated hotels and how much capital will be provided for independent hoteliers to acquire single hotel assets from hotel chains. In Europe, at an average development cost of circa €100 000 per room, the total capital needed for the projected new rooms over the next 10 years will be in the region of €70 billion. The provision of this capital is not assured. However, the most efficient way to meet the demand growth is through hotel chains rather than unaffiliated hotels and this is also the lowest risk basis on which the capital can be provided. On our estimates the 220 000 new unaffiliated rooms will require capital of around €20 billion. Although this is a significant reduction in the rate of growth it is still a material amount of capital and Otus expects more than 85% of it to be concentrated on the citizenship service, industrial and subsistence economies where unaffiliated rooms will grow by 7% over the period. Otus anticipates that the experience and market service economies will be quicker to reduce the capital available to build new unaffiliated hotels and Otus projects that such capital will grow by only 4% over the period amounting to around €3 billion. The lower the capital invested in unaffiliated hotels the better the performance of the industry and the higher the returns to capital providers.

The question of the capital available for unaffiliated hoteliers to acquire single hotel assets, either from other unaffiliated hoteliers or to buy redundant hotels from chains is problematic. Bankers in Europe have sustained the unaffiliated segment by providing capital for such acquisitions. The UK experience is notable. Most of the hotels that change hands are old, with fewer than 50 rooms, are mid-market or lower, full feature or basic hotels in tertiary or quaternary locations. Many in country and coastal resorts have heavily seasonal demand while those in other areas face strong competition from the chains. By definition, these hotels have no brand infrastructure, invariably they are owned and managed by amateurs and they experience the highest levels of bankruptcy and liquidation in the industry by far. The more this practice continues the longer the hotel industry will be under-demolished and the higher the risk attached to hotel debt. The problem will be resolved only by cutting-off of capital. The solution is in the hands of the banks.

The second issue in estimating the changes over the period is the extent to which there will be a migration from existing unaffiliated hotels to chains. The limits on this process include the low propensity of unaffiliated hotel owners to award management contracts or franchises on their hotels to hotel chains and the low rate of single hotel acquisitions by the chains. It is anticipated there will be a relaxation in the current entrenched positions on these issues and it has been estimated that these processes will migrate almost 100 000 rooms, less than 3% of the current unaffiliated stock, to the chains over the period.

The European hotel industry 2011

Otus's net projections Europe-wide are that hotel chains, through growing share of new build rooms and, migration of existing rooms from unaffiliated to chains and after accounting for the disposal of redundant hotels to the unaffiliated market, will grow room stock by 50% to 1.62 million and that unaffiliated rooms will grow by 4% to 3.76 million rooms. The outcome of the projected developments is that by 2011 hotel concentration in the region will grow from 23% to 30%.

In the current EU countries Otus expects the processes to grow chain room stock by 44% to 1.38 million while in the rest of Europe there is an anticipation of hotel chain exposure doubling to 240 000 rooms as Table 4.4 records.

For the longer-term Otus projects a doubling of global room stock by 2030 to 30 million rooms, a compound annual growth of 2.5%, not enough to keep pace with the long-term projections for growth in world travel demand. By that date it is projected that, of the 30 million rooms, 15 million will be affiliated, which entails that over this period the total number of unaffiliated rooms will grow by nearly half while the number of rooms affiliated to hotel brands will grow more than three times. Consistent with this trend the forecast is that within ten years the first hotel chains with one million rooms will emerge.

The development process in hotel chains

From the perspective of hotel development the first difference between chains and unaffiliated hotels is in the starting point. There is no standard starting point, but for unaffiliated hotels the development process typically starts with a site, which means that the city, the country and the economy in which the venue is located is determined. The formation of the concept stage of development then seeks to establish the most effective market level, hotel configuration, room configuration and size for the proposed hotel.

In contrast, hotel brands start with concept formation typically by identifying the market level and the configuration of facilities for the brand. The chain's approach to hotel configuration has been to improve the financial structures of hotels mainly by increasing the proportion of turnover derived from rooms, which in turn produces higher margins and higher returns. In upmarket hotels such as those in the Hilton, Intercontinental and Sheraton brands this has been achieved by locating hotels in the larger cities and increasing the number of rooms per hotel. At the mid-market level this has been achieved through the creation of limited feature brands such as Holiday Inn Express and Courtyard by Marriott. At the economy lodging and budget levels the improvements have been achieved by developing brands such as Travelodge and Formula 1 as room-only hotel brands.

Country	Year end			
	Total rooms 2011	Chain rooms 2011	Unaffil. rooms 2011	Chain share % 2002
Experience				
United Kingdom	408 100	223 150	184 980	55
Experience	408 100	223 150	184 980	55
Market services				
Denmark	45 000	15 330	29 660	34
France	677 250	280 360	396 910	41
Netherlands	88 120	30 890	57 240	35
Sweden	109 680	38 530	71 140	35
Market services	920 050	365 110	554 950	40
Citizenship service				
Austria	104 450	23 380	81 070	22
Belgium	70 120	22 000	48 110	31
Finland	59 720	24 600	35 120	41
Germany	696 320	201 370	494 960	29
Italy	775 530	87 610	687 920	11
Ireland	55 780	15 200	40 580	27
Luxemburg	7 900	1 950	5 960	25
Spain	713 850	272 440	441 410	38
Citizenship service	2 483 670	648 550	1 835 130	26
Industrial				
Greece	246 150	39 700	206 450	16
Portugal	116 290	27 010	89 290	23
European industrial	362 440	66 710	295 740	18
EU	4 174 260	1 303 520	2 870 800	31
10 New states	453 960	97 710	356 250	22
Rest of Europe	745 350	120 240	625 100	16
Europe total	5 373 570	1 521 470	3 852 150	28
EU room migration		74 000	−74 000	
New States room migration		8 520	−8 520	
Rest of Europe room migration		13 920	−13 920	
Net total European rooms	5 373 570	1 617 910	3 755 710	30

Sources: WTO, IHRII, Otus & Co.

Table 4.4
European hotel supply 2011

Investment in non-room facilities in full feature hotels has been reduced progressively by limiting the number of restaurants and simplifying the logistics of restaurants. The main impact has been the reduction of non-resident demand for such hotel restaurants and the reduction in restaurant usage by hotel customers at lunch and dinner. The exception has been in the conference market, which is a captive meal market for full feature hotels and is logistically easier for the hotel to manage, since delegates invariably arrive to eat at the same time and have a set menu. The resultant higher percentage of hotel turnover derived from rooms has produced higher hotel EBITDA (Earnings Before Interest, Taxes, Depreciation and Amortization) margins and higher returns.

The innovations with most impact in the configuration of hotels have not come from the development of single hotels, but from the conception of hotel brands. Brands are conceived to meet the twin goals of attracting both demand and capital and thus to grow the length of the brand. The longer the hotel brand the more the corporate infrastructure is designed to capture demand for the portfolio rather than for individual hotels. The longer brands deal in wholesale markets, which are beyond the reach of unaffiliated hotels. In contrast, the conventional wisdom about hotel development has assumed demand capture to be more reliant on the inherent features of the hotel. The recent fashion for boutique hotels is the most notable example. Invariably, they are small hotels trading at the deluxe and upmarket levels in major and primary cities, with a high investment cost to create their style and no brand infrastructure.

When hotel brand specifications are established a rollout programme is planned within which hotel size is a function of location. For hotel brands a higher priority is attached to the rollout programme than to fretting over the unique facilities or design that might be developed on any given site. The countries, economies and cities that are target markets for the brand are then identified and the rollout programme progresses by finding sites and capital. However, for any hotel brand the brand length potential is inversely related to market level. Deluxe brands need the fewest hotels and budget hotels need the most to generate brand power.

For the rollout of hotel brands the conventional wisdom on the development process is too slow and too expensive. Hotel chains are more than the sum of their venues and have the right to insist on economies of scale in the development process, which involves reducing the time and the cost required for development. In brands this is achieved in their approach to concept formation. The rollout simply adapts the brand specifications to the conditions of each site. The faster the rollout programme the more the economies in planning and construction.

An implication of the accelerating rollout of hotel brands is not only that hotels in any brand bear a family resemblance to each other, but also that the performance of hotels within a brand is not uniform. For instance, Post House Hotels, the mid-market full feature brand with 77 hotels in the UK, was sold to Six Continents in 2001 for £810 million. Twenty per cent of its rooms were in London, 23% in the primary provincial cities, 54% in the secondary and tertiary towns and cities, 3% in quaternary locations and the average size of a Post House was 158 rooms. The RevPAR range across the portfolio in 2000 was £62.63 to £16.55 and EBITDA per room ranged from £18 951 to £3 125. The value of each hotel was not uniform. On the basis of 8 × EBITDA (Earnings Before Interest, Taxes, Depreciation and Amortization) the hotels ranged in value from £155 000 per room to £25 000. Typically, the construction cost for a mid-market full feature hotel in the UK could be circa £60 000 per room, which indicates the potential gap attached to the value of existing hotels and the replacement cost of equivalent hotels. The diversity in performance and in values is not untypical in mid-market and upmarket chains.

Many brands, particularly those at deluxe, upmarket and mid-market levels grow by acquisition as well as new build. Holiday Inn, owned by Six Continents and the brand to which Post House Hotels were converted is an example. In a formal auction process for a hotel chain the limits on time and information available to potential buyers before their bids have to be submitted is controlled and in the case of hostile bids only publicly available data can be examined before the company is acquired.

The logic of hotel development practice is based on venues. When the focus is raised to the corporate level the development process has to be adapted. The conventional approach to development assumes little or no knowledge or understanding of the hotel market by the client, but as hotel brands have developed so the extent and the reliance on feasibility studies has reduced and the roll-out programme has routinized the rest of the development process. Banks and other institutions progressively are using independent feasibility studies as a validation of the decision to lend or invest in hotel projects. This process parallels the growth in the proportion of the capital available to chain hotels. The more that the development process delivers hotels and chains that produce returns on capital that meet the demands of investors as well as the demand of customers then the higher will be the level of concentration in the hotel industry. It is a critical step in the progress of the industry.

Conclusion

The strong prospects for the European hotel industry in the medium to long term will propel hotel concentration to more effective levels. This requires thinking about the industry to be elevated from the level of the hotels to the level of the brands and this in turn requires the hotel development process to adapt to the rhythm of the brand rather than to be constrained by the possibilities of individual venues. Of course, there are many other challenges for the chains, such as, the access to capital, the distribution of demand through the Internet and the development of corporate executives with an effective understanding of the hotel business. The growth prospects are the fundamental driver that demands solutions to the challenges and the prize is a more concentrated, more successful and more professional hotel industry.

References

Armitstead, M. (2000) Development strategy and brand management, in Ransley, J. and Ingram, H. (eds) *Developing Hospitality Properties and Facilities*, Chapter 2, pp. 22–36, Butterworth-Heinemann, Oxford.

World Tourism Organization (2001) *Compendium of Tourism Statistics*, Madrid.

World Travel and Tourism Council (2002) *Global Tourism Projections*, London.

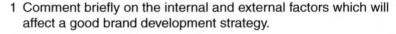

Review questions

1 Comment briefly on the internal and external factors which will affect a good brand development strategy.

2 Considering the headline projections for European hotel growth to 2011, what are the key implications for hotel development?

3 Outline ways in which European hotel chains might react to the strong projected growth by Otus and other consulting firms.

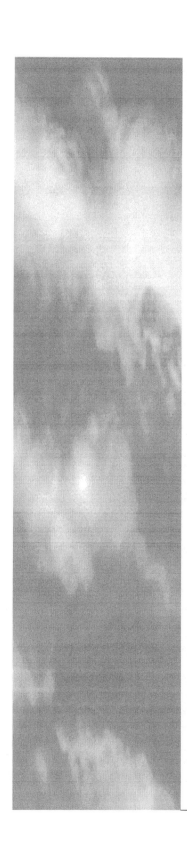

CHAPTER 5

Project finance

Jan deRoos

Project finance is the art and science of securing the funds necessary to develop, acquire, renovate, and recapitalize hospitality assets. In this chapter, the discussion will focus on the financing of individual projects, as distinct from corporate finance, which seeks to finance the activities of the firm as a whole. The chapter contains the following topics:

- Overview of project finance
- Capital markets' view of the hospitality industry and hospitality property
- Risk and returns in real estate
- Raising development funds
- Elements of permanent debt financing
- Recent innovations in debt financing
- Elements of equity financing
- Evaluating return on investment
- Project finance – stylized examples
- Refurbishment, defensive spending, and repositioning
- Conclusion.

Overview of project finance

There are two fundamental sources of capital for the hospitality industry: debt capital and equity capital. Debt capital comes from a variety of sources, but the business is dominated by the banking industry. The defining difference between debt and equity capital is the fact that debt capital does not represent a direct ownership interest, while equity capital is synonymous with ownership. Debt capital for project financing is almost universally originated as a mortgage. The use of the mortgage provides debt capital with an indirect claim on the ownership of the project should the equity owners fail to meet their obligations to pay their debt. In addition to private sector debt and equity capital, some projects make use of public sector funds in various ways, in exchange for meeting goals that are in the public interest. These public sector funds can be important and sizable portions of a project's capital structure.

In its broadest sense, project financing is used for four activities:

- *Project development*. The process of securing the funds required to create new venues or to redevelop existing ones. The lender in these cases, called the construction lender, often makes a commitment for a very short time frame, usually only for the time required for building and opening the improvements. The construction lender expects the owner to secure so-called permanent financing upon the completion of the development phase. In fact, many construction lenders will not commit to a project until the permanent lender has made a firm commitment to fund the project upon completion.

- *Acquisition financing*. The process of obtaining the funds required to acquire an existing building. In the case of the acquisition of a stable business, the owner will often secure a long-term commitment from a lender to facilitate the acquisition and provide permanent debt financing. In the case of the acquisition of a 'turn-around' story, the owner will attempt to secure both the funds needed to acquire the asset, as well as the funds needed to reconfigure, rehabilitate, or reposition the building. Again, the owner will seek a long-term commitment from the lender.

- *Refinancing*. Two motivations drive most refinancing decisions. The first is to replace existing financing arrangements with new arrangements of lower cost. The second is to 'harvest' unrealized gains for projects that have appreciated in value. Refinancing provides a way to get access to or monetize this value, as an alternative to selling the building.

- *Renovation and repositioning*. Hospitality assets require constant renovation and refurbishment; in addition, assets require a major renovation and/or repositioning from time to time to maintain their income producing ability. Owners seek financing to help fund the costs of these programmes.

Capital markets' view of the hospitality industry and hospitality property

Whether it is a restaurant, hotel, or other hospitality venue, the capital markets view hospitality projects as inherently more risky than other real estate investments. This risk is separated into two broad categories, business risk and development risk. Hospitality properties have significantly more business risk than other projects that seek mortgage financing. In addition to understanding the real estate risk of projects, lenders and investors must understand the business plan and have confidence in the ability of the management. Contrast a typical hotel to an apartment investment. In a typical full-service hotel, approximately 75% of the revenues support the operation, the costs of labour, food, materials and supplies, leaving 25% of the revenues to support capital. In the apartment, less than half of the revenues support the operation, leaving over 50% of the revenues to support capital. This business risk, known as high operating leverage, leaves hospitality assets exposed to market risks, management risks, and pricing risks. In addition, the fact that customers do not sign long-term contracts for the use of space means that management must constantly be developing new business and offering their products for sale on a daily basis.

The second source of risk is development risk, which incorporates a wide variety of factors such as the risk that a project is started and not completed, the risk that if completed that the project is significantly over budget, or the risk that the project will not be built according to approved plans and specifications. New entrants come into the business with good ideas and some capital, but little experience. Experienced firms expand their operations into new markets without completely understanding those markets. In a significant number of cases, many factors conspire to create a situation in which the project is abandoned or the project requires significant additional funds to be properly completed.

Given the discussion above, the capital markets have a 'love/hate' relationship with hospitality assets. Capital loves the industry because projects can produce returns that are significantly greater than the returns to other investments. Capital hates the industry because it is quite risky. In general, the capital markets attempt to strike a balance in which the conditions of the commitments and rates charged compensate for the risks taken. All capital market participants impose conditions on the capital employed to minimize the perceived risks. The controls include limits on the amount of debt financing relative to value and relative to annual cash flow, required property insurance, required annual spending on renovations, assignment of cash flows to a third party for distribution to lenders and owners, strict limits on the ability to change brands or managers, and controlled disbursement of capital.

Risk and returns in real estate

Project sponsors look at the risk and returns to the underlying project and the risk and returns to their invested equity capital. This is best illustrated by an example. Consider a project in need of funds. The sponsor has worked hard to create a project that produces an overall return or yield of 12.0%; the sponsor is confident that the overall yield will not be less than 8.0%, and it is highly unlikely that the project yield will exceed 16.0%. The sponsor asks whether this return is acceptable or if a higher return is desirable. If the sponsor desires a higher yield, it is possible to use debt capital to increase or 'leverage' the equity yield. Assume the sponsor is successful at obtaining a loan equal to 50% of the required funds at an overall cost of 7.0%. As part of the loan terms, the sponsor is required to deliver a constant 7.0% yield to the lender and absorb the fluctuations in cash flows. As a result, the lender obtains a 7.0% yield with (almost) 100% certainty. The sponsor now can receive a 17.0% yield on his 50% equity investment. This is the benefit of financial leverage. However, the sponsor obtains this 17.0% yield with a confidence interval of $\pm 8.0\%$ rather than the $\pm 4.0\%$ confidence interval on the overall project. Thus, adding debt capital has the potential to increase returns, but it also adds to the risk remaining with the sponsor's equity capital. Investors need to manage this trade-off carefully when determining the optimal capital structure for projects.

Raising development funds

There are three general structures used to secure development financing:

1 Property investors seeking stable returns work with developers willing to take development and start-up risk. In this case, the developer obtains a commitment from the investor to purchase the building upon completion, called a 'take-out' commitment, typically in the form of a permanent loan plus equity. Once the developer has secured the 'take-out' commitment, he is then able to secure a construction loan from a lender to help carry the project from inception through completion. While it is not easy to obtain a construction loan once the 'take-out' is in place, it is nearly impossible to secure a construction loan without the 'take-out'. While the developer would like the construction loan to equal the costs of development, it is rare for construction loans to exceed 75% of project costs.

2 Many property owners develop their own projects with the intent to hold them for an extended period. In this case, debt financing consists of two loans, the permanent loan and the construction loan. The owner first obtains a permanent loan commitment, much like the 'take-out' commitment outlined

above. The owner then shops for a construction loan, using the commitment for the permanent loan as evidence that the capital market believes in the project; the permanent loan commitment significantly reduces risk for the construction lender.

3 Owner/developers having a short-term holding period obtain a construction loan to carry the project from inception through completion. The owner combines the construction loan with a commitment from the construction lender to carry the project for a short period after opening, typically one to four years. Note that the construction lender is taking both development and operating risk in this case. This type of loan is called a 'mini-perm', taking the name from the fact that the operating loan carries a short time commitment. Once the project has reached stabilization, the owner goes back to the capital markets to secure long-term permanent financing or the owner will seek to sell the project or a portion thereof.

As can be seen, the process of securing development financing is complicated. The reason for the 'take-out' plus construction loan or the separate construction and permanent loans is that the risks of development are very different from the risks of operating the building. Lenders willing to take operating risk are generally unwilling to take development risk and vice versa. Construction loans are relatively expensive, because development risk is a significant problem for developers. In general, interest rates on construction loans are 1.0% to 3.0% higher than rates on permanent loans.

Elements of permanent debt financing

While many types of permanent loans are used throughout the world, there are enough similarities to provide a framework for understanding how the system works. The process and requirements outlined below are based on the acquisition of a property, but a similar process and requirements are used for all long-term, permanent financing of new developments and for refinancing. Fundamental to the process is the concept of a mortgage, in which the building and its contents are pledged as collateral for the loan, called a security interest. The essence of this pledge is that the lender obtains the right to sell the property to satisfy the loan if the borrower fails to meet the obligations of the mortgage.

The process starts with the borrower approaching a lender, seeking a loan. The borrower prepares a loan application package, which is reviewed by the lender. If the lender would like to proceed, the lender prepares a 'deal-sheet', containing a summary of the major terms of the proposed loan. A typical 'deal-sheet' would have the following items:

- *Loan term*. The number of years the borrower has to use the lender's funds. The first thing to keep in mind is that a permanent loan is not permanent. Loan terms range from 5 to 15 years, with a 10-year term being by far the most common. This does not mean that the loan is fully paid in 10 years, but it does mean that the lender requires any remaining mortgage balance outstanding at the end of the term to be repaid.

- *Loan amount.* The size of the loan. Typically based on two important underwriting criteria, the Loan-to-Value ratio (LTV) and the Debt-Coverage ratio (DCR). In the case of the LTV ratio, the loan is sized as a percentage of the appraised value of the property. For example, if the lender imposes a maximum LTV ratio of 60%, the maximum loan size is €6 000 000 for a property appraised at €10 000 000. In the case of the DCR, the loan is sized as a function of the net operating income (NOI) expected from the property. For example, if the lender imposes a DCR of 2.0, this means that there must be €2.00 of NOI for each €1.00 of annual debt service. If a property expects €1 000 000 in NOI, the lender will allow €500 000 to be used as the annual debt service, resulting in a loan of approximately €5 825 000, given a 7% interest rate and 25-year amortization of the loan.

- *Amortization* (or depreciation). The number of years used to calculate the annual debt service. Most loans use an amortization term of between 15 and 25 years.

- *Interest rate.* There are two types of interest rates, fixed rates and floating rates. Fixed interest rates are just that, they are fixed for the loan term. Floating interest rates adjust monthly, based on an increment or 'spread' over some benchmark rate. The benchmark rate most typically used is 30-day LIBOR (the London Interbank Offer Rate). If a floating rate is used, the borrower and lender may agree to a cap and a floor on the rate to be used; the cap is the maximum interest rate charged, the floor is the minimum interest rate charged.

- *Loan fees or points.* Quoted as a percentage value. Most lenders charge a fee of between 0.5% and 3.0% of the loan amount to originate a loan on a property. This is in addition to the loan application fee.

- *Prepayment.* The ability of the borrower to pay the remaining mortgage balance prior to the end of the term. This is often severely restricted, limiting the borrower's flexibility. It is common for a loan with a 10-year term to have an absolute ban on prepayment for the first 3 years, and then a requirement that the borrower pay a penalty to prepay for the remaining 7 years.

- *Assumption.* The ability for a new owner of the building to assume or take over the loan upon sale of the building. Lenders rarely allow a loan to be assumed.

- *Secondary financing.* The power of the borrower to place an additional loan on the property. A highly negotiated item, borrowers desire the ability to borrow additional funds for a variety of reasons, lenders are reluctant to add additional debt to a project, undermining their security interest. At a minimum, lenders will be very clear about who gets paid first, second, third, etc. in case of a borrower default. The general term for the highest priority claim is the first mortgage.

The borrower evaluates the loan terms and makes a decision to proceed with the loan or not. If the borrower elects to continue, loan terms are finalized, the lender then performs a variety of due diligence activities. These include a review of ownership and title to the property, a physical inspection, a review of the major contracts, a market study and appraisal, and a review of agreements that might affect the loan. Once these activities are completed a closing date is set and the loan is funded.

At the time of writing this chapter, interest rates for hospitality projects are at historical lows over the past 30 years; a 65% LTV first mortgage on an established 3 to 4-star hotel in a large urban setting would be in the range of 6.0–7.0%. Companies that regularly track the cost of debt and equity capital are HVS International and Jones Lang LaSalle Hotels.

Recent innovations in debt financing

Readers should be aware of two innovations that have significantly influenced the debt markets in the past decade. The first is the so-called mezzanine debt market. Due to significant loan losses during the 1980s and 1990s, first mortgages have become smaller. It was common for a borrower to obtain a first mortgage loan with an 80% LTV or even 85%. Today, it is quite rare for the first mortgage to exceed 70% of value, in most cases it is sized to be between 50 and 60% of value. A direct result of this practice is that equity requirements have increased; remember that equity must provide the funds not supplied by debt capital. Certain lenders have entered the debt market, providing incremental debt that brings total debt financing from (say) 60% of value to 80% of value. This additional debt is called a 'mezzanine loan'. It is usually much more costly than the first mortgage, but less costly than equity capital.

Consider the following example, using the logic from the earlier section on returns and risk. A property producing a 10% overall return can obtain a 60% LTV first mortgage that costs 7% per year. This means that equity must fund the remaining 40% of value, and equity will obtain a 14.5% return. Now consider an alternative. The property still qualifies for a 60% LTV first mortgage that costs 7% per year. A mezzanine loan of 20% is available at a cost of 12% per year. This means that equity must fund the remaining 20% of value, and equity will obtain a 17% return. Thus, mezzanine debt serves to reduce the equity requirements as well as increase the overall return to equity, if properly structured.

Equity must determine if the increase in return (from 14.5% to 17%) is adequate compensation for the increase in risk.

The second innovation is the commercial mortgage-backed securities (CMBS) market. As the name implies, securities (bonds) backed by mortgages on commercial property have been created. Investment banks aggregate a set of mortgage loans into a portfolio, and the bank creates a set of bonds that receive the cash flows derived from the mortgage portfolio. Using financial engineering techniques, a wide variety of bonds can be created from a portfolio of similar mortgages. For example, a set of mortgages with a uniform 10-year maturity can be transformed into one set of bonds with a 3-year maturity, another with a 5-year maturity, and yet a third with a 10-year maturity. In addition, certain of the bonds can be isolated from the risk of mortgage defaults, making them much less risky than the portfolio as a whole. CMBS broadens the potential appeal of mortgages as an investment; CMBS bond investors can now choose between a variety of maturities and risks rather than hold the relatively uniform risk of commercial mortgages. The CMBS market removes the mortgages from the balance sheet of lenders and replaces them with bonds in the hands of investors, allowing the lenders to originate additional loans.

The CMBS market has two important implications for borrowers. First, the CMBS market is made more efficient by reliance on uniform underwriting standards, thus borrowers will see more uniform requirements from lenders in the future. Second, the CMBS market imposes significant restrictions and penalties on borrowers who wish to prepay their loans before the end of the loan term. Borrowers are well advised to understand these restrictions prior to closing on a loan that will be securitized.

Elements of equity financing

Equity capital is generally the most difficult capital to raise and the most expensive. As outlined in the section on risk and return, equity capital is the residual claimant on a project; equity receives the left over cash flows after all other claims are paid. As a result, equity participants work hard to understand the precise nature of the risk and returns to their investment.

In seeking other equity capital for a project, the project sponsor is looking for a partner or partners. Potential partners, especially those who will invest more than half of the equity capital will impose significant requirements on the sponsor and in many cases will insist on control of the project. It is difficult to reconcile the viewpoint of the sponsor and the investors. The sponsor has spent months if not years assembling a project, whether it is an acquisition or a new development. The sponsor has a significant investment of both funds and time in the process. However, the mere fact that a sponsor is looking for an equity capital is an admission that the sponsor does not have sufficient funds to complete the project or an admission that the sponsor would like to share the risk of the project with others. In either case, potential equity participants understand that they are vital to the realization of the project and that they have significant negotiating power.

The most common sources of equity capital are:

- *Friends and family.* For many small projects and for most initial ventures, this source is the only source available.

- *Real estate funds.* Generally of two types, pension funds and life insurance companies provide long-term equity commitments to established, stable operations with low risk; opportunity funds provide short-term equity capital to risky ventures such as undercapitalized projects, assets in need of renovation or repositioning, or failed projects with good market potential under alternative management.

- *High net worth individuals.* Real estate, especially hospitality real estate can provide significant tax benefits to equity owners. Individuals in high tax brackets can benefit from investment in projects that generate these tax benefits. Investors should be wary and be sure to understand both the before-tax and after-tax returns to a project.

- *The public market.* Many times projects or interests in projects can be sold to property funds. The property share companies in the UK and the Netherlands and the REITs in the USA are examples of these investors.

- *Investment banks.* Banks have shown recent interest in becoming the equity owner of a project rather than simply lending funds. These transactions are typically structured as sale-leaseback agreements.

It is well beyond the scope of this text to detail the tax benefits of equity ownership, but students should be aware that hospitality projects have the ability to generate significant tax benefits. This is primarily because taxable income is much smaller than the cash flow from a project. Depreciation, a non-cash expense, is deducted from cash flow to determine taxable income. For hospitality assets, the depreciation deduction is enhanced by the large quantities of FF&E inherent in running an operation. In highly leveraged real estate investments, it is often the case for taxable income to be negative, but to obtain a positive cash flow. For investors with other taxable income, the negative taxable income generated by their hospitality investments can be used to reduce other taxable income.

Evaluating return on investment

Investors use two fundamental metrics when evaluating projects, the Net Present Value (NPV) of a project and the Internal Rate of Return (IRR). These metrics give investors a single figure to compare with other investments and to facilitate decision-making by introducing a set of simple rules to a complicated decision process.

The Net Present Value of a project is the sum of the present value of the project inflows and the present value of project outflows. Present values of project inflows and outflows are calculated using a discount rate. The proper discount rate to use is that rate that the investor could obtain on projects of similar risk and maturity; this rate is called the desired rate of return, the desired yield, or the hurdle rate.

Decision rules for the NPV metric:

- If the NPV is equal to zero, the investor obtains exactly their desired rate of return. In this case, the investor would accept the investment.

- If the NPV is greater than zero, the investor obtains the NPV in addition to their desired rate of return. In this case, the investor would also accept the investment.

- If the NPV is less than zero, the investor does not obtain their desired rate of return. In this case, the investor would not accept the investment.

The Internal Rate of Return is that discount rate that makes the present value of project inflows equal to the present value of project outflows. The IRR is then compared to the desired rate of return.

Decision rules for the IRR metric:

- If the IRR is equal to the desired rate of return the investor would accept the investment.

- If the IRR is greater than the desired rate of return, the investor would also accept the investment.

- If the IRR is less than the desired rate of return, the investor would not accept the investment.

Consider the following simple example, which calculates the overall project IRR as well as the NPV and IRR of the equity investment. The investor purchases a 120-room hotel property for €10 000 000 and anticipates selling it for €12 000 000 five years hence. The investor can borrow €4 661 443 and would invest €5 338 557 in equity, which requires a 14% before-tax yield. Property level net operating income is €800 000 in the first year and increases at 3.0% per year. The assumptions are summarized in Figure 5.1.

Figure 5.2 shows that the overall project IRR is 11.25%. The equity IRR is 14.43% and the equity NPV is €88 983. Given the inputs, the investor would make the decision to invest as the project IRR is greater than the desired rate of return and the NPV is positive.

NPV and IRR Example

Purchase Price	€10 000 000
Net Operating Income in Year 1	€800 000
Expected Annual Increase in NOI	3.00%

Equity Parameters
| Holding Period | 5 years |
| Desired Before-Tax Yield | 14.00% |

Loan Parameters
Debt Coverage Ratio	2.00
Loan Interest Rate	7.00%
Amortization Term	25 years
Payments per Year	1
Annual Debt Service	€400 000
Loan Amount	€4 661 433
Remaining Balance at end of Holding Period	€4 237 606

Selling Assumptions
| Sale Price | €12 000 000 |
| Selling Expenses | 2.00% |

Figure 5.1
NPV and IRR example: assumptions

	Year 0	Year 1	Year 2	Year 3	Year 4	Year 5
Initial Investment	(€10 000 000)					
Net Operating Income		€800 000	€824 000	€848 720	€874 182	€900 407
Loan Amount	€4 661 433					
Equity Investment	(€5 338 567)					
Annual Debt Service		€400 000	€400 000	€400 000	€400 000	€400 000
Before-Tax Equity Cash Flow		€400 000	€424 000	€448 720	€474 182	€500 407
Sale Price						€12 000 000
Selling Expenses						(€240 000)
Net Sale Price						€11 760 000
Remaining Loan Balance						(€4 237 606)
Before-Tax Equity Reversion						€7 522 394
Overall Project Cash Flows	(€10 000 000)	€800 000	€824 000	€848 720	€874 182	€12 660 407
IRR	11.25%					
Equity Cash Flows	(€5 338 567)	€400 000	€424 000	€448 720	€474 182	€8 022 801
IRR	14.43%					
NPV	€88 983					

Figure 5.2
NPV and IRR example: calculations

Note from Figures 5.1 and 5.2 that both the project IRR and the equity IRR are calculated. Prudent investors calculate both figures. The project IRR is compared to yields on similar buildings. The investor wants to be sure that the project is competitive with other similar investments. In addition, the equity IRR and NPV are calculated. Here the investor seeks to maximize the risk-adjusted return on invested capital. This can be done two ways, holding risk constant. First, the investor can purchase a building with superior project level returns. Second, the investor can seek lower cost debt capital. Given that debt capital is quite efficiently priced, it is difficult to convince one lender to lend at lower cost than another; thus the best strategy for superior equity returns is to seek superior project level returns.

Project finance – stylized examples

Each of the examples outlined below is representative of successful acquisitions. The examples are based on projects that are located in major urban markets of the European Union. Returns and costs are averages based on the experience of seasoned professionals in each area; they do not represent any particular project. The analysis will focus on costs per unit of revenue production, characteristic capital structures, and average return requirements.

Independent restaurant – leased premises

A restaurant in leased premises does not need to invest in the structure, but does need to construct and furnish the front-of-house and back-of-house to meet the needs of the operation, and for the small-wares, supplies, and working capital needed to start operations. Costs range from €8000–€10000 per seat, so a 100-seat restaurant would require an investment of €800000 to €1000000. Since the restaurateur does not own the building, securing debt financing is difficult, as a failed restaurant does not hold much of value for the bank. Seasoned operators are able to borrow 50–60% of the funds needed; these loans are expensive, with an interest rate of between 10% and 12% in today's market. Equity funds the remainder of the costs and requires a return of between 25% and 33%. Table 5.1 shows how unit-level economics work on a per seat basis.

Note the high cost of capital and the cost of the lease. Restaurants need high revenues to be successful; the inability to maintain per seat revenues impacts only the equity return, as rents and debt service are typically fixed payments.

Overall cost	€9500 per seat	
Debt capital	€5000 per seat, 11% cost of debt	
Equity capital	€4500 per seat, 30% cost of equity	
Revenue per seat	€22000	
	Net income before occupancy cost	€3740 (17% operating margin)
	Rent	€1760 (8% of revenues)
	Debt service	€550 (11% of €5000)
	Equity return	€1350 (30% of €4500)
	Remainder	€80 (approx. zero)

Table 5.1
Independent restaurant – leased premises

Chain restaurant – stand alone facility

Very similar to a leased facility, except now the operator has to acquire the land and build the structure. These costs make total costs approximately €13 000 to €20 000 per seat. Debt capital is available for seasoned chains at a cost of 8.0–10.0% on up to 70% of total project costs. Equity funds the remainder of the costs and requires a return of between 20% and 30%. Unit-level economics work on a per seat basis as shown in Table 5.2.

As Table 5.2 shows, a chain restaurant offers the potential for superior returns, relative to an independent operation. This is fundamentally due to the fact that rents for leased premises are priced above the cost of building similar quality space. The problem for restaurateurs seeking urban locations is that there are very few empty sites or buildings available for purchase in locations that generate the business needed to support the operation.

Small hotel

A small hotel offers the potential for long-term returns if operated properly. The example shown is a two-star operation without a restaurant in an urban location. Costs per room will be in the range of €50 000 to €80 000, depending on the city and the relative location. The owner would be able to borrow up to 65% of project costs at interest rates of between 7% and 9%. Equity would require a return of between 14% and 20% on the remaining investment. Unit-level economics work on a per room basis as shown in Table 5.3.

Note that 2.0% drop in revenues or a 1.0% drop in the operating margin completely eliminates the remainder; thus equity returns are highly dependent on the operator's ability to generate revenues and operate the facility efficiently.

Full-service hotel

Consider a traditional 4-star hotel in a large urban setting. This facility has guestrooms, several food and beverage outlets, meeting

Overall cost	€18 000 per seat
Debt capital	€12 000 per seat, 9% cost of debt
Equity capital	€6 000 per seat, 25% cost of equity
Revenue per seat	€20 000
Net income before occupancy cost	€3 000 (15% operating margin)
Debt service	€1 080 (9% of €12 000)
Equity return	€1500 (25% of €6 000)
Remainder	€420

Table 5.2
Chain restaurant – stand alone facility

Overall cost	€60 000 per room	
Debt capital	€36 000 per room, 8% cost of debt	
Equity capital	€24 000 per room, 14% cost of equity	
Revenue per room	€16 500	
	Net income before occupancy cost	€6 600 (40% operating margin)
	Debt service	€2 880 (8% of €36 000)
	Equity return	€3600 (15% of €24 000)
	Remainder	€120

Table 5.3
Small hotel

Overall cost	€150 000 per room	
Debt capital	€100 000 per room, 7% cost of debt	
Equity capital	€50 000 per room, 14% cost of equity	
Revenue per room	€56 000	
	Net income before occupancy cost	€14 000 (25% operating margin)
	Debt service	€7 000 (7% of €100 000)
	Equity return	€7 000 (14% of €50 000)
	Remainder	€0

Table 5.4
Full-service hotel

rooms, a business centre, and some recreational amenities. Acquisition costs per room will be in a range from €100 000 to €250 000; the reason for the wide range is that gateway cities (London, Paris, Brussels) command significant premiums over similar hotels in the secondary markets. The owner would be able to borrow up to 75% of project costs at interest rates of between 6% and 9%. Equity would require a return of between 12% and 18% on the remaining investment. Unit-level economics work as follows on a per room basis as shown in Table 5.4.

Again, note from Table 5.4 that equity returns are highly dependent on the operator's ability to generate revenues and operate the facility efficiently. Illustration 5.1 shows the Savoy Hotel, London, which, at the time of writing is being marketed at one million £UK (€1.3 million) per bedroom.

Refurbishment, defensive spending, and repositioning

The costs of renovation are not trivial, in a 4-star hotel it will cost approximately €7 000 to perform a full renovation of each guestroom; this includes replacement of all furniture, renewal of floor, wall and ceiling finishes, and a modest refreshing of the toilet and bathroom facilities. A thorough renovation of a restaurant dining room will cost approximately €2 000 per seat to replace all

Illustration 5.1
Savoy Hotel, London
(Source: the Grand Hotel,
Chartwell Books, 1984)

furniture and renew the floor, wall, and ceiling finishes. These examples do not consider the costs to maintain and replace equipment in the back-of-house; kitchen, laundry, technology infrastructure, and building systems.

It is common for hotels and restaurants to set aside a portion of overall revenues for periodic renovation, refurbishment, and equipment replacement. It is widely acknowledged that this amount should be approximately 5.0% of total revenues in hotels and approximately 3.0% of revenues in restaurants. This is the level necessary to maintain the revenue producing capability of the business; if this amount is not set aside, the owner of the business will be faced with the need to renovate but will have to secure the funding to do so.

In addition to the ongoing needs for renovation simply to preserve the relative competitiveness of a hospitality business, owners often use two strategies to strengthen their investments. The first is called defensive spending. An existing hotel faced with the prospect of significant new competition may renovate to improve or change the facilities. For example, a meeting oriented hotel might significantly upgrade the technological capabilities of the meeting facilities, as the new competition will undoubtedly come to the market with the latest in technology. Alternatively, the room mix (mix of single bedded and double-bedded rooms) might be changed to develop new markets or to change orientation of the property, so as to avoid competing directly with the new competition.

The second strategy is a repositioning. Consider a 3½-star hotel with significant new competition coming into the market. It might make sense for the hotel to reposition itself as a true 4-star property to maintain profitability. This repositioning can take significant funds to achieve.

The same analysis framework is used to determine the appropriate level of funding for renovation, defensive spending, or repositioning. Lenders asked to consider funding a renovation will insist on a feasibility study that compares the value of the building without renovation to the value of the building with renovation. The difference between the two values is the greatest amount that should be rationally spent, irrespective of the costs of renovation. Renovation funding can be secured as a standalone commitment or can be combined with a recapitalization of the property. A recapitalization is especially warranted when the property will have a significant increase in value as a result of the renovation. As with development loans, the lender will impose strict controls on the disbursement of funds, to insure that funds are used to pay for the renovations and to exercise control over the quality and pace of renovations.

Conclusion

It has been shown that project finance is a complex topic that requires knowledge of building economics and the capital markets. One must become familiar with the rudiments of project finance to become a successful hospitality professional. The ability to use 'other people's money' to enhance the returns to equity is a fundamental concept, as well as an understanding of the risk that comes from adding debt financing to a project.

Review questions

1 What are the four activities that require project finance?

2 Why is equity capital difficult to raise?

3 How are IRR and NPV used to evaluate projects?

CHAPTER 6

Legal agreements and contracts

Chris Rouse

As hospitality developments become more complex in a global economy, it becomes more important to ensure that legal agreements protect the parties involved against undue risk or litigious activity. This chapter considers some of the aspects of management agreements, beginning with a historical perspective and discussing issues in negotiating management contracts today. The structure is as follows:

- Historical perspective
- The current market
- Negotiating management contracts today
- Matters of principle
- Other detailed matters
- Current legal issues
- Future issues
- Conclusion.

Historical perspective

The concept of investors and developers engaging professional managers for hotels is not new. Managers such as Cesar Ritz or Marcel Escoffier were hired in the 19th century to run famous new hotels across Europe. Then, as now, the identity of the 'manager' could be crucial in raising the finance for the construction of a new hotel. Essentially, however, these managers were servants of the owners of the particular hotels. The rise of the corporate hotelier, essentially a company selling hotel management services for fees, rather than a salary, is a development which occurred after the Second World War.

This was essentially a US phenomenon, closely allied to the growth of intercontinental air transport and the recognition of global brands. In a world which required re-building, skilled corporate hoteliers, with access to capital, with links to global airlines and with recognized, glamorous brand names, had enormous negotiating power. The number of such corporate hoteliers was small and almost exclusively American. ITT Corporation owned Sheraton. Hilton had long-standing links with TWA (Transworld Airlines) and Inter-Continental Hotels was a creation of Pan-Am (Pan American Airways). In addition to their transport connections, these companies, in a pre-internet age, were at the cutting edge of communications technology, usually led by their associated airline reservation systems.

A common characteristic of ITT Corporation, TWA and Pan-Am was that hotels were not the core activity of the group parent companies and the hotel company subsidiaries had to compete internally for investment funds. The emergence of third party investors and owners, prepared to develop and own hotels was a huge benefit to these hotel companies with global aspirations. This new breed of third party investors allowed the hotel operating companies to liberate themselves from the draining constraints of owner-occupation, with its enormous demand for capital and, in return, acquired the benefit of the operator's brand name and the credibility which an association with those brands conferred.

Hilton International is generally credited with inventing the corporate management contract, creating a legal form that replaced the contracts of employments available to Ritz and Escoffier. The early post-war contracts were often structured as profit-sharing agreements, with Hilton often taking a fee denominated as 33% of gross operating profit. It is worth pointing out, of course, that this was operating profit and not the considerably smaller post-debt free cash flow. As competition for management contracts increased, the industry settled upon a two-tier management fee structure.

All the major operators began to quote fees in the form of a base fee, usually calculated as a percentage of turnover and an incentive fee, usually calculated as a percentage of gross operating profit. In a significant number of cases, operators would take a

Illustration 6.1
Hilton Hotel (Courtesy
of Hilton International
Hotels)

minority equity interest. This investment, often of a 'token' nature, had the very useful advantage of making a project look robust, which could be a significant factor in raising debt finance. Some equity investors also continue to find reassurance in co-investment by an operator. One effect however can be to grant the operator an extraordinary degree of security of tenure, which may not necessarily be in an owner's best interest.

Most, but not all major international hotel groups also provided that their expenses directly attributable to the operation of the hotel would be reimbursed in full and instituted procedures whereby 'common costs' such as marketing, brand development, system development and other costs, would be allocated across all the hotels in the chain, often on a per room basis. In addition, as reservation systems became more sophisticated, separate charges would be levied for reservations made through the operator's systems.

The current market

Since the last major recession in the global hotel market in the early and mid-1990s, the nature of hotel ownership has been transformed. There has been a significant shift from combined operation and ownership of hotels and in the last five years alone the proportion of their hotels owned by major operators such as Accor and Hilton International have declined from almost half of their estates to a quarter. The new owners are banks, public and private investment funds, venture capitalists, property groups and institutions. In many cases the preferred operating and investment structure has been based on leases, but there is increasing evidence that management contracts, often with a minimum return guaranteed by the operator are again becoming popular. Three new UK hotels – The Marriott, Park Lane in London, the Radisson SAS in Liverpool and the new Hilton in Manchester – have all been developed (or are being developed) on the basis of management contracts and not lease structures.

Despite these changes there are more operators than there are opportunities, and situations where major international hotel companies can acquire management contracts on large hotels in major city centre locations remain relatively rare. The balance of negotiating strength has moved away from the hotel operator to the owner or the developer and operators now have to be sympathetic to the particular needs of their business partners. Twenty-five years ago the standard management contracts of InterContinental Hotels and Hilton International were pre-printed and essentially non-negotiable. Hilton, indeed, had to be paid a fee even to release a copy of their standard agreement. In today's market, the negotiation of these agreements can be extremely time-consuming, often preceded by detailed negotiation of letters of intent and heads of terms.

Negotiating management contracts today

In order to put the relationships under a management agreement into context, it is helpful to list the most important issues which need to be addressed as 'matters of principle'. If agreement can be reached over these issues it should not be too difficult to agree the other detailed points and it will be for the lawyers to ensure that the commercial agreements are properly documented and cross-referenced.

Matters of principle

The commercial terms should reflect the reality of the respective positions of the owner and the operator and it is of crucial importance that the parties are clear about their objectives and aspirations. A developer, who may be planning to sell the completed hotel will certainly have a different set of objectives to the owner of a theme park or resort, who will be focusing on long-term infrastructural benefits, with little thought about the separate sale of the hotel. The developer of an hotel in a mixed-use scheme, where it is usual to review and change the component mix of a retail element every 10 years, will clearly be unused to dealing with the issues raised by an 80-year hotel management contract. Many management companies attempt to exercise a quasi-ownership role and it is not unusual to see this in the way they prepare the draft management agreements. It is important that the respective roles are made absolutely clear and, as will be shown later, there has been significant litigation in the USA about the precise nature of the legal relationship between the two parties.

In order to achieve a proper balance of the legal and commercial realities, the following matters should be addressed as a priority:

(a) Owner to approve budgets

It has to be agreed that the operator will provide detailed operating budgets, capital expenditure budgets and a marketing plan for the owner's approval, each year. The owner must have the right to approve these budgets. It is possible to have a mechanism to arbitrate on disputes, but the fundamental principle must be acknowledged – the hotel is the owner's investment and the money is the owner's money.

(b) Owner to approve general manager and financial controller

The owner should have the right to approve the appointment of the hotel's general manager and, it is also recommended, the financial controller or chief financial officer. It is quite extraordinary how often this has to be negotiated and not granted in draft agreements.

(c) Bank accounts to be the property of the owner

The bank accounts must be in the name of the owner and not 'held in trust by the operator'. It should always be spelt out that the owner owns the bank accounts. This has to be established beyond doubt. It is not acceptable in our view that the cash from a managed hotel should be merged with the cash of hotels owned by others. Similarly, bank statements, on a daily basis, should be held at the hotel itself and not at an operator's head office. The owner should also have the right to approve the signatories to the accounts.

(d) Owner's right to deal with the hotel

The owner must be able to sell the hotel without the operator's consent. This right may be of fundamental importance to a developer, whose business plan assumes a sale to new investors. If the operators are concerned that the hotel may be sold to subversive organizations such as the Cosa Nostra or to Al Quaeda, then suitable wording may be found. If a new purchaser has a favourite management company, or is itself a management company, there should be a negotiated right to terminate. There should, of course, be a compensation package with the operator in these circumstances.

Many old agreements imposed a blanket restriction on the owner selling the hotel without the operator's approval. Most modern agreements usually contain detailed provisions, giving the operator first right of refusal in the event of the owner wishing to sell the hotel. In some cases the operator even has a right of pre-emption and can take over the deal after it has been negotiated with another party. Even more damagingly, many investors will not accept the risk of fruitlessly spending time and resources in negotiating a deal, when these rights exist. This can have a serious effect on the saleability of a hotel. It is recommended that a right of pre-emption should never be given. A right of first refusal would be a relatively common and acceptable fallback position. Under this arrangement, the owner has to offer the hotel to the operator, at a specific price and for a specific period. If the operator does not buy the hotel, the owner is then free to sell the property in the open market, on identical (or broadly similar) terms.

An owner may also care to ask for a right to terminate the agreement in the event of there being a change in the ownership of the operator or its parent company. Most operators will hate the idea of a provision like this, but it can be a very useful bargaining point in negotiations.

Linked with these provisions are the attempts by the stronger operators to impose 'non-disturbance' clauses, which provide that the management contract may continue, despite the owner of the hotel suffering receivership or liquidation. Banks may often find the continuation of the brand to be a source of comfort in such circumstances, but others have very strong objections to such clauses. It can be a delicate area.

(e) Restrictions on competitive use of the operator's brand name

The operator should give the owner specific undertakings about the use of the operator's brand name. The name of the operator is often of considerable value, but an owner is paying handsomely for it. There is nothing in most drafts to prevent the operator operating three or four hotels in the same locality, which could have a serious effect upon a particular hotel. It is usual to suggest a geographical restriction for the use of the operator's name.

Alternatively, or in addition, the owner should seek a priority listing in the operator's reservation system (i.e. always first choice) or the right to approve any additional use of the operator's name. For the purposes of negotiation, the owner could seek restrictions on the whole operator's name in a location or town. The owner may, as part of the compromise, offer the operator the first right to operate any additional hotels which the owner develops in the restricted area. This can be a useful trade-off.

(f) Performance criteria

Most draft management agreements contain no performance criteria at all. It is perfectly reasonable for the owner to have the right to terminate the agreement, without compensation, should the operator consistently fail to meet the budgeted targets. The difficulty arises in trying to define the terms of an acceptable test.

Long experience has led to the conclusion that the use of an independent expert, acceptable to both sides, is the most practical way to solve these issues. The test often used is one of 'material under-performance' against a defined and agreed competitive set. It is often advisable not to specify hard tests for 'material under-performance', but rather allow the expert to recognize it when it occurs.

It is not unusual in most of the major hotel markets, for operators to share information on room rates and occupancy. Many operators refer to this practice as the 'ring round', because the information is traded, unofficially, by telephone. In a number of cities, Amsterdam being an example, the local tourist authority circulates information on rate and occupancy to the city's hoteliers. This practice has always run the risk of being deemed anti-competitive under EU Competition law, but since the Enterprise Act came into force in June 2003, there has been a new focus on these activities, which are now defined as criminal offences, with draconian penalties.

It is suggested that it is of great importance that these issues are addressed in a management contract and that proper procedures are put in place for the sourcing and provision of market information. Under the Enterprise Act, the directors of the owning company can easily be as liable as the employees of the operator. It is perfectly lawful to arrange for a hotel to participate in benchmarking surveys, and to have the benefit of the results, which are either published, or provided on a tailor-made basis by a number of the leading hospitality consultants such as Deloitte & Touche, PKF, TRI and Smiths Travel. The recommendation is that this should be agreed as an operator's responsibility, with the costs treated as operating expenses of the hotel.

(g) Asset management

With the rise of hotel owners and investors who have no direct hotel operating experience it is increasingly important that they have the benefit of independent expertise in monitoring the performance of their hotel assets. This need has given rise to the existence of the independent asset manager.

There are four particular areas which provide the cornerstones of asset management. These are property, operational and budget reviews; contract compliance; sales and marketing reviews; and monitoring of capital expenditure. Experience shows that a regime of annual budget reviews, monthly analysis of operating numbers and quarterly face-to-face discussions between owner, asset manager and operator provide a solid basis for effective relationships.

The asset manager should have the right to receive budgets, reports, attend meetings and generally act as the owner's representative. The fees and expenses of an asset manager may be agreed to be operating expenses, although this will be a matter of negotiation.

(h) Opening date and term

Some draft agreements provide that, at the operator's option, the relationship will last for 80 years. This may have a totally unacceptable effect upon the value of the hotel, although a term of this length can only properly be assessed in relation to the strength and attraction of the hotel brand. This is an area where views are changing. As little as 10 years ago it was the accepted wisdom that a hotel with vacant possession would have a higher value, on sale, than a hotel 'encumbered' by the existence of a management contract. In an environment where the buying and selling of hotels was largely led by operating companies, who were driven by the need to expand their brands, it is understandable that an hotel which could not be re-named would not attract significant market interest. Now, however, few hotel operators are driven by the desire to own all their assets and the investment market is beginning to appreciate the value inherent in a strong brand. Is a luxury hotel more valuable without an operator, or with a Four Seasons flag? Is a budget hotel likely to be more valuable with an Express by Holiday flag, or managed anonymously, by a local entrepreneur? An owner would be well advised to take a realistic view of the value of a brand and decide whether the brand adds value, compromises value or is value-neutral. Decisions on the length of term then become somewhat easier.

It is usual for property investors to value their future income by discounting the income stream back to achieve a present value. There are some major operators, on the other hand, who do not discount future fees when valuing their contracts and, for these operators, the length of term can have a disproportionate importance. The majority of property investors are relatively indifferent as to whether a lease is for 50 or 75 years, but experience has taught that major concessions may be won from these operators in management contract negotiations by the offer of a relatively modest number of additional years.

A term of less than 10 years will clearly not be acceptable to most operators. The normal recommendation is that, unless the financing calls for a longer term, the initial term should be for at least 10 years and each subsequent additional term (5 years each) should be by mutual agreement of the operator and the owner. The principle of mutual agreement to extensions of the original term is crucial.

The opening date (and the pre-opening budget) should all be agreed with the owner and not imposed by the operator.

(i) Restrictions on redevelopment

The operator should have no right to insist that the hotel is rebuilt in the event of destruction, although every operator tries to secure this position. The owner may have many better things to do with the site. The recommendation is that owners have freedom to do as they choose, with an agreed compensation payment to the operator if a more commercially attractive alternative is found. The most common compensation formula would be where the past year's fees (or a multiple) are multiplied by a fraction representing the number of years remaining under the agreement, divided by the original term.

(j) Fees

It is still common for the major chains to base their fee quotations on a perceived industry standard of a base fee of 3% of total revenue, with an incentive fee of 10% of adjusted gross operating profit (the 'adjusted GOP' is usually the result of deducting a repairs and renewals provision and a base management fee from the GOP). Some groups classify their base fees as licence or royalty payments for the use of a brand name and a structure of 2% of total revenue as a royalty fee and 1% of total revenue as a base fee would not be unusual, but the reality remains a deduction of 3%.

In a competitive environment, management companies are prepared to compromise on the standard fee structure, particularly where there is no requirement that they invest in the enterprise. In circumstances where management companies do invest, either through equity, through loan guarantees or through promises of a guaranteed owners return, then there is marked reluctance to deviate from a standard fee format. As a general rule, the higher the perceived standard of the brand, the greater the reluctance to deviate from the fee structure. In this regard, companies such as Hyatt and Four Seasons are traditionally the most inflexible and Hyatt even requests an incentive fee of 12%.

On the basis of discussions with Four Seasons, Hilton International, Hyatt, Le Méridien, Mandarin Oriental, Marriott, Radisson SAS, Sheraton and InterContinental Hotels, the following represents a generally agreeable fee structure for international operators:

a) A base fee (including royalties and licence fees) of 2.5% of total revenue

b) An incentive fee of 8% of adjusted gross operating profit

c) Re-charge of head office costs limited to no more than 0.5% of total revenue

d) A contribution to central and chain marketing expenses of no more than 1.5% of total revenue.

Further, a number of companies would probably agree to a base fee of 2% of total revenue and a number would agree to a cap of 1% on central and chain marketing expenses.

It is increasingly common for the incentive fee to be calculated on an 'adjusted gross operating profit' (GOP) or 'adjusted income before fixed charges'. The adjustment is made by including the cost of the replacement reserve in the operating expenses, before calculating the GOP or income before fixed charges. This is in the owner's interest and most operators will agree, even though very few actually volunteer the arrangement.

Depending upon financing needs (and the competitive environment) it would now be common to seek a stand-aside arrangement with the operator, whereby significant elements of the fee package – certainly the 'incentive' fee – are subordinated to debt service or some other agreed performance criteria. Subordinated fees may be waived or accrued, depending on the relative strength of the negotiating parties. It is however important to ensure that unpaid fees do not become debts, chargeable upon the property. One well-known management company seeks mortgage rights in respect of delayed fees, which is never normally recommended.

(k) The operator system fees

There is always a temptation to concentrate upon management fees and not give sufficient attention to other fees and costs. Many draft agreements do not define how these are to be calculated other than 'on the same basis as other hotels operated by the operator'. This is not good enough. Is this calculated on a cash or percentage basis, pro rata by the number of rooms or on another basis? It must always be specified. Do operators re-charge all telephone calls relating to the hotel back to the property or do they bear the cost from their fees as an overhead of the own business? It can be an expensive question.

The owner should also beware of marketing and reservation charges made by reference to reservations and not to cash. For example some companies charge a fixed fee ($25 or whatever) per reservation, irrespective of whether the stay is one night or one month. It is always preferable to have an agreed percentage of the room charges actually paid and not a flat fee. If the hotel is a resort, it is always advisable to negotiate specific arrangements for room-nights sold either wholesale or specifically allocated to tour operators.

Care should be taken in establishing exactly how reservation fees arise. Some companies adopt a 'hit' method, where the charge arises at time of booking. Others only charge a reservation fee when the guest arrives at the hotel and there is no charge to the owner for a 'no-show'. The latter method is preferable and a well-advised owner will not allow the operator the option of changing the method of calculation.

Other detailed matters

The above 'matters of principle' are the items which it will generally be necessary to settle in order to form the basis of an agreement which will survive for many years. Many of these matters are not addressed in initial draft agreements provided by operators. The following are detailed matters which consistently need to be addressed.

Reliance upon forecasts

From the perspective of an owner or developer, the operators being considered for a management contract should be experts – they must have explored and investigated the market. Any studies should be at their expense and should have been presented to the owner prior to finalization of the contract negotiations. The owner should be entitled to rely upon the operator's forecasts and not vice versa. It is invariably recommended that a prudent owner should request forecasts from the operator, if necessary giving them an exclusive negotiating period so that the work may be carried out and assessed. Depending upon the competition for the particular opportunity, the owner may or may not contribute to the costs of an independent study, but this does not obviate the need for operator forecasts.

Country risks

The operator will have decided to do business in a particular jurisdiction and must accept the realities of doing business in that country. Withholding taxes should be at the operator's own risk and should not involve the owner in extra expense.

Confidentiality clauses

Confidentiality clauses invariably appear at the end of agreements and are often considered as legal strengthening. Such clauses usually look innocuous and provide that information about the hotel and about the contract itself should not be revealed, without the express agreement of both parties. These clauses should however be treated with care and with as much thought about their commercial implications as the other terms of the agreement. A confidentiality clause may look reasonable at the beginning of an agreement, but an owner should always ensure that he or she has the right to share the operating numbers with a prospective replacement operator. One very high profile change of operator has recently been made extremely difficult, due the owner's inability to share this information with the existing operator's competitors.

Third party fees

All consultants' fees and the terms of their engagement should be subject to owner's approval and the owner should receive copies of any consultant's reports. In a recent case, the operator sought legal advice from the hotel's lawyers about the tax treatment of its fees and put the bill through the hotel's books as an operating expense. Vigilance at the drafting stage can avoid these problems.

Policy approvals

The major points have been dealt with above, but some operating standards should be introduced into any agreement, particularly relating to credit control. The owner should have approval of the operator's credit policy, for example and it is strongly recommended that the operator's policies on staff discounts and its various marketing arrangements, such as loyalty schemes, reward cards and Internet marketing policies, are attached to any management contract, as exhibits, with a proviso that they may only be changed with the owner's agreement.

Shared services

The owner should have approval of those services which are to be shared with other hotels operated by the operator. These services should be detailed in the agreement and it is largely the lack of any detail on shared services, particularly shared purchasing services that has led to an outbreak of litigation in the USA.

The ability of hotel brands with a famous name, or with a multitude of hotels, to achieve significant discounts from suppliers by using bulk purchase orders is a very attractive inducement to an independent owner in seeking an association with that brand. If a hotel manager is legally the agent of an owner, as the US courts seem to be deciding, then the operator must pass on the full benefit of all discounts to the owner and not take a fee, or the benefit of an undisclosed group commission for itself in providing these services. This whole area has the potential for creating mistrust and bad blood between owners and operators and needs to be dealt with on the basis of total disclosure to avoid the creation of a legal 'minefield'.

Other points on fees

Fees have generally been dealt with above. It should however be determined whether the books of account are to be maintained on an accrual basis for the fee calculations. This may mean that the revenue-based element of the management fee may be payable before the cash has been received. The recommendation is that payment of the fee should be determined by reference to cash actually received.

Agreements are still to be seen in which the revenue-based element of the fee is payable monthly and the owner's profit distribution is payable every six months. In our opinion both payments should be paid at the same time.

Severance payments and staff benefits

It is recommended that the owner has approval of severance payments, insurance, incentive and pension benefits. These should, of course, be included in a proper budget presentation each year.

Branded operator's equipment

The practice of branding operating equipment is usually not dealt with in draft agreements provided by operators. The use of the operator's name on operating equipment is a difficult area and the owner may not care to be put to the expense of replacing this equipment in the event of termination. The owner should seek the operator's advice on their practice in this regard and seek confirmation that branding will be minimized on non-consumable items. At termination of the agreement, the operator should be obligated to re-purchase branded equipment from the owner.

Replacement reserves

Hotels are a unique class of real estate, in that they retain a strong residual value. Most major European cities have flagship hotels that are at least 100 years old. There are very few office blocks of which the same is true The secret in preserving this residual value lies in maintenance, repairs and renewals and a proper programme

Illustration 6.2
Breidenbacher Hof Hotel
Dusseldorf (Courtesy of Jones
Lang Lasalle)

of re-investment and capital expenditure. The usual method of regulating this crucial aspect of a hotel property is by making sure that a sufficient proportion of the hotel's revenue is set aside for these purposes.

Operators like to see this percentage of the revenue kept low in management contracts (with the major burden being borne by capital budgets) because sums transferred to the replacement reserve usually have an impact on the incentive fees which the operators receive. It is recommended that a proper analysis should be made of the likely re-furbishment and capital expenditure and that an agreed policy should be agreed and documented accordingly. It will be obvious that a resort hotel, in a temperate climate, with an average length of stay of 4 or 5 nights will require considerably less expenditure than a city centre hotel in a location with a climate like Moscow, or an airport hotel with an average length of stay of one night. Proper and appropriate provision should be made with a realistic analysis of both the type of hotel and the characteristic of the location.

One other point which some operators try to achieve and which can be overlooked concerns the distribution of the replacement reserve at the termination of the contract. It should go without saying that any balance remaining at the end of the contract should be transferred to the owner, but some operators try to argue that they are entitled to that part of the replacement reserve that has reduced their incentive fees. In our opinion, this ought to be resisted and the balance of a replacement reserve should not be credited to gross operating profit in the final year and shared between owner and operator. In a perfect world it should probably be spent, as it is in the owner's interest to have a properly maintained hotel, rather than experience an underspend, with fees being paid on the amounts 'saved'.

Independent external auditors

It is recommended that the owner should have the right to appoint the accountants/auditors. Management companies can be very sensitive about this, but an owner needs to be aware of the extent of the global business relationships between an auditor and an operator and should take some trouble to ensure that its own interests are protected. It is an acceptable fallback in negotiations for the owner to have the right to approve these appointments.

Insurances

In a world increasingly aware of the risks from terrorism, insurance has now become a major cost item. The negotiations over placement of insurances should really be a question of economic benefit. If the owner can arrange comparable insurance cheaper than an operator, then the owner should keep control of this item. In view of the costs involved, this is now an area where an owner should obtain the best advice available in the market.

Additional insurance and deductibility should not be left to the operator's discretion. These matters should be agreed with the owner after proper investigation.

Arbitration

It is astonishing how often 'neutral' countries are chosen as seats of arbitration, which will involve undue expense on one of the parties. It is hoped that a sensible agreement will choose a jurisdiction which will not involve either translation of material evidence or expert witnesses to give evidence on an applicable law.

Indemnities

These matters are properly the province of the parties' legal advisers, but based on reasonable business principles there is usually no reason why the owner should indemnify an operator against the result of the operator's negligent acts. This is a sensitive area as there is an increasing number of laws which create a personal liability on the directors of an enterprise which can result in imprisonment or disqualification as a director for actions committed by employees or agents. Breach of Competition Law is just one area mentioned previously.

Current legal issues

The most noteworthy cases of recent years involving hotel management contracts have been in the USA and the most famous, or infamous case was decided in 2000 and is called *Woodley Road Joint Venture v ITT Sheraton Corporation*. In the Woodley Road case a jury awarded $51.8 million in damages – almost $15 million in actual damages and over $35 million in punitive damages – against Sheraton. The jury also concluded that the owner was entitled to terminate Sheraton's management contract (with more than 30 years remaining) without cost or penalty. The damages and free termination resulted from a finding that Sheraton breached its management agreement and its fiduciary duties to the hotel's owner, a joint venture owned primarily by John Hancock and Sumitomo Life.

Without being too technical, it will now be almost impossible under US law for almost any hotel operator to avoid the legal status of an 'agent' ... and every agent is a 'fiduciary.' A fiduciary is in the position of a quasi-trustee or a director of a company who owes the first duty of loyalty and care to the principal. A fiduciary cannot take rebates or kickbacks (bribes), cannot use or profit from its principal's property (which includes free rooms), and must prefer the principal's interest to its own. The US courts recognize English common law, which was extensively quoted in the judgement. The Woodley Road jury found that Sheraton received various discounts, rebates and other consideration from vendors and that these constituted 'kickbacks' and 'commercial bribes', which were a breach of contract and of Sheraton's fiduciary duty.

In the middle of May 2002, New World, the group which sold the Ramada and Renaissance brands to Marriot started legal proceedings against Marriott (who are the managers of these properties) making similar allegations to those in Woodley Road, with the additional charges of racketeering and bribery. Marriott have rigorously denied any such charge. As might be expected in a period of downturn, unhappy owners are sometimes minded to blame their managers. In another high profile case, Strategic Hotel Capital launched proceedings against Marriott, citing Marriott's alleged failure to provide detailed bank statements and unauthorized use of guest records. Strategic's claim that guest records belong to the owner of a hotel and not to the operator is an interesting point.

Future issues

There is a contemporary momentum, which may well prove to be unstoppable, for the harmonization of accounting principles across the leading economies of the world. One effect of this is likely to be a harmonization of the treatment of on- and off-balance liabilities, such as guarantees given to support rental payments under leases. At the moment, European regulators (and stock market analysts) are rather more liberal than their US counterparts in the treatment of such liabilities, which goes a long way to explaining why, in general, European operators are much more willing to give such guarantees than those subject to the US general accounting principles (commonly known as GAP). This will be a fascinating evolution and if the US philosophies prevail, which is by no means certain after the major dot.com accounting scandals of the recent past, the future may well see a preference for management contract structures, as opposed to leases.

In the budget proposed for 2003/4 the UK Chancellor of the Exchequer proposed radical revisions to the stamp duty payable on commercial leases. These proposals have now become law. Without going into great detail, the effect on a standard form hotel lease in the UK will be to increase this duty, or tax, by a factor of 10. In a typical case this will increase stamp duty on the lease of a 100-room budget hotel from £20000 to £200000. In future, the structure of management contracts may become increasingly attractive to tax planners and entrepreneurs in structuring new hotel real estate deals.

Conclusion

Management contracts flourished between the end of the Second World War and the mid 1990s when investors and operators both began to see the value inherent in leasing structures. In the more turbulent world, which began on 11 September 2001, the question of risk assessment has become respectable and operators and investors are coming to terms with the need for a new set of ground rules. As has been shown, there are many complex questions, where the strength of a hotel brand has to be weighed against the ability of a developer or hotel owner to deliver vast amounts of relatively illiquid capital. These conflicting interests will need to achieve equilibrium and the flexibility inherent in a management contract structure has the potential to be the vehicle that can deliver these solutions.

Review questions

1 What are the main factors in the current hotel market which affect legal issues?

2 What are 'matters of principle'?

3 Outline some restrictions on development of which hospitality developers might need to be aware.

Construction

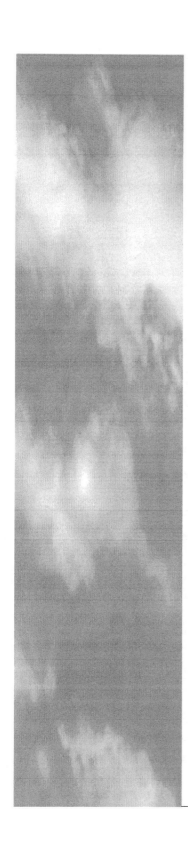

The design team

Josef Ransley

This chapter aims to increase awareness of those involved in the management of design as part of the hospitality development process. The structure is as follows:

- Project brief
- Project requirements
- Professional team appointments
- Duties and services
- Statutory approvals
- Design development
- Procurement
- Construction
- Handover and occupation
- Conclusion.

Once the client brief has been articulated and the project requirements appraised, then a team of specialists is usually appointed
to advise the client and deliver a set of specific services to assist
the client to realize the project objectives. Generally, such specialists will consist of, but not be limited to, an architect, structural
and building services engineers, a cost consultant, interior designer
and construction management group. All these individuals or
their respective companies will be required to be suitably qualified and registered with appropriate professional institutions or
industry associations. Most such bodies will publish a minimum
standard of professional practice, and their members have to
comply with, and subscribe to, a standard list of duties and services as well as information on indicative fee values.

This collective group of specialists is then contracted by the
client to carry out the design development for the project as well
as be responsible for the delivery of the physical product. The
steps in the process of design to post-occupation appraisal are
described in Figure 7.1.

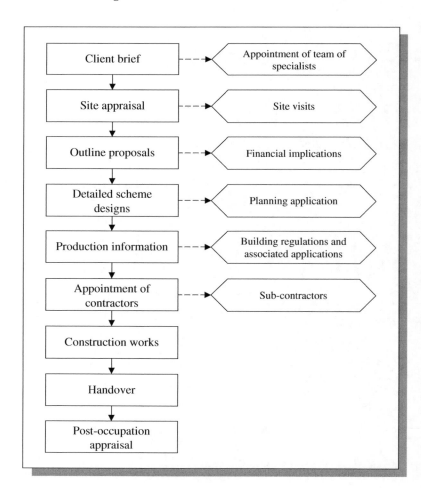

Figure 7.1
A model of the hospitality
design process

Project brief

As has been shown in previous chapters, the project brief forms the basis of turning the concept into a written description of the idea and prescribes its requirements. The brief then is utilized to carry out an initial project viability study which, if positive, is then extended into a more detailed market and financial study and appraisal. If the project passes these hurdles it is then funded and released for implementation. At this stage of the project's development the level of detail, normally undertaken with a specific application to a given site, will not have been extensive, primarily due to the not unnatural desire for the developer or operator to minimize expenditure until the project has proved viable in principle and has been funded. If the project has reached the stage for implementation and the initial stages have been carried out in an appropriate way, the most critical issue that arises is to set up the structure and team for its implementation in the best manner. If the project is set up and structured correctly, it has a chance of being implemented and realized in a satisfactory way. If this critical stage is not addressed correctly then the chances of realizing the project objectives are severely restricted. Importantly, the brief will have set out the requirements of cost, time and quality and, as has been shown, these are critical to the financial feasibility of the project. Equally important and often forgotten is the establishment of the client team, whose normal structure is shown in Figure 7.2.

The client team establishes the reporting structure and, more relevant, the decision-making entity for the project. All development projects benefit from a speedy and clear decision-making process and whereas time is always critical on most projects, it is all too rare for the decision-making process to be defined at the outset. Those responsible for delivering projects do well to define this process at the outset and clarify the terms of their authority, the format, references and timescales for obtaining decisions involving other parties. Equally, those assigning responsible parties for delivering projects should have due regard and confidence in the abilities of the people they are charging with such obligations. Delay in confirming decisions can prove very expensive and disruptive and are one of the main causes of projects failing in terms of cost, quality or time.

The project requirements

The project manager is usually the first person charged with the responsibility of delivering the project's objectives. Normally the project manager will either be an internal employee or external appointment and, in all cases, he or she should be knowledgeable of the financial and operational criteria of the hospitality industry and not just property construction. If the project manager is an external appointment, the same criteria should be utilized. In determining the consultants to be employed, the first consideration is

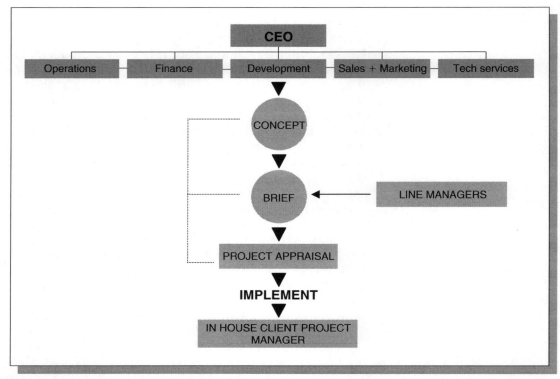

Figure 7.2
The normal structure of the client team

the nature and scope of the project, and these generally fall into the following categories (Table 7.1):

- Soft refurbishment
- Soft and hard refurbishment
- Full refurbishment
- Repositioning
- Repositioning and extension
- Building use conversion
- New build.

Different projects require different skills and the manner and form of contract used for their implementation will all influence the number and type of consultants utilized. For example, a soft refurbishment normally involves the replacement of curtains or drapes, bedspreads, upholstery coverings and wall decorations. This type of refurbishment will often be internally funded and dealt with by the company's in-house interior designers and implemented by the maintenance team or local interior decorators

Construction	Content	External consultant
Soft refurbishment Bedroom and public areas	Soft furnishings Carpets Floor and wall finishes Artwork	Interior designer Planning supervisor Cost consultant*
Hard refurbishment Bedroom and public areas	Soft furnishings Furniture Floor and wall finishes Lighting Artwork Bathrooms Minor building work Building permits	Interior designer M&E services engineer Architect or building surveyor Cost consultant Planning supervisor Project manager*
New build, repositioning or enlargement Bedroom, public areas and back of house facilities	All interior elements Exterior building fabric New build areas Landscaping Branding/signage Building permits	Project manager Interior designer Architect M&E services engineer Structural engineer Cost consultant Planning supervisor Specialist consultant**

*Optional consultants
**Specialist consultants used for issues such as planning, lighting, environmental, traffic, studies

Table 7.1
Specialist consultants used on various development options

or suppliers. A repositioning and extension project, however, will be much more complex involving obtaining permits or local and statutory approvals, external finance, party wall negotiations, provision of utilities, complete replacement of the building services infrastructure and major construction works. In the case of the latter we can envisage that the range and skills of the consultants will be extensive. However, the knowledgeable project manager will, before defining the range of consultants and services required, reflect and discuss the method of procurement and construction relevant to the cost, quality and time attributes of the project brief. For example, if time is less critical than cost and quality, then there may be justification for seeking to ensure that the project is fully designed and costed before works are commenced. On the other hand, if time and cost are more critical than quality then the detail of the design is not so crucial. The first example would require a comprehensive design team providing a full range of services to detail extensively and specify all the elements of the project information for supply and construction, whereas in the second the requirement would be to secure a fixed price and completion date normally allowing the contractor/supplier greater freedom to determine the specification of the elements.

(i)

Illustration 7.1
Carlton Hotel, Edinburgh: a
refurbished hotel (Courtesy
of Paramount Hotels)   (ii)

Chapters 8 and 9 consider these issues in greater detail, but
clients invariably seek the best in terms of cost, quality and time.
These are not unreasonable aspirations, as development is generally undertaken in a competitive environment with declining
resources, and this requires a focus on attaining value for money.
This includes applying the requisite design resources as the procurement of these can equate to 12–15% of the overall project cost.

Another area becoming more relevant to determining the selection of design skills and services is the changing nature of the
construction industry from skill based to factory manufactured

Illustration 7.1
(*Continued*)   (iii)

based. Historically, bathrooms in hotel projects were part of the architect's design scope. However, this element of the product has evolved from the architect undertaking the planning with decorative input by the interior designer to one where now the interior designer generally does the detail planning and design and produces the detail design drawings and specifications. Considering the range of different room types and configurations that can be involved in a refurbishment this can be an extensive and time consuming exercise, nevertheless, while the client may include and pay the interior designer for doing this work, it is still quite common for the construction cost of this element to be included in the total value of works used to calculate the percentage fee charged by the architect. Similarly, it is not unknown on a new build project wherein the bathrooms are procured and installed as a pre-manufactured pod for both architect and interior designer to receive the full fee for this element even though one party only will prepare a greatly reduced set of detailed drawings and information. The latter example applies to more and more building elements and components and, in certain highly regulated countries such as Germany, where such products require national certification, manufacturers' control of the marketplace is such that variances no matter how desirable for aesthetic reasons are not financially viable. Admittedly, the architect or designer will still be responsible for the coordination and integration of such pre-manufactured elements in the overall building design and construction but that is a different service element covered separately in any good agreement. Other areas to be considered in evaluating the project requirements and determining the design team resources to be applied include:

Planning applications. Where these involve monuments or listed buildings or development in sensitive areas, the use of a specialist planning consultant in the early stages, before the appointment of other teams can save time and resources to secure agreement in principle for the permissible development. In the USA, consultation with a land agent can attain the same results.

Cost. Sensibly utilized in the preliminary stages of a project's viability stages for establishing benchmark costs, cost consultants do just that, establish a project's likely outturn cost based on industry benchmark information. This is often confused with the cost of a specially designed property and can lead to projects starting on an erroneous basis.

Unrealistic timescales. A common error driven by naivety or unrealistic aspirations at the outset, time and resources are applied to defining the brief but not the time to realize the objective realistically. Similarly, time is expended on detail design production information without thought to the time required or remaining to procure and construct the specified elements. Alternatively, skill based elements will be incorporated into fast track projects where the time is not available to realize them.

Resources. Clients will resource the project internally to realize it to the implementation stage and then fail to allocate adequate resource to manage the delivery. Consultants' and contractors' skill sets, resources and current workload will not be reviewed or analysed to see if they are adequate.

Quality and complexity. Is the project complex and requiring a high degree of quality in specific areas? The input of professional skills in a limited service hotel is far less than a quality resort, as should be the method and systems of procurement. Does the provision of building services require a full mechanical and electrical design service or would a performance specification suffice?

Definitions. Do all the parties understand the content of FF&E and OS&E? (see glossary of terms for explanations). These are probably some of the most misinterpreted elements of a project cost estimate and ones that lead to most cases of cost overruns or omissions on hospitality projects. Similarly in Europe there is a tendency to define quality in terms of star ratings even though there is no European standard for hotel quality ratings and those that do exist nationally are inadequate in terms of definition for use in any contractual way.

International variants. As consultants practising in most English speaking nations or those that historically formed part of the British Empire will have a similar background in training and basis in the scope of services and of terms of engagement they publish, there is a wide variety in the detail of the definitions worldwide. Those engaging consultants are advised to research the local definitions and systems before making assumptions about the meaning of the commonality of the terminology utilized.

Professionalism. Professional status, methods, character, or standards in a modern world where everyone from a sewage worker (not to demean their contribution to society) to a physician

(i)

Illustration 7.2
Elysium Hotel & Resort,
Paphos, Cyprus
(Courtesy Scott
Brownrigg)

(ii)

(iii)

Illustration 7.2
(*Continued*)

(iv)

is a professional, surviving in a very competitve marketplace, the term has lost much of its meaning and standing in society. Most professional bodies write their own standards of professional practice and control the training, qualification and monitor compliance of standards of practice of their membership. Enforcement of standards is as difficult for them as is that of most hotel franchisers or franchisees, so perhaps the old motto of 'buyer beware, seller not fair' is becoming more applicable to our selection of the professional consultant. Personal references, even though they take time and energy, are still the most valued way of selecting those that you will be entrusting to advise you on spending large amounts of your or your company's capital funds.

Experience. Some would argue that the scribbles of a young child are as creative as those of our renowned modern artists and, irrespective of the validity of such a view, determining the creative skills one is seeking to procure is different to the technical skills needed to deliver a complex construction development. Many examples exist of separating the two in attaining the requisite skills and undoubtedly there can be no substitute for experience and a proven track record in hospitality development that is so sensitive to attaining a balance in cost, time and quality for realizing a return on investment. Experience, it is well to remember, is vested in the individual and rarely in the corporate body, so select and secure the individual and not just the corporate body.

The above is by no means an exhaustive list of the items to be considered in establishing the requirements for the skill and service levels of the design team members on any given project, but hopefully provides sufficient insight to demonstrate the need to investigate carefully the terms and provisions required for any relevant project in the particular location.

Professional team appointments

The number of consultants to be appointed on projects, especially large or complex ones can be extensive as illustrated in Figure 7.3.

The most realistic way to address the issue of professional appointments is to consider the professional in the same light as the employment, for instance, of a chef or maître d'hôtel, both are essential to your business's success and in determining their employment the nature, scope and standard of service to be provided will be critically evaluated. For an existing restaurateur or someone new to the restaurant business he or she will expend time to understand the role they will play and to define this and the services they will be required to deliver in a written contract of employment, the same service requirements and terms need to be resolved for any consultant's appointment. Whereas most professional institutes or bodies will publish standard terms, these need to be aligned to suit the project's requirements and not automatically assumed as suitable. All contracts need to define in detail the

125

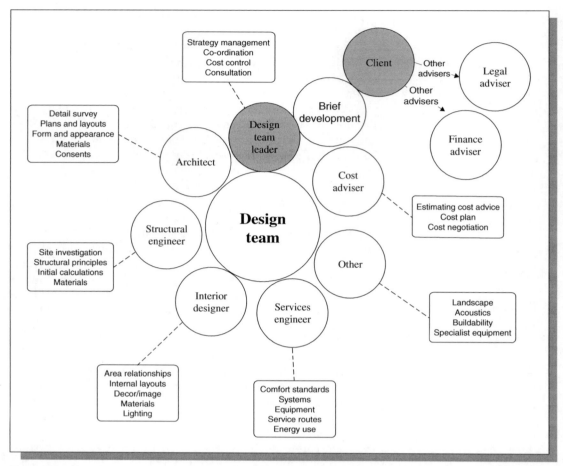

Figure 7.3
The design team

scope of works involved, the schedule of services to be provided, the project's stages and duration and the applicable fee agreed. Separately the contract should identify the level of professional indemnity insurance cover required to be secured by the consultant and any additional warranties needed to be put in place by the client to satisfy the requirements of his funders. Good contracts will address the coordination responsibility between the differing consultants' appointment, the seniority and order of authority, sequential order and flow of information as well as the reporting structure. Clients should require the project manager or lead consultant, historically the architect, to publish a coordinated schedule of services, preferably accompanied with a consultant's services matrix. See Figure 7.4 for an example of a schedule of services.

The objective of the schedule of services on a complex or large project is readily to determine that all the necessary responsibilities and tasks have been allocated. Interestingly, the best examples of

JV Ref No.	Annex 2 Architect	Annex 2A Interior designer	Annex 4 Structural engineer	Annex 5 Building services engineer	Annex 8 Lead consultant
Stage 2					
2.1	(A.2.2.8) In cooperation with the other members of the Project Team, complete the design of the Project up to tender stage.	(A.2.2.8) In cooperation with the other members of the Project Team, complete the design of the Project up to tender stage. Issue the Contractor Client with a set of tender drawings, specification sheets and workmanship specifications for the interior elements, in the agreed tender works package format.	(A.2.2.8)(A4.2.7) In cooperation with the other members of the Project Team, and in accordance with the Contractor Client's brief complete the structural design element (including, if necessary bar bending schedules) of the Project up to tender stage.	(A.2.2.8)(A5.2.11) In cooperation with the other members of the Project Team, and in accordance with the Contractor Client's brief complete the building services design element of the Project up to tender stage.	(A.2.2.8) In co-operation with the other members of the Project Team, complete the design of the Project up to tender stage.
2.2	(A5.2.3) Work closely with the Contractor Client and the Project Team to ensure that the building services design is fully integrated with the overall design of the Project and that the works can be completed within the amount allocated for building services in the approved cost limit and within the programmed time.	(A5.2.3) Work closely with the Contractor Client and the Project Team and use best endeavours to ensure that the building services design is fully integrated with the overall interior design of the Project and that the interior design can be realized within the allocated budgets and programme period.	(A5.2.3) Work closely with the Contractor Client and the Project Team to ensure that the building services design is fully integrated with the overall design of the Project and that the works can be completed within the amount allocated for building services in the approved cost limit and within the programmed time.	(A5.2.3) Work closely with the Contractor Client and the Project Team to ensure that the building services design is fully integrated with the overall design of the Project and that the works can be completed within the amount allocated for building services in the approved cost limit and within the programmed time.	(A5.2.3) Work closely with the Contractor Client and the Project Team to ensure that the building services design is fully integrated with the overall design of the Project and that the Works can be completed within the amount allocated for building services in the approved cost limit and within the programmed time.
2.3					Lead the Design Team and coordinate

(Continued)

JV Ref No.	Annex 2 Architect	Annex 2A Interior designer	Annex 4 Structural engineer	Annex 5 Building services engineer	Annex 8 Lead consultant
					spatially and technically all elements of the design including the work of other Consultants, Contractors and Suppliers and integrate into the overall design of the works during the tender process.
2.4					Lead the Design Team and coordinate a response to any Contractor Client queries that may arise during Stage 2 (A8.2.10)
2.5					Coordinate all design work, ensure that the designs are fully integrated and are tested throughout the design phase against costs targeted and planning or other controls and take any action necessary to rectify deficiencies. (A2.2.1)
2.6	(A2.2.1) In cooperation with the other members of the Project Team, develop the scheme design within the approved cost limit and	Prepare preliminary schedule of drawings and specification sheets to illustrate scope of information to be provided	(A2.2.1) In cooperation with the other members of the Project Team, develop the scheme design within the approved cost limit and	(A2.2.1) (A5.2.7 part) In cooperation with the other members of the Project Team, develop the scheme design within the approved cost limit and	(A2.2.1) In cooperation with the other members of the Project Team, develop the scheme design within the

	submit to the Contractor Client for approval giving details of proposed specification and Services.	and agree tender works packages with the client and Project Team. In cooperation with the other members of the Project Team, develop the scheme design within the approved cost limit and submit to the Contractor Client for approval giving details of proposed specifications and details.	submit to the Contractor Client for approval giving details of proposed specification and Services.	submit to the Contractor Client for approval giving details of proposed specification and Services.	approved cost limit and submit to the Contractor Client for approval giving details of proposed specification and Services.
2.7					Prepare and agree a resource loaded design programme for the remainder of the design process on a package-by-package basis with the Contractor Client and incorporate the programme requirements of the other Consultants to ensure integration with the Project Programme.

Figure 7.4
An example of a schedule of services

consultant's appointments are to be found as prescribed by turnkey or design and build contractors who themselves will be contracted direct to the client to deliver the project's design and complete construction and fitting-out on a fixed price and timescale basis. Their attention to the detail of consultant's appointments is in some cases extreme but nevertheless reflects their understanding of the risk of failure on any part of the process.

The other aspect worth consideration in reinforcing in any consultancy agreement or contract is that of professional duty of care. This imposes an automatic duty of care on each individual specialist consultant arising from the law of tort, which is concerned with conduct, which causes harm to a party's personal, proprietary or financial interests. While responsible for their own area of expertise, all consultants regularly engaged in working in construction have a duty of care to warn of any omission on the part of the other that comes to their attention.

Negligence claims require three essential elements: namely the existence of a legal duty of care, a breach of that duty, and consequential damage. It should be noted that consultants can only be held responsible for negligent acts or omissions and not for failing to satisfy the clients objectives, for example if an architect or designer presents his design proposals and the client rejects them, if it can be demonstrated that the requirements of the brief have been addressed, the client has to pay for the work done. This example clearly demonstrates the contractual importance of the brief in appointing consultants; note though that as the client is deemed in law not to be expert, the consultant has a duty to develop and agree the project brief with the client. Whereas there has been a tendency in recent years for consultants to move towards providing the client with what he wants, it should be remembered that the function of a professional person is to provide what the client needs, the agreement on a developed and detailed brief is of paramount importance within the consultant's agreement and to realize the client's project objectives.

Other aspects of the terms of appointment that need to be addressed include provision for:

Collateral warranties. A fundamental principle of contract is that only the contractual parties have any rights or duties under that contract, therefore for any third party, such as the party providing the loan finance for the project, which commonly can be 70% of the total finance, to have any claim any third party would require the benefit of a prescribed form of warranty to create a contractual relationship and provide for the rights to seek a remedy if design defects became apparent after completion.

Copyright. In general, copyright remains with the originator or creator for his or her lifetime and for 50 years thereafter. It is unusual to transfer copyright, but more normal to grant a licence to use the copyright material for a particular purpose or for a particular period of time. In hospitality projects where it is common to develop multiple units of a successful product it is important to resolve this provision in agreements.

Simple or speciality contract. A simple contract is executed under hand, whereas a speciality contract, which can and normally is the same document, is executed as a deed. The important difference between the two is that the former requires a consideration present between the parties to be valid and an action for breach between the parties is limited to a period of six years after the date of the breach. The latter does not require a consideration to make it valid and the limitation period is twelve years from the date of the breach.

Expenses. There is no automatic right to expenses and fees quoted should clearly state these are excluded otherwise the client can assume they are included.

Design stages. It is advisable for all consultants' agreements to set out the different work stages, with the proviso that no stage is progressed until the precedent stage has been completed and the subsequent authorized. Reference should be made to the coordinated design services matrix, as different consultants' work stages are inter-dependent on the performance of the other.

Design programme. A detailed programme setting out the different consultants' work stages, timescales for performance and deliverables is recommended to ensure that the overall project programme is maintained.

Duties and services

To cover the full range and scope of all the different consultants' duties and services that can be involved in differing projects internationally is beyond the scope of this chapter. Each project and location will have special requirements and it is in this area that the project manager can be of significant benefit to the client. A prerequisite requirement of the definition for a project manager in construction is that he has a broad experience of the industry and its various requirements. While the primary role is one of communication and coordination, he or she has the prime duty to advise the client on the different expertise required for a given project, and the content of services and duties to be provided. It is accepted practice that all other consultants also have a duty to advise the client of any specialist they consider necessary to be appointed at the beginning or during the project's design development stage. Simple examples include the appointment of a planning supervisor in the UK on effectively any construction project. The planning supervisor's role in simple terms is to advise the client on all aspects of health and safety and ensure that it is considered in the development process from the start of the design stage of the project through to its completion. I cite this example, as it is the only statutory regulation for construction work that exposes the client to a potential jail sentence in the case of non-compliance.

The services that specialist design consultants in the construction industry may offer as part of their normal or additional services will cover every facet of their specialist area of expertise: the architects will cover building work and the care and maintenance of buildings in use; the structural engineer will cover structural design from foundations to roof including advice on the ground conditions; the mechanical and electrical engineers address all aspects of the building services including IT; the interior designer will deal with all aspects of the buildings interior fitting out and FF&E; and the cost consultant will advise on all aspects of costs, contracts and in some cases taxation and financial planning. Other specialists such as landscape, lighting and acoustic consultants provide services that are specific to their more limited areas of speciality.

Normally the essential appointments for most hospitality projects consist of the cost consultant, architect, structural, mechanical and electrical engineers and interior designer. In the case of refurbishment works involving minor building works this team could be reduced by omitting the architect and limiting the services of the M & E consultants to the preparation of a performance brief and review of the contractor's proposals and inspection of the completed works including attendance of the commissioning on site. If the building to be refurbished is an older property the additional services of a building surveyor, with his specialist knowledge of such properties could be procured to augment the interior designer skills at a lower cost than that of an architect. Whereas architects and interior designers may share similar design skills for this type of work there would only be a requirement for one designer.

An important human consideration in framing the duties of the consultant is that different consultants, not unnaturally, will have a different viewpoint as to their duties and greater responsibilities to society in general. Much as such viewpoints are laudable sentiments, they need to be shared with the client as in the end it is he or she who is paying for the project's development costs. To illustrate this point, it is not unusual for an architect to resist maximizing the density of a given development below that which would be approved by the requisite authorities to provide for, in his opinion a more pleasant aspect or environ, similarly the mechanical engineer may wish to enhance the environmental performance beyond that envisaged by the client. In both examples the costs of the project would undoubtedly increase and albeit that the long-term benefits might be viewed as desirable it is nevertheless incumbent on the consultant to explain and persuade the client to address the issues and vary his brief and not accept for the matters not to be disclosed. Clients and consultants need to be sensitive to these issues but in the final analysis the consultant must respect the fact that he or she is providing a service and not determining the project content. Equally, there are instances where the client will endeavour to influence the consultant to ignore specific requirements relative to procedural requirements, compliance with regulations or other aspects that he or she considers expensive and unwarranted, it is incumbent on the consultant in such situations to resist and refuse to implement such requests.

Development of highly cost sensitive projects such as hospitality projects should more readily be structured in the preparation and presentation of cost plans to reflect its nature and recognize that the hospitality industry analyses elemental expenditure in a different way to most other forms of development. When the development constitutes a product that requires to appeal, attract and satisfy its customer it is not surprising that certain aspects are considered of greater importance than normal. Equally, as most mainstream hospitality projects, to be financially viable inevitably require some sort of balance to be established on expenditure on the elements of building, services, interiors (FF&E) and operating supplies and equipment, it is surprising that rarely are cost plan reports structured to reflect these categories of planned expenditure. Not surprisingly, this lack of communication has often led to problems with the planned project expenditure at the latter stages of the design development and or implementation, normally resulting in a compromise on the aspects to which the customer readily relates.

Statutory approvals

All countries, states or regional authorities will have in place planning or development policies governing the control of new development and for the alteration of existing buildings. Most will also have specific regulations relevant to the retention and maintenance of important buildings of historical merit or monuments. Such policies will vary in terms of content as they will express and reflect national or local aspirations to protect the existing environment, or to limit or alternatively encourage development. In all cases they will be empowered by means of national or local statutory regulations and require approval of any proposed development to be obtained by means of a formal application and approval process.

Approval is generally divided into two separate stages: first outline approval confirming permission to develop or alter an existing building in principle based on very limited information having been submitted to support the application. Normally this stage is the most difficult as its objective is to agree the principles of the nature, use and scope of the new development. It will also address issues such as highways, infrastructure, general zoning of the site, density, employment generation, parking, tourism and hotel accommodation requirements and any other relevant local requirements or constraints. Outline or consent in principle will not permit the development to proceed until more detailed information has been submitted for separate approval. The second stage of approval will entail the submission of much more detailed information relating to the design, layouts, style, finishes, landscaping and other specific aspects that the planning or development policies have deemed to require control by the relevant authority. Historically speaking the more developed the country you are seeking to develop in, the greater and more controlled the planning or permit requirements will be. This is changing; often in areas in the world where new tourism potential is identified the government has specified that controlled development is more sustainable in the longer term – a reaction to some of the short-term boom and bust cycles that have been part of some excessive tourism development in the past.

Considering that planning or development policies are of a local nature, politically relevant and constantly evolving, it is usually imperative to have local advice to secure a principal permit or outline consent. Separately, there will also be a requirement to satisfy the requirements of the local building control regulations; these will primarily be concerned with life safety and therefore most relevant to the design detail of the properties structure and means of protection of and the evacuation of occupants in case of fire. Secondly, and a more recent development, building control regulations are starting to impose more stringent requirements in respect of energy conservation in building design and use as well as the use of environmentally safe materials. Unlike planning or development permit approvals, building control permits are normally not finalized until the building is complete, the authority will therefore seek for the developer to undertake a consultation process during construction that progressively reviews the design as it progresses ahead of the construction. Building control regulations must be regarded as limited in their objective and not assume they qualify or underwrite the quality of the broader detail design of the building or its construction. Importantly for hotel projects, these normally require a fire certificate before occupation is permissible and are only issued after the building has been inspected at completion by the local fire department. If the building does not comply with their requirements then no guests can be checked in until it does comply. Such certificates are normally renewable every few years.

Other significant regulations that will impact on new development or use of existing buildings is the impact of the requirements of the disability discrimination laws recently introduced in the USA, European countries and other parts of the world. These laws impose a complete change in the provision of access for the physically disabled, which can involve a high degree of alteration to existing public buildings including hotels and restaurants. Similarly, the health and safety law in construction introduced in Europe relating to buildings being designed in a way that ensures they can be constructed and maintained in a safe manner have, it was calculated in the UK, added approximately 2% to the total construction cost of projects. These are only the main regulations that deal with development in its broader sense, and there are many and varied requirements of a simple or complex nature. As all regulations and laws constantly evolve and generally have regional or even more local interpretations applied, consultants have to have a good understanding of current requirements before addressing the concept design for any development proposal let alone the detail stage. Lastly, one prediction for the future that can be relied on is that regulations will continue to increase in number and become more complex and demanding, even in a free world economy, that is the price we pay for globalization, overpopulation and disregard of the environment.

Design development and procurement

Having secured the required outline or principal development permits, the design team progresses the detail design and specification for the development. Subject to the planned procurement route the control of this will remain with the client or the contractor. In all cases this stage relates to the production of all design drawings, workmanship and material specifications, provision of samples, prototype bedrooms, cost checking, value engineering and determining construction methods, systems and timescales required to obtain competitive pricing for the overall construction and installation cost of the project.

While costs, procurement and construction will be addressed in more detail in Chapters 8 and 9, the key issues to be addressed by the project team in this stage are:

- Coordination and communication

- Detailed integration of the operational requirements

- Maintain objectivity in respect of the brief

- Control projected costs

- Maintain programme and reasonable requirements

- Quality and comprehensive nature of information

- Consolidation of all information.

The reference to the 'project team' rather than the 'design team' was intended to reinforce the need for clients to understand that their input and interaction in this detailed design stage is essential if the content of the information being produced is to reflect their needs in detail. Changes to information at this stage is inexpensive as opposed to change when the work is on site, however, there is a misconception that this stage is for the design team to do their work, leading to the client making changes when the work is being implemented on site. Detailed design information forms the basis of the contract with the contractors and suppliers in that it defines

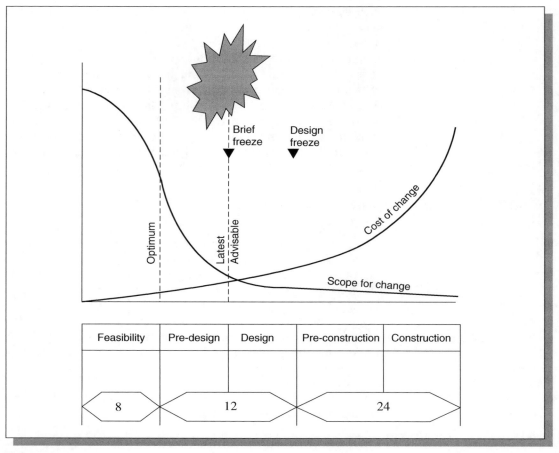

Figure 7.5
Change cost diagram

the content and quality of what is required to be produced, changes to this on site result in delay and extra costs as they constitute a variance to the agreed contract.

This is also the time to integrate fully the detail of the operational requirements, ensure that all the requirements have been integrated and coordinated between the different design consultants' information and importantly for the cost consultant constantly to check and review the project costs. All these aspects and especially the latter require a constant management, communication and interaction between the client and design team if the maximum efficiency and value for the project is to be realized. The devil is in the detail and equally important the detail must flow from the project objectives, without constant interface with the client it is surprising how easily the agreed objectives and concept designs can be lost.

As any experienced manager will confirm, without the appropriate leadership and direction, those employed in different departments can quickly lose sight of a company's strategy or plan, in the case of specialists with different priorities this can readily be compounded. Without appropriate leadership and prompt management decision making the team, usually under pressure at this stage, can introduce short cuts in the quality and comprehensive nature of the information resulting in the imposition of unreasonable expectations on the construction team that will be building the project, aspects for which the client will incur additional cost. Lastly, a common failing is for information not to be properly consolidated before tendering, resulting in tenders being returned incomplete, in a format that cannot be properly analysed or worse include a wide range of provisional sums all of which put the project cost, time and quality at risk.

Construction

On a properly managed project, when all the previous stages have been correctly carried out and the selection of a contractor has been based on more than the lowest price, then resource, skill, ability, experience, financial status and performance plus a realistic programme have been agreed to attain best value. This stage of the project should be the least demanding for the design team, their role being limited to visit the site regularly to see that the work is being done in compliance with the quality and detail set out in the design information and requirements of the permits or statutory approvals. If your design team members are spending excessive time on site to clarify or provide additional information, it is either because the design information was not complete, poorly coordinated or the client is imposing late changes. The net result of any of this is usually delay and additional cost. In simple terms, building contracts are based on the contractor undertaking to carry out a specified scope and quality of work in an agreed period of time for an agreed price for the client, any variation or change to the agreed scope or quality is a change to the contract. Change in any form is demanding, change to any contract is demanding and negotiable and therefore, not surprisingly, expensive.

Handover and occupation

Hospitality properties are very complex, and it has become normal for such buildings to be handed over in phases. This is primarily caused by the fact that it is in the financial interest of the operator to start to earn revenue from the property as soon as possible after the building is practicably or fully complete. Equally relevant is the fact that the operator will have pre-sold a level of the accommodation from a specific date. Usually this 'soft' opening date is planned some months in advance of the completion date, when there is a contractual duty to provide this accommodation.

In order to satisfy these requirements it is sensible for the operator to take partial possession of the building to facilitate training

- Handover – partial or full
- Quality control – inspections/alterations
- Practical completion – commissioning/defects/remedial/manual/ certification/*de minimis*
- Occupation – maintenance/latent defects/adjustments/certification
- Final account and certificate
- Liability – 6, 12 or 15 years

Figure 7.6
A typical handover sequence

of staff, install operating supplies and equipment and thoroughly clean and prepare the facilities for rental to guests. A typical handover sequence is shown in Figure 7.6.

Partial possession involves the client accepting part of the building as complete and suitable for use – of 'practicable completion'. This means that there is an acceptance that the contractor has fulfilled obligations under the contract and that the owner or operator as agent will take full responsibility for that area of the building. Responsibility involves such issues as insurance, security, health and safety and particular attention should in such circumstance be paid to access for staff, suppliers, and goods and in some instances potential or paying guests. The other meaning of the term 'practicable completion' is that it recognizes that the area or building is not fully complete. Therefore the design team members under the direction of the contract administrator (normally the architect) will have prepared a schedule of defects or incomplete works. The contract will provide for this in that the client, while having possession of part or the whole of the building must still provide the contractor with reasonable access to carry out remedial or complete outstanding works. All this is simple in concept but imagine having to provide reasonable access to large numbers of let bedrooms or working kitchens for building tradesmen to carry out work! This is quickly where definitions of 'reasonable' start to differ.

Conclusion

It is the brief which captures the essence of the project and establishes its objectives, as it inherently defines the requirements and skill set that are necessary to realize the objectives. The analysis and extrapolation of the project requirements will generally prescribe the procurement method and the nature and number of consultants to be utilized. Membership of professional bodies only guarantees a minimum standard of practice, and therefore consultants should be carefully selected for those particular skills which apply to the project. Duties and services require detailed clarification and coordination to ensure that all the aspects of the project's design and specification requirements are covered and best value fee agreements are attained. The design and construction team are effectively the manager's tools to do the job and, like a good craftsman, will take great care in selecting the best or most appropriate available for the task.

Natural, regional, cultural, climatic and economical factors will give rise to variance in regulatory requirements that have to be satisfied. It is resolving these aspects and numerous others that combine to make designing and developing hospitality projects internationally so complex. This creates a need for excellence in communication, coordination and the integration of operational requirements in the design development stage. Construction is a sequential activity which is extremely time sensitive, as the completeness and quality of the design information directly links to the success of the construction process. Once construction commences, change should be avoided and when required, managed in a manner to minimize the impact on time, quality and cost. The contractor should be regarded as the head chef, preparing a five-course banquet starting at 7 p.m. With speeches scheduled for 10 p.m., what would happen if it was decided to change the third course at 7.15 p.m?

Finally, completion should be recognized as a process of a sequential transfer of areas rather than an instant possession of the total. The important aspects of handover relate to the transfer not only of part or whole of the building, but also the information relative to its management and maintenance in a safe and appropriate manner. This involves training of staff, provision of all as-built and installed specifications, drawings and installation information together with maintenance manuals and instructions. For all those involved in the development process and the resultant operation, enormous benefit can be accrued by undertaking a post-project review involving client, design, construction and operational personnel as well as operational team members, providing for future improved performance on other and not necessarily similar projects.

References

Chappell, D. and Willis, C. J. (1992) *The Architect in Practice,* seventh edn, Blackwell Science, Oxford.

Reader's Digest Universal Dictionary (1986) Lexical Databases, Houghton Mifflin, Boston.

Speaight, A. and Stone, G. (2000) *Architects' Legal Handbook*: *the law for architects,* seventh edn, Architectural Press, Oxford.

Review questions

1 Outline the various stages in the hospitality design process.

2 What roles might design team members play in the process?

3 Explain the elements of negligence.

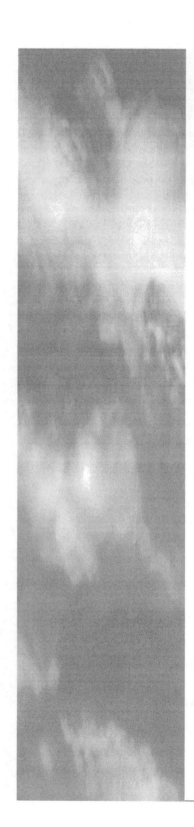

Building costs

Simon Rawlinson

The hospitality industry is cost and value driven and most capital projects need to be delivered within tight financial constraints. This chapter explains how cost and value are managed on construction projects and outlines the key processes and players involved. This chapter considers:

- Introduction
- Cost and value: securing high development returns from hospitality projects
- Cost management: key processes in securing project value
- The cost, time and quality equation
- Cost drivers: why hotel costs vary
- Refurbishment: considerations for works in existing buildings
- Adding value to construction. Value and risk management
- Procurement strategy. Buying the building
- Conclusion
- Case study.

Introduction

This chapter also examines formal techniques used to optimize value on projects, including risk and value management, together with methods of buying and managing construction. The procurement arrangements and roles described are common in the UK, but many of the principles can be applied to other global markets. Although the main focus of the chapter is upon new build construction, many of the issues are also pertinent to refurbishment work. The case study illustrates how an innovative approach to procurement and effective team working can help to deliver high quality construction within challenging time and cost constraints.

Cost and value: securing high development returns from hospitality projects

Capital projects are complex, and their successful development is dependent upon a wide range of influences. Clients in the hospitality industry are cost driven and projects are typically delivered to challenging budgets and programmes. While the success of a project may be assessed by the rate of return achieved, in reality there is a much wider range of benefits that the project will deliver, which in turn are affected by design and construction. As construction costs form such a large proportion of initial capital costs, accounting for 50–70% of the capital costs of a hospitality project, it is important that these are managed in the pursuit of maximum project value. The key players responsible for the management of capital costs are quantity surveyors (QSs), the client, design team and contractor.

- *Quantity surveyors* (QSs) are construction professionals who forecast and manage construction costs throughout the project lifecycle, advising the client and design team so as to focus investment on elements of the project that deliver the greatest benefit to the client, or which minimize risk. Also known as cost consultants, they also manage the financial implications of changes introduced during the design and construction programme to ensure that the budget is met.

- *Client*. The client sets the brief and budget, appoints the project team, signs off the design and ultimately determines the cost levels of a project. Ways in which clients can contribute to the effective control of costs include:
  - Providing a comprehensive brief
  - Sticking to the brief, signing off the design and avoiding design and specification 'creep'
  - Avoiding changes to design and construction at later stages of a project.

- *Contractors.* Contractors are typically employed to construct a project based either on designs prepared by the client's consultants or a scheme for which the contractor is responsible. As contractors secure work through price competition, there can be pressure on them to recover profit by the rationalization of the design or through securing additional payments. Fully designed schemes constructed with the minimum design change give the contractor the best opportunity to secure a reasonable return and for the project to be delivered on budget.

- *Design team.* The design team, typically comprising architect, interior designer, structural and services engineers, cost consultant and other advisers, is responsible for the development of the design to meet a brief, budget and programme, based on an analysis of the client's needs and wants. Cost and value on a project will be affected by the match between the design solution and the client's brief. Other areas of performance that can affect the outcome of a project include the management of the design process and the supervision and approval of the contractor's work.

Cost management: key processes in securing project value

Value in hospitality is derived from services provided rather than from bricks and mortar. It is based on location, strength of brand, management and quality of service and ambience. On construction projects, the role of cost management is to set an appropriate budget, to ensure that funds are focused on elements which add value, and to avoid erosion of value caused by the escalation of project costs.

Cost management is led by the QS, but if it is to be effective, should be carried out as a team activity, providing positive advice and input tailored to the circumstances of the project. The key cost management processes are as follows:

1 The production of initial estimates

2 The development of the cost plan

3 Procurement, contractor selection and tendering

4 Progress and cost reporting and agreement of the outturn cost of the project.

1 *Initial estimates* are prepared ahead of any detailed design work, enabling a client to assess project costs without investment in detailed design work. Initial estimates can be used to identify options for further development, or for investment appraisals, and are prepared using costs taken from similar projects, adjusted for size, quality, location, price levels and

other cost drivers. Initial estimates are typically within ± 15 to $\pm 20\%$ of the outturn cost of a project.

2 *Cost plans* are prepared by the QS as the design is developed in greater detail. A cost plan is a highly structured and detailed estimate used to confirm that a design meets the client's budget. It also establishes a clear relationship between the design, specification and cost. Clients will use cost plans to secure project funding, and in some cases, as the basis for agreeing a price with a contractor. Used effectively, it is a tool for setting and monitoring expenditure targets for particular parts of the building, highlighting instances of disproportionate over or under expenditure or potential areas for cost saving. The accuracy of the cost plan increases as the design is developed, and as an increasing proportion of the costs are based on market testing. At the time of tender, the cost plan will predict the final outurn cost to an accuracy of $\pm 7\frac{1}{2}\%$.

3 *Procurement, contractor selection and tendering*. Construction differs from many industries in that it has a highly fragmented supply chain and the selection of the right team is an important factor in project success. Construction offers a wide range of options for the purchase and management of projects, dealing with the following aspects of organization and administration:

- *Method of project procurement*. The managerial and contractual arrangements which determine responsibility for design, the balance of risk between parties, arrangements for dealing with changes, payment and so on.
- *Method of contractor selection*. Concerned with the selection of a preferred contractor from a shortlist based on cost, time and quality criteria.
- *Method of agreeing the project price*. Balancing price competition, speed and timing of cost certainty.

From a cost management perspective, key issues associated with procurement, contractor selection and tendering include:

- Ensuring that the contractor has the skills, experience and supply chain in place to deliver the project
- Ensuring that the project can be built for the proposed contract sum
- Utilizing effective use of competition to secure advantageous prices without compromising programme or specification
- Securing appropriate financial commitment, such as an agreed lump sum, to meet the client's funding requirements
- Obtaining price information at an appropriate level of detail to support the agreement of the cost effect of changes
- Ensuring that the contract documents properly reflect the client's preferred level of risk exposure.

4 *Progress and cost reporting and agreement of the outturn cost of the project*. Construction involves a degree of uncertainty, and once

work on site commences, factors including unexpected site conditions, the completion or coordination of design work, or changes to client requirements can alter the scope or sequence of work, potentially affecting progress on site, final costs and the date of completion. In most building contracts, the risk of design change rests mostly with the employer, so in many instances the contractor can be entitled to extra payments for additional work. Transfer of these risks involves the transfer of a degree of control to the contractor, and can also involve the payment of an additional 'risk premium'.

As construction projects are dynamic, rigorous management is required, and it is common practice for clients to receive progress reports on a monthly basis, summarizing progress and changes to the scope of work together with a projection of cashflow, out-turn cost and completion date. This report is a vital management tool and should be used by the team and client to initiate any actions required to ensure that time, cost and quality objectives are met.

Once the works are completed, the contractor and the client's team will negotiate the final costs of the project, incorporating the cost implications of approved variations and potentially add-itional payments related to the prolongation of the programme. Financial penalties could also be applied if the contractor were judged to be responsible for some or all of the delay.

The cost, time and quality equation

On all construction projects, the client and the project team are faced with balancing three critical and interrelated factors: con-struction costs, the available development programme and the desired quality and specification of the end product. Balancing these three factors requires a degree of compromise, although in the case of the hospitality sector, projects frequently have both fixed budgets and opening dates. These three factors overlay other issues, including the size of the building, its function, plan and location which also drive the cost, programme and specifica-tion. Experienced hotel project teams have well developed skills relating to working under tight budget and programme con-straints to meet expectations of high quality.

The effect of a very tight budget, an exceptionally challenging programme or a very high level of quality is likely to be detrimental to the achievement of objectives associated with the other factors. For example, a restricted budget will not only affect the level of quality that can be achieved, but may also dictate that a complete design is required before construction commences, potentially extending the overall project programme. Similarly, negotiating the contract sum for a project to shorten overall duration may result in the building being constructed at a premium price, without any corresponding increase in the achieved level of quality.

Cost drivers: why hotel costs vary

The UK domestic hospitality development sector is very diverse. Table 8.1 illustrates the wide range of costs for typical UK developments. The range of costs shown is determined by a range of factors including, among others; the facilities provided, sizes of bedrooms and quality of finish. These factors are termed cost drivers.

Cost drivers can be specific to a type of building, a client or a procurement strategy. Consideration of a project's cost drivers is particularly important at the earliest stages of a feasibility study, when the client and project team have the greatest freedom to opt for alternative sites or design options.

Current construction cost (inclusive of furniture, fittings and equipment)	Average gross floor area per room (m² gifa)	Unit cost	
		£/m² gifa	£000s/ bedroom
Luxury city centre hotel, multi-storey, conference and wet leisure facilities	70–130	1 500–2 000	135–200
Business town centre/provincial hotel 4–6 storeys, conference and wet leisure facilities	70–100	1 200–1 750	90–130
Mid-range provincial hotel 2–3 storeys, conference and leisure facilities	55–70	1 100–1 500	55–85
2–3 storeys, bedroom extension	35–45	800–1 250	30–45
City centre aparthotel 4–7 storey apartments with self-catering facilities	50–60	900–1 200	45–75
Budget city centre hotel (new build) 4–6 storey, dining and bar facilities	35–45	950–1 050	35–50
Budget city centre hotel (office conversion) 4–6 storey, excluding dining facilities	32–38	750–1 150	22–45
Budget roadside hotel 2–3 storey lodge, excluding dining facilities	28–35	850–1 150	26–33

Notes: Costs are for mid-range schemes for chain or affiliate hotels in outer London, with prices current in October 2003, assuming competitive tendering. Indicative costs include furniture, fittings and equipment, but exclude costs of drainage, external works and any necessary site preparation and demolitions. Cost of professional fees and VAT are also excluded

Table 8.1
Indicative costs in hotel developments

The figures set out in Table 8.1 provide indicative costs and require adjustment to account for the characteristics of specific projects.

The following twelve cost drivers are particularly significant in determining overall cost levels:

1 Site conditions and characteristics

2 Building plan, layout and massing

3 Quality levels

4 Building services installations

5 Extent of prefabrication

6 Furniture, fittings and equipment (FF&E) expenditure

7 Leisure facilities

8 Extent of external works

9 Requirements of local and statutory authorities

10 Unforeseen work and change to client requirements

11 Speed of construction

12 Location.

1 Site conditions

Site conditions such as unstable ground or requirements for decontamination will drive costs up, with no prospect of a return through increased revenue. The topography, layout and location of the site may also drive costs. A steeply sloping site will require extensive excavation and levelling works, while access problems or noise restrictions in a populated area will slow construction and add to demands on management resources. As part of the feasibility estimate, additional costs associated with these constraints and others, such as planning requirements, the impact of adjacent buildings, party walls and rights of light, may also need to be considered, possibly reducing the sum paid for the land.

2 Building plan, layout and massing

The interrelationship of the plan of a hospitality property, its room layout and the massing of multi-storey developments can have a marked effect on the costs of the development, influencing the overall floor area, the achievement of optimal room sizes and circulation allowances, and the cost of building elements such as external walls and windows.

For hotels, the most efficient floor plan is a rectangular or 'U' shaped block with double loaded corridors, that is, rooms on both sides of the corridor. This layout minimizes circulation and fire escape requirements and optimizes the number of rooms served from a single maid's station. This layout is commonly found on lodge and business hotel developments. This same building plan also results in a relatively low wall to floor ratio.

Site constraints, particularly on existing urban sites, commonly limit the opportunities for designers to devise an optimal floor plan. Relatively inefficient floor plans will be acceptable in prime locations, so long as the viability of a proposal can be demonstrated in the feasibility study.

The massing of the building, and in particular the number of storeys, can have a major effect on cost and programme. For example, guestroom blocks in excess of 4 or 5 storeys will require a structural frame and a non-load bearing external wall cladding system. This requirement, together with the need for enhanced life safety systems on taller buildings, will generally increase costs by 7–8%.

3 Quality levels

Quality levels are determined by the project's target market, and affect space allowances, facilities and staffing levels, along with standards of décor and service. Achieving the appearance of high quality at moderate cost, and focusing investment for maximum impact, in bathrooms for example, is a key area where specialist hotel teams can add value to their client's businesses.

4 Building services installations

Building services installations control the internal environment and their specification and performance is a key determinant of development quality.

The main cost driver affecting building services in guestroom blocks is the installation of comfort cooling into guestrooms. In the UK there is a growing trend for cooling to be provide in 'high grade' budget accommodation as well as business hotels. Full comfort cooling installations with fresh air supply will typically add £6000–7000 to the costs of a business grade guestroom, whereas the more simple systems in lower grade hotels will cost between £3500 and £4000. The increased intensity of services installations can also have a 'programme penalty', related to the complexity of air, water and power distribution and requirements for testing and commissioning. Use of prefabricated bathroom pods or service risers can reduce this problem. Other elements of services specification where quality is driven upward in response to client expectations include environmental controls, fire detection and telecommunication systems.

5 Extent of off-site manufacture

Techniques of off-site manufacture are increasingly applied at all levels of hospitality development. Lodge hotels have for some time been associated with off-site manufacture, either using load bearing modules or the assembly of panels. As the quality standard of the hotel rises, the opportunities for wholesale prefabrication are reduced and the application of off-site manufacture technologies is concentrated upon areas with intensive services and finishes such as bathrooms.

The economics of prefabrication are complex. Modular bathrooms have a cost premium of 5–10%, whereas use of prefabricated services can save money if there is an economy of scale. Other benefits associated with the use of prefabrication include improved quality, better site management, elimination of risks and simplified commissioning. Large scale off-site assembly such as the use of bathroom pods involves long lead-in times and tight dimensional coordination, and the design has to be frozen at an early stage to permit manufacture to programme.

6 Furniture, fittings and equipment (FF&E)

Furniture, fittings and equipment (FF&E) expenditure is closely linked to quality levels. These costs are usually under the control of the operator and there can be confusion between the scope of the interior design and FF&E elements of the building work. FF&E can drive up the developer's costs if not properly controlled. However, if the needs, characteristics and expectations of the target market are fully understood and a clear brief is established at an early stage, the FF&E budget can be set accurately and more effectively controlled. Table 8.2 sets out indicative rates for FF&E for a range of hotel developments.

7 Leisure facilities

The costs of specialist space associated with leisure facilities differs significantly from the cost of standard hotel space and may have implications for the design of the whole hotel. The inclusion

Hotel grade	Cost of FF&E (£/m² gross internal floor area)	
Budget	150	185
Mid-range	300	340
Luxury	360	500+

Costs include preliminaries but exclude contingencies, professional fees and VAT

Table 8.2
Indicative costs for furniture, fittings and equipment

of banqueting facilities may, for example, require a transfer structure to provide column-free space, which will increase structure costs and possibly the height of the building.

Since the scope of leisure facilities varies from hotel to hotel, these are best considered on a case-by-case basis, priced separately at the early stage of a project using functional unit rates. A guide to suitable rates for these facilities is given in Table 8.3.

8 External works and service

The requirements for external works and services are almost wholly site related and are typically excluded from the comparison of hotel cost benchmarks. These costs need to be considered on a case-by-case basis. Factors that cause variations include the

Functional area	Cost (£/m² functional area)	
Front of house and reception	920	1 300
Restaurant areas	1 030	1 600
Bar areas	900	1 450
Function rooms/conference facilities	770	1 450
Dry leisure	710	860
Wet leisure	1 500	2 000

Unit rates are inclusive of preliminaries, but exclude costs of site preparation, FF&E, external works, contingencies, professional fees and VAT. The rates were current in October 2003, based on a business sector hotel located in Outer London.

Table 8.3
Indicative costs of leisure and ancillary accommodation

Illustration 8.1
Royal Savoy Resort, Madeira
(Courtesy of Royal Savoy
Resort)

extent of site, the need for access roads, and the balance between hard and soft landscaping and requirements for the reinforcement of the local services infrastructure. External services such as drainage, power and water are connected by statutory providers. There is little competition for these services and costs have to be negotiated.

9 Requirements of local and statutory authorities

The influence of external stakeholders can affect overall project costs. Planning requirements can, for example, dictate the appearance of external elevations, which could result in the use of relatively expensive materials. External works, such as road layouts and junctions, parking provision, preservation of existing landscape features and emergency access, are all subject to the requirements of local statutory authorities. Costs associated with an authority's requirements can sometimes be reduced through negotiation, but are largely unavoidable.

10 Unforeseen work and changes to client requirements

As discussed in connection with cost management processes, allowances need to be made for the costs of design development and unforeseen work. Typically this is calculated as percentage of estimated construction costs and can vary from 3 to 5% for new build to 6 to 10% for refurbishment, depending on the complexity of the project. A larger contingency is generally included in early stage estimates for design development, for complex work or for refurbishment projects, where the full extent of the work may be less certain than for new build.

11 Speed of construction

Speed is important to developers and operators in order to respond to market opportunities, to generate early income and to reduce finance costs. The construction industry has developed a number of techniques to reduce construction time. These include the use of standardized components and off-site manufacture, the integration of design and construction and the development of strategic alliances with the supply chain. Setting a rapid programme without considering these issues could bring a cost or quality penalty.

12 Location

The geographical location of a hospitality project can influence the level of pricing, caused by differences in wages and material costs and local market conditions. Table 8.4 details regional location factors that were current in June 2003.

Region	Adjustment factor
Inner London	1.06
South East	0.94
South West	0.87
East Midlands	0.86
West Midlands	0.86
East Anglia	0.89
Yorkshire and Humberside	0.83
North West	0.86
Northern	0.85
Scotland	0.86
Wales	0.86
Northern Ireland	0.72

Table 8.4
Regional variation of
construction costs in the UK

Refurbishment: considerations for work in existing buildings

Regular refurbishment of hotels is necessary to maintain service quality, customer loyalty, room rates and market share. Broadly there are two categories of refurbishment, distinguished by the extent of works required:

- Guest room refreshment, required every five to seven years and aimed at maintaining a hotel's competitive position within its marketplace. The scope of works will include redecorations, replacement FF&E and minor improvements works.

- Guest room re-branding, aimed at moving a hotel into a higher market sector. The scope of works will be extensive and intrusive, including the creation of additional rooms from redundant space, the changing of room layout and replacement of bathrooms and services.

Refurbishment projects are often difficult, combining the problems of working in an existing occupied building with the pressures of fixed budgets, tight programmes and a site-based client. Particular problems that need to be addressed on refurbishment projects include:

- *Building condition*, including problems with the building structure, fabric and services as well as difficulties caused by the absence of as-built details and a legacy of ad hoc maintenance.

- *Working in occupied buildings* usually means working in phases, which results in additional costs related to temporary works and services diversions. The keys to successful phased working are:
  - maintaining speed of construction
  - maintaining the sequence and continuity of work

(i)

Illustration 8.2
A typical hotel plant room   (ii)

- managing safe, segregated access
- minimizing the impact of noisy and disruptive activities on guests

● *Constraints caused by the building fabric*. The project team will need to work around a wide range of constraints, including:
- Structure, including restrictions on room layouts, services routes and the position of openings
- Floor plans and window openings, influencing the re-planning of guestroom layouts

- Plant rooms and services routes, including the size and location of existing plant rooms and the availability of additional space.

Adding value in construction: value and risk management

Value management

Value management (VM) is used to enable a client to focus limited resources on the key objectives of a project, identifying lower costs or higher utility design solutions. VM techniques can be used to select the best project, establish the client brief, optimize the design or, if necessary, reduce costs without affecting function. The principal benefits of VM to the client are:

- Selection of the right project based on analyses of the client's objectives
- Maximization of project benefits
- The elimination of waste in design and construction
- The reduction of project duration
- Improving communication within the project team.

The benefits are obtained by identifying and eliminating causes of poor value or unnecessary cost drivers such as poor project definition, bespoke design solutions or inappropriate levels of specification.

VM is most effectively carried out as a team based process, typically facilitated by a specialist. The most important elements of the process are:

- *Function analysis*. The development of a model based on what a building does, and how the building benefits rather than the construction materials.

- *Ideas generation*. Identifying ways in which building functions can be delivered at a lower cost, greater speed or with a reduced level of risk.

- *Proposal development and implementation*. Developing, validating, planning and implementing selected changes.

Clients are advised to invest appropriate resources into VM processes and the implementation of workshop recommendations. The process recommended by a VM specialist should be followed closely. As opportunities to introduce change on projects reduce over time, the maximum benefit from VM is derived at the earliest stage of a project.

Risk management

Construction involves risk. Many projects are one-offs, involve long development programmes, a large number of stakeholders and inevitably expose the client to the uncertainties of working 'on site'. Risk management (RM) techniques enable the project team to plan for and reduce the impact of risks, improve the overall management of a project and increase the certainty of achieving the client's objectives. Using a formal risk management process, risks are identified, an assessment is made of the cost, time and quality consequences of a risk occurring and, where appropriate, mitigation actions are identified. The principal benefits of risk management are:

- Greater certainty of project outcomes
- Improved control of risk through pre-planning and early remedial action
- Encouragement of 'right first time' thinking
- Allocation of responsibility for risk mitigation to the party best placed to manage the risk
- Implementation of cost effective risk mitigation measures
- Effective control of the contingency sums and other risk allowances.

In common with value management, risk management is a team based process, utilizing the knowledge and experience of the whole project team to manage the client's exposure to risk. The principal stages in the process are:

- *Identification*. Utilization of team experience to identify and prioritize risks on a project which require further analysis and active management
- *Analysis*. Assessment of the time and cost consequences of major risks and the probability of their occurrence
- *Management*. Identification of the party best equipped to 'own' the risk and selection of the appropriate management strategies. Proactive management of risk is the key to a successful strategy. It is easy for a project team to 'go through the motions' of risk management and a member of the team should have clear responsibility to ensure that agreed actions are undertaken.

Procurement strategy

Project procurement is concerned with the purchase, management and delivery of design and construction. Methods of managing and delivering construction projects vary around the world, determining, for example, the degree to which design is undertaken by the constructor or the extent of project risk retained by the client. The choice of procurement strategy will affect how a client's goals are met but will not by itself determine project outcomes.

Some of the key issues that need to be considered when selecting a strategy include:

- The client's contractual relationship with the design team and contractor

- The need for single or multi-point responsibility for project delivery

- The necessity for direct professional accountability

- The apportionment of responsibility between client and contractor for time and costs risks

- The need for, and timing of, a contractor's commitment to a fixed price

- The need for the lowest possible price

- The client's ability to vary the scope of works

- The degree of complexity of the project

- The apportionment of responsibility for standards of workmanship and materials

- The allocation of responsibility for finished quality standards.

The three most common strategies for project procurement used in the UK are:

1 Lump sum contracting

2 Design and build

3 Management routes.

These three alternatives offer a range of options characterized by different design outputs, methods of pricing and detailed contractual arrangements. Full discussion of this is beyond the scope of this chapter. Consequently, the basic alternatives are outlined below and compared in terms of their contribution to the delivery of the client's cost, time and quality targets.

1 Lump sum contracting

Traditional contracting is based upon the split of design and construction work. This method of procurement is associated with competitive tenders, ideally based on practically complete design information. Competitive lump sum tenders tend to be economical and importantly provide an indication of the client's total cost commitment before construction starts. However, the requirement for the preparation of complete design information and detailed tender documentation extends the design programme. A variant involving two stages of tendering enables, at the cost of reduced price competition, the appointment of the main contractor ahead of the completion of design. Lump sum contracts can also be negotiated.

The advantages of lump sum contracting include:

- Appointment of contractors on the basis of price competition

- An early cost and time commitment

- Ability to define clearly quality requirements at tender stage

- Facility to change the scope of works without excessive cost and time penalties.

The disadvantages of lump sum contracting include:

- Split of design and construction activities and limited continuity between design and build phases

- Undermining of cost and time certainty due to the ease with which the scope of works can be changed

- Sharing of risk of cost and time overruns between client and contractor

- Absence of single point responsibility for overall project delivery.

Lump sum contracting is particularly suitable for refurbishment and conversion projects, where the two-stage tender variant is widely adopted. In such cases, the combination of early cost commitment and flexibility to deal with a varied scope of work is invaluable.

2 Design and build

The main feature of design and build procurement is the allocation of single point responsibility for both design and construction. Most of the risk for cost, time and quality is transferred to the design and build contractor, along with sufficient control to enable effective management of the risks. Design and build contracts can be let on the basis of conventional, two-stage or negotiated tenders. Tenders are prepared in response to a set of employer's requirements, which vary widely to the extent in which the design is prescribed.

When obtained competitively, design and build tenders return the lowest construction costs, although this may be at the expense of achieved quality. Cost and time of delivery are relatively certain with design and build, but construction quality is more difficult to define in the brief and to control on site unless the client invests in design team resources to review the contractor's proposals.

The principal advantages of design and build contracting include:

- Low cost, relatively fast construction
- Time and cost certainty
- Single point responsibility for design and construction
- Early cost and time commitment.

Some of the disadvantages of design and build contracting are:

- Reduced client control over design and quality standards
- Variable standards of design work from design and build organizations
- Limitations to the design liability offered by design and build organizations
- Limitations on the client's ability to change the scope of works, together with high cost and time penalties.

Design and build is particularly well suited to the budget market where hotel clients seek standardized solutions. Properly organized design and build can also be used to deliver projects of the highest quality. It is less suitable for conversion and refurbishment projects due to difficulties associated with the establishing of the scope of the work.

3 Management routes

Management routes are distinguished by the main contractor taking an exclusively managerial role. Specialist contractors undertake the construction work. Management routes provide the opportunity for early input into the design from the contractor, and permit an overlap of design and construction, reducing the overall project duration.

However, on management routes, no single lump sum price for construction is agreed and as a result, no contractual cost or time commitment is given to the client before the start of construction. There are two principal variants of the management route in the UK: construction management and management contracting. Construction management is distinguished by the employer being required to contract directly with all the separate trade contractors, thus increasing client control but also increasing the burden of risk and the requirement for management input.

The main advantages of management routes are:

- Reduced project durations due to the overlapping of design and construction and the improved management of the construction process
- Early contractor involvement in design development
- Increased project control for hands-on clients
- Specialist design input from trade contractors.

The disadvantages of management routes include:

- Lack of cost and time certainty at the beginning of works
- Relatively high cost of management routes
- Increased burden of administration and risk carried by the client.

Management type contracts are best suited to complex projects where additional management and coordination resources are necessary to retain project control, or to projects where the client is willing to accept greater cost uncertainty to achieve early completion.

4 Partnering

One problem area for construction is the confrontational nature of many projects. The client and contractor have very different objectives and, if major problems do arise, relationships can become distracted by disputes related to cost or liability for changes. In an effort to reduce the level of confrontation, some clients have used 'partnering' approaches, involving the adoption of common objectives, shared decision-making processes and managed problem resolution, enabling the team to concentrate on building rather than disputes. Partnering agreements typically overlay conventional construction contracts, although some collaborative contracts have recently been made available in the UK. There is no guarantee that partnering arrangements will deliver more effective projects, and considerable management time needs to be invested in their establishment. The application of partnering is best suited to extended development programmes rather than one-off projects.

Conclusion

This chapter has focused on the relationship between value and cost and how projects can best be managed to meet the client's objectives. Hospitality projects are generally delivered to tight cost and programme constraints. Value can be added by focusing the budget on elements which enhance service quality and the guest experience or by ensuring certainty of delivery. Rigorous application of cost management processes from the outset of the project will increase the likelihood of meeting these objectives. Value and certainty can also be enhanced by the application of management techniques related to value and risk.

Hospitality and construction are both complex businesses and the employment of experienced design and construction teams that understand the needs of the sector will provide the best opportunity to add value to the client. The specialist contribution of the QS, in forecasting and managing costs, advising on project procurement and in applying value enhancing techniques will contribute to keeping a project on track to meet the client's cost, time and quality objectives.

Review questions

1 Outline the key processes of cost management as a means of securing project value.

2 Explain the cost, time and quality equation.

3 What are the basic reasons for why hotel costs vary?

Case Study

Introduction

This case study illustrates how innovative procurement and a focused, team based approach to project delivery enabled the successful delivery of a five star hotel to challenging time and cost targets. It illustrates how an experienced contractor and design team can add significant value to a project and also demonstrates that the client has an active role in ensuring its successful delivery.

Background

The case study involved the construction of a new build, five star 140 bed hotel, incorporating ballroom, business centre and fitness suite. The hotel forms the centrepiece of a larger mixed use development and it was vital to the client that the hotel was trading before the Millennium celebrations. In order to assure that completion was achieved on programme, the client decided to procure the hotel via a separate contract. At this stage, planning drawings and an outline building services specification were available, but no operator had been signed up and there was no agreed interior design concept. The challenges for the design team were:

- To create conditions in which an extremely challenging 66-week design and construction programme could be met

- To communicate and secure the client's expectations in terms of quality, ahead of the appointment of the interior design team
- To ensure that the client's quality expectations were met within cost and time constraints.

Procurement

Owing to the compression of the programme and the importance of cost and programme certainty, design and build was chosen to enable rapid mobilization of design and construction and to provide single point responsibility. The client and cost consultant adapted details of the procurement strategy to enable the quality objectives to be met by:

- Appointing the contractor on the basis of experience and the quality and organization of the team as well as by price
- Providing benchmark cost information for undefined fit-out elements to enable tenderers to include auditable allowances in their tenders
- Reviewing tenders to ensure that the contract sum was sufficient to build the project to the expected quality standards
- Employing a peer review team of designers and engineers to review and check the work of the contractor and its team.

The successful tenderer was appointed within six weeks of the initial instruction on the basis of agreed adjustments to their tender. The contractor signed up to a 66-week programme on the basis of a lump sum tender totalling £29 million.

Management of construction

Once the contractor was appointed the key to the success of the project was effective motivation of the team and control of the design and construction process. On the project, the QS was appointed as the 'Employer's Representative' (ER), with delegated rights

to undertake most contractual roles on behalf of the client. In this instance the ER and contractor established a common purpose, avoiding disputes that can negatively affect performance on projects. Key elements of this approach included:

- Collaborative working. The client and contractor teams exchanged information and resources to facilitate early completion of design tasks
- Proactive management. The project was managed on the basis of a sequence of structured meetings, clearly identifying actions and avoiding delay caused by extended correspondence
- Escalation procedure. A clear procedure was put in place to escalate problems or disputes to project principals for early resolution. This kept the team focused on delivering the project
- Change management. A formal system was put in place to evaluate changes before instruction, identifying variations that could cause significant delay or extra cost ahead of instruction.

The contractor had a well integrated supply chain and most work packages were delivered to programme. Off-site manufacture of bathroom pods, complete with the room air-conditioning system were utilized to maintain quality, and to simplify site works and on site inspection. Where difficulties did occur, either related to the availability of design information or cashflow issues, the employer intervened to maintain project momentum.

The problem focused approach used on the project is well illustrated by the solution adopted to enable inspections to be completed without compromising the handover date. Normally these are the contractor's responsibility and can get squeezed into the last weeks of a programme if there are delays. The project team realized at an early stage that additional resources would be required to meet the programme and the client invested additional fees to employ the peer review team to provide a dedicated inspection resource. This action eliminated one round of inspections and enabled the process to be managed effectively. It epitomizes the actions of a client and contractor team fully focused on the key project objectives, able to identify effective solutions to problems as they arose.

Summary

The hotel was finally delivered at a cost below the tender sum within a period that enabled opening ahead of the critical millennium trading season. The project was a major success in that it achieved all of the client's principal objectives. The keys to this successful outcome were:

- Effective and focused teamworking by an experienced and well integrated project team

- The establishment of a realistic budget, enabling the team to focus on achieving appropriate quality standards within the client's programme constraint

- Focusing of appropriate resources on quality, helping the contractor to know what was expected at an early stage and providing the review resources to ensure that the client's expectations were met

- Focused management systems

- A problem solving culture.

This scheme is not a typical project and it illustrates the importance of the teamwork aspects of construction. However, it also shows how standard approaches to construction such as design and build procurement can be adapted to meet specific needs, and the importance of the role of client, consultants and contractor in the successful delivery of a project.

CHAPTER 9

Managing construction

Josef Ransley and Kevin Pearce

Construction represents the physical manifestation of all the hard work which has occurred in planning and organizing the development project. The construction process is a complex one which can be affected by a variety of factors affecting handover, such as quality, budget and operational capability. This process must, therefore, be carefully managed and understood to avoid potential problems. This chapter addresses the following issues:

- Context
- The building team
- Public perception
- Planning and programming
- Compliance
- Conclusion.

Context

The construction industry has experienced many changes during the last century, and none have been more far-reaching than development changes over the last 25–30 years. Some examples include the de-skilling of trades and crafts, the almost wholesale introduction of subcontractors, and as a result, the inevitable increase in factory-type produced preformed units constructed off-site using, in the main, semi-skilled labour, the increase in regulation of health and safety legislation at work, and the massive influx of environmental directives in Europe and elsewhere. This chapter considers some of those changes, their impact on designers and building contractors alike, and the builder's rise (or demise?) to becoming a manager of subcontractors, consultants and processes, to control and coordinate the building process. Also, as a result of these changes, the chapter provides an insight into the public's perception of builders, together with the builders' own examination of doing best what matters most for the public and clients. Such an examination may lead to the conclusion that improvements are needed in:

- Planning, programming and monitoring to achieve on-time completion

- Procurement, supervision and inspection to produce a compliant and quality product.

The chapter focuses on some of the processes building contractors employ to manage these 'performance gaps'.

Illustration 9.1
The design model on site

Trade	Activity
Bricklayer	Laying brickwork
Carpenter	Structural and carcassing work
Joiner	Timber work to finished carpentry
Concreter	Placing concrete
Drainlayer	Providing below ground drainage
Steel fixer	Cutting, shaping and positioning steel reinforcement

Table 9.1
Construction trades and
activities

The building team

A study of building workers carried out by the UK Building Research Establishment listed over 50 separate occupations associated with construction. Therefore, construction is an industry where total reliance is placed on the diverse attitudes, abilities and adaptability of its workers. Conventionally, these workers were grouped under 'trade' headings according to their skills, as shown in Table 9.1.

Twenty-five to thirty years ago most tradespeople were directly employed by building contracting companies who managed and directed all works on a site using a general supervisor or trades foreman to coordinate the work of each trade. More recently, most, if not all, trades are employed as subcontractors; relatively few if any artisans or tradesmen are employed directly by the building contracting company. The medium to large building contractors have now become building construction managers, responsible for the coordination of the construction of a building using only subcontractors and/or suppliers. The main reason for this change in employment is the fact that the continuous employment of their own artisans could not be guaranteed during periods of economic recession.

De-skilling of trades

The training of skilled building workers has traditionally been a matter for employers and unions. In order to compete with the other employment areas in terms of time-related earning power, the basic apprenticeship period for skilled building workers has been reduced, and this has resulted in a gradual but continuous 'de-skilling' of traditional trades. Furthermore, greater emphasis is now being placed on more academic subjects in schools, and this, together with the unattractiveness of working and weather conditions on generally exposed construction sites, has resulted in far fewer recruits than previously.

The effects of this move away from the traditional skilled building workers on site has caused designers to concentrate much more upon the selection, and the implementation of alternative

(i)

Illustration 9.2
Prefabricated bathroom
units

(ii)

construction methods. Therefore, there is now an ever greater need than before for close consultation with the design team and building contractor. Notwithstanding the above, in recent years mechanization has become universal on- and off-site. The increased use of plant and factory-type produced preformed units has meant that semi-skilled operatives are often in the majority on a building site.

Organization: contract management

In general, the building contractor's organization must generally be divided between office and site activities. Offices will often be concerned with estimating/tendering, site planning, construction process and planning, quantity surveying, cost control and bulk purchasing of materials and hire of plant. A typical regional building contractor's office organization chart is shown in Figure 9.1.

The work on site will be under the control of a contracts or construction manager/director, who may coordinate many other

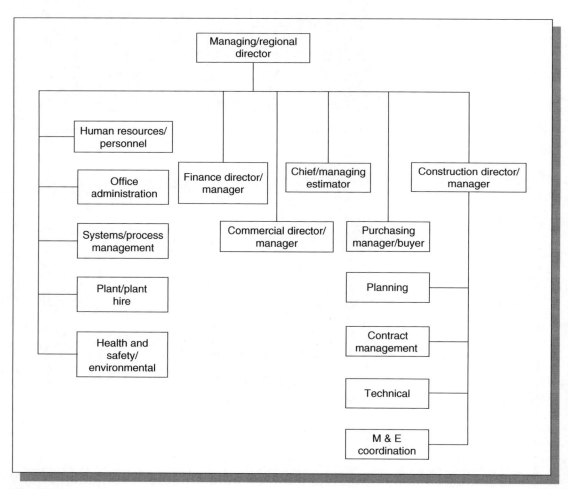

Figure 9.1
Regional building contractor's office organization chart

projects on different sites. The resident or direct contact on a particular site will be the site or project manager, who will be responsible for the building contractor's own employees and subcontractors.

A site organization chart for management responsibility for a medium- to large-sized contract is represented in Figure 9.2.

Most medium- to large-sized building contractors now provide for both the design and construction of a building project. This combines the services of the design team with those of general contracting. In effect the building contractor provides a 'package deal' in which he is responsible for all the major decisions on design and technical matters, prepares plans and specifications, obtains approvals and carries out the construction. The building contractor most often employs independent design practices for a fee, also 'contractor' design subcontractors, together with building control and planning specialists. The role of the design manager or design and build manager has become more prominent in this type of project and more often it is this individual who now

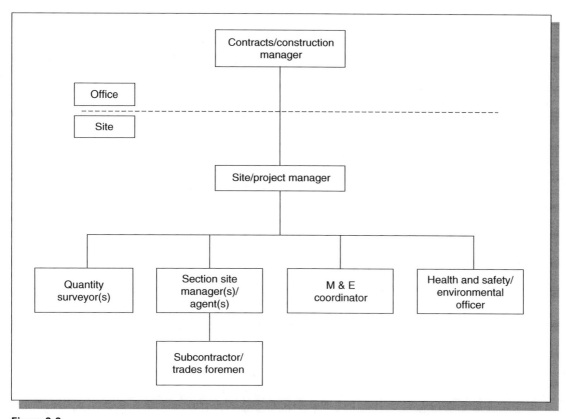

Figure 9.2
Site organization chart for a medium- to large-sized contract

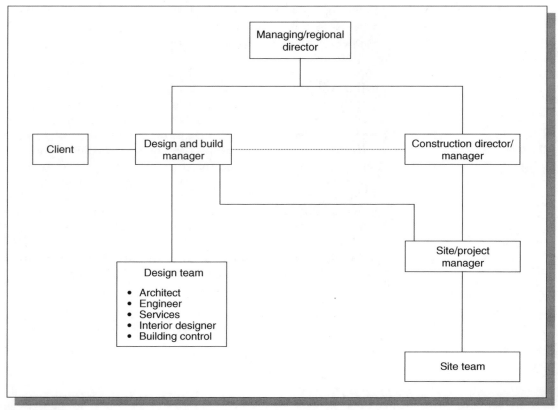

Figure 9.3
Organization chart for a design and build contract

provides the main or single point of contact, both technically and commercially, with the client and appointed agents.

An organization chart for a typical design and build contract is depicted in Figure 9.3.

Public perception

There is a commonly held perception by the public at large, private and public sector clients that many builders never finish on time, fail to do a 'good job' or put right their mistakes. Customers' perception of the performance of building contractors may differ from reality. Customers or clients may be behind the times, they may be slow to change their attitudes, they may label builders as unhelpful, uncaring when, in reality, the modern building contractor now usually offers a much better level of customer service. But that is what many customers may think. It is their perception, however accurate or inaccurate, on which they will base their decisions to purchase the builder's product.

Most building contractors have now come to accept this perception as reality. Most large building contractors have now carried out their own customer surveys, and not surprisingly, customers have identified a distinct dissatisfaction with the builder's ability to:

- Complete projects on-time, and
- Provide a quality product with few snags (defects).

Customer surveys

The initial aim of most of these surveys is to identify 'what matters most to customers', and to measure the customers' level of satisfaction with the builder's performance. The customers are those clients and their professional advisers who have worked with the building contractor over the previous 2–3 years. To achieve this aim, a survey is preceded by explanatory research involving depth interviews with a varied selection of customers, in order to identify what matters most to them. Having done this, a questionnaire is designed covering the 20 most important issues. These surveys are usually carried out via telephone interview, with a level of response needed from around 80–100 interviewees, in order to obtain a representative sample. A typical mix of respondents is 60% professional advisers and 40% customers.

Priorities for improvement

The respondents answer the following questions against each of the 20 most important issues:

1 How important are these issues to you, the customer?
2 How do you rate the performance of the building contractor? (They score their answers on a ten-point Likert scale, where 10 is high and 1 is low.)

All responses are analysed to produce a table showing the gaps in order of size between importance and satisfaction, the key factors used to identify priorities for improvement being the size of gap set against the most important issues. A typical 'priorities for improvement' chart is shown in Figure 9.4.

While building contractors are continuously trying to improve in all aspects of their services, they have in general decided to address each of the following by improving current methods and management procedures through process control. Some aspirations for satisfying customers more effectively include:

- On time completion
- Good quality with minimum snag

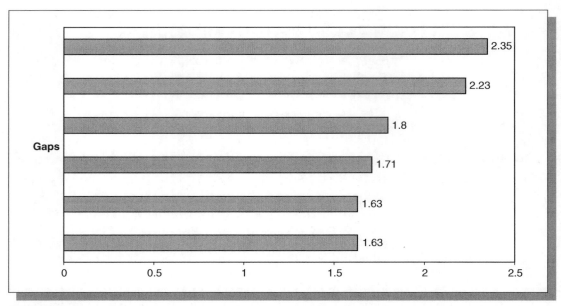

Figure 9.4
A typical 'priorities for improvement' chart

- All defects made good
- Prompt attention to snagging
- Quality of service
- Ability to plan and programme a project.

The remainder of this chapter will focus on some of the processes building contractors employ in order to improve their ability to manage these aspirational quality standards.

Planning and programming

The planning and programming of work for a typical medium to large design and construction building project involves the coordination of many human and material resources to ensure economy and efficiency. The more detailed the planning and programming, the less likely it is that unforeseen circumstances may upset either the intentions or timetabling of a project, thereby reducing the chances of frustration and delays.

The processes adopted to control, coordinate and monitor these many human and material resources are complex. The following processes are considered:

1 The 'master' programme

2 Design information

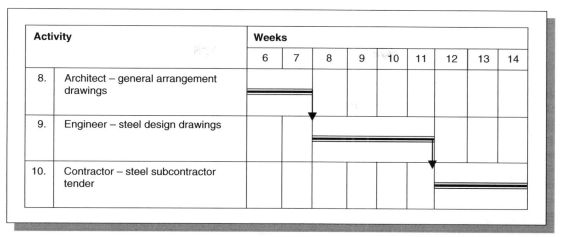

Activity		Weeks								
		6	7	8	9	10	11	12	13	14
8.	Architect – general arrangement drawings									
9.	Engineer – steel design drawings									
10.	Contractor – steel subcontractor tender									

Figure 9.5
Example of a logical link in a critical path

3 Subcontractor procurement

4 Material purchasing

5 Plant and plant hire

6 Temporary works

7 The construction programme

8 Contract review.

1 The 'master' programme

Highly sophisticated programmes can be produced to provide a visual representation of the interrelationships between design information production, material and component deliveries, subcontract and trade related work. These can provide more accuracy and are based on the critical path method. This method is sometimes considered too complicated for practical use in small to medium sized projects because of the frequent reconstruction, which may be necessary as a result of updating. Nevertheless, the critical path method reflects actual site techniques more accurately than bar charts.

Presently, there is almost across-the-board use of specialized computer programs which offer ease of updating by continuous feeding of data. However, bar chart programmes are often still preferred by building contractors, clients and professionals alike. These bar charts are often produced within 'logic links'. In its simplest form, a logical link is an arrow depicting that a programme activity cannot start without the completion of another. Figure 9.5 shows an example extract of a logical link as a visual aid of the critical path of a project.

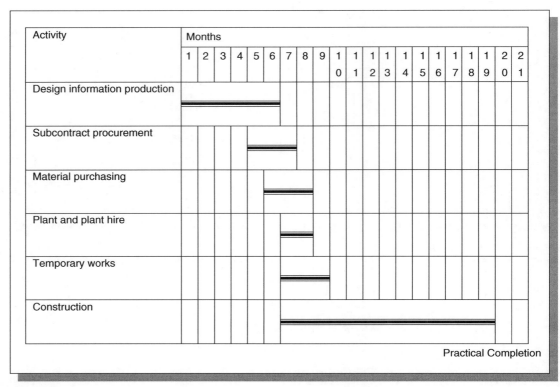

Figure 9.6
Example of a master programme

The 'master' or contract programme combines and coordinates all the other planning and programming activities, and is the main network programme, with the other (for example design information, subcontract procurement, material purchasing) being the sub-network programmes. Therefore in simple terms this can be represented via a 'master' programme chart, an example of which is shown in Figure 9.6.

2 Design information

Design programmes can take the form of a bar chart and are often called pre-contract programmes. They are prepared by the design team in order to establish how long it will take from the beginning of the design process in order to start (procurement, purchasing etc.) and construction activities on-site. They allow the design team to assess accurately the demands on staff and the effects which the new project may have on other concurrently running work. When tendering for a project, the contractors will have often submitted an outline or tender programme. This will have indicated the approximate periods of time required for each major construction activity, together with the total period indicated for

Item	Details	Date information requested	Date information required	Date information received	Remarks
	External openings				
25	Setting-out drawings	18.02.02	16.06.03		
26	Lintel schedule	26.03.02	28.07.03		
27	Window schedule	24.03.02	13.05.03	20.05.03	Window details 07 and 08 incomplete
28	Door schedule	24.03.02	23.05.03		
29	Ironmongery schedule	12.04.03	17.07.03		

Figure 9.7
Extract from a drawing and information required schedule

the proposed project. The total period for construction is very often the critical factor in deciding the planning and programming strategy for all other elements, and especially design information.

Building contractors often prepare and monitor an 'information required schedule', which provides the design team with a programme for the release of drawings and information to enable the builder to construct the project in line with the construction programme, the subcontract procurement and material purchasing schedules and also to comply with the contractual obligation, under most forms of contract, to request information.

The 'information required schedule' can in its basic format take the form as shown in Figure 9.7.

The amount of 'detail' will be contract specific and full consideration is needed of the following:

- The full scope of the project

- All activities listed on the construction programme

- All major procurement and 'purpose-made' items

- All 'provisional sums' in detail

- Specialist subcontractor requirements.

The 'date information required' will initially be taken from the construction programme, and will allow a suitable period in advance of the work on-site, allowing for all lead-in requirements including:

- Period of procurement (materials and subcontractors)

- Design approval and manufacture

- Client approval periods

- Integration with other activities on the programme

- Mobilization and administration.

The schedule may be revised and updated from time-to-time, but the 'date information required' is not to be relaxed.

3 Subcontract procurement

The preparation of 'subcontractor procurement schedules' has, for the modern-day builder, become one of the more important tools to ensure the project is completed on time. This schedule gives the site team a programme with which to place subcontract orders, providing a control framework for design information production in accordance with the construction programme. The 'subcontractor procurement schedule' in its basic format can take the form shown in Figure 9.8.

The building contractor will determine how the construction activities will be divided into subcontractor trade packages.

The 'start-on-site date' will be taken from the construction programme, with the 'subcontractor lead-in (weeks)' period allowing for all lead-in time requirements including:

- Drawings and approval

- Manufacture

- Delivery periods

- Integration with other trades.

On design and build contracts the 'lead-in' time needs special consideration, with particular consideration being given to the overall design. The 'latest enquiry date' is derived from

Item	Subcontractor trade	Latest enquiry date	Tender period (weeks)	Latest order place/date	Subcontractor lead-in (weeks)	Start on-site date
9	Structural steel frame	14.01.02	5	18.02.02	14	27.05.02
10	Pre-cast concrete floors	15.04.02	2	29.04.02	8	24.06.02
32	Plastering and tiling	22.07.02	3	12.08.02	4	09.09.02
33	Painting and decorating	16.09.02	2	30.09.02	2	14.10.02

Figure 9.8
Extract from a subcontractor procurement schedule

subcontracting the lead-in and 'tender period', in weeks, from the 'start-on-site date'. This 'latest enquiry date', being the date information is required from the design team.

4 Material purchasing

The preparation of 'material schedules' is similar in principle to that of preparing the 'subcontractor procurement schedule'. However, with more and more subcontractors now providing a complete service (providing labour, plant and materials) the volume of material purchasing by the building contractor has somewhat diminished. Those subcontract trades who, in the main, provide only labour and plant, not materials, are usually limited to the following:

- Groundworkers
- Bricklayers
- Carpentry and joinery.

Although joinery, especially in building hotels, is now subcontracted to specialized labour, plant and material subcontract joiners, or 'fitting-out' subcontractors. Again, this schedule gives the site team a programme with which to place orders (this time purchase orders) providing a control framework for design information production, especially written specifications of materials, in accordance with the construction programme.

The 'materials schedule' can take the form shown in Figure 9.9.

The 'required on-site date' will effectively be the 'start-on-site date', taken from the construction programme, with the 'delivery period (weeks)' being the period in which the supplier needs to procure and deliver the materials from stock or from works. The 'latest requisition date' is a reminder for the site team to compile

Item	Material	BoQ/spec reference	Quantity	Unit	Latest requisition date	Latest order place date	Delivery period (weeks)	Req'd on site date
7	100 mm ∅ hepseal pipes	A37	240	M	04.02.02	11.02.02		11.03.02
8	100 mm ∅ hepseal collar	A38	142	Nr.	04.02.02	11.02.02		11.03.02
26	140 mm dense conc. block	D8	470	M²	17.06.02	24.06.02		08.07.02
27	100 mm insulating block	D9	810	M²	06.05.02	13.05.02		10.06.02

Figure 9.9
Extract from a materials schedule

Illustration 9.3
Interior fitting out in progress

their 'materials indent' or 'material requisition' detailing what materials and quantity they require. The site team will use the 'materials schedule' to establish priorities for the provision of these indents with due consideration to extended delivery periods and pending increased cost dates.

5 Plant and plant hire

As with material purchasing, the volume of purchasing and/or hiring plant has diminished, with more and more subcontractors providing a service which includes labour and plant. The site and/or project manager and quantity surveyor will examine all plant and transport requirements for the project and establish whether a case can be made for purchasing rather than hiring, taking into account the services normally provided by plant hirers (for example servicing and maintenance) and submit this case as a course of action to the contracts manager/director or plant manager for a decision – similarly for plant which cannot be hired.

The site team will initiate the hire of mechanical and non-mechanical plant for their project via a 'plant hire order,' with the conditions of hire of mechanical plant being very different to that of non-mechanical plant. All plant on-site is scheduled, with details including the type of plant, owner, number and to whom it was issued being recorded, and reconciled weekly, against the tender/budget allocation. With the exception of tower cranes, on most large, or even medium-sized building projects, the only plant a building contractor would use, would be associated with the site set-up and the preliminaries element of the project, such as generators for lighting and power, road sweepers and small tools.

6 Temporary works

Depending on the size, type of structure, location and complexity of a project, temporary works can form a large part of the planning and programming of a project. Construction operations considered as temporary works, and which are subject to strict requirements, both legislative and in design and engineering terms, are as follows:

- Falseworks for horizontal and inclined soffits for the support of in-situ and pre-cast concrete and other elements requiring temporary support

- Temporary steelwork, timber and reinforced concrete, including temporary members required during the erection of permanent works

- Sheet piling both in temporary works and the construction stages of permanent works

- Temporary working platforms, bridges and site roads

- Excavations and trenches, both shored and strutted and open cut battered excavations

- Embankments

- Temporary roadworks (highways) and access arrangements requiring design input

- Effects of construction operations and methods on permanent works

- Formwork

- Special supports for services

- Plant foundations

- Demolition provision and sequence.

The above list is not exhaustive and all require careful consideration and examination before they are implemented within the project planning process. The site or project manager will have overall responsibility for temporary works on a project, however, a trained temporary works coordinator (TWC) is now appointed on most construction sites to help plan and coordinate all temporary works.

The TWC will prepare a schedule of temporary works requirements, including a preliminary programme(s) for design, checking or certificating, ordering and erection. Execution of the temporary works, loading and dismantling of falseworks are carried out under supervision only when designs and procedures/processes have been approved and previous stages have been approved in writing. These stages, in brief are as follows:

- *Design brief and design*. The TWC will prepare a design brief for each item of temporary works, the intention being to identify the overall parameters of the work and to advise the designer of particular aspects if relevant. The TWC will issue with the design brief a programme identifying times for design, checking, ordering, delivery, erecting, certifying, loading, dismantling and removal of equipment from site.

- *Design check*. All sections of the temporary works design will be checked by an independent person not involved in the original design process. Design elements prepared by a subcontractor or equipment supplier must be provided with a valid and accredited independent design check certificate.

- *Design check and/or construction certification*. Where any design is carried out the TWC will ensure the designer and checker provides a suitable certificate and/or set of design calculations. When construction of the temporary works is checked, the TWC will ensure the checker completes suitable signed documentation that the check has been completed.

- *Method statements*. The TWC will ensure that any method statements required for the construction, loading, unloading and dismantling of temporary works are produced.

- *Temporary works register*. The TWC will maintain a register of certification, and will initial each stage to certify that designs and design checking are known by him to have been satisfactorily completed, and that erection and erection inspections are known by him to have been satisfactorily completed by an independent suitably experienced person, other than himself.

- *Permits to load and unload*. Permits to load will contain the relevant loading constraints and sequence, including partial loading. Permits to unload will include what criteria or sequences are required for unloading or dismantling temporary works. All permits must be approved by suitably qualified persons and checks signed by the TWC before loading, unloading or dismantling.

Failures in temporary works are caused by poor planning and can result in serious injury or death to operatives, wasted material and labour time, and severe delays to programme.

7 The construction programme

A well-prepared programme is essential to every construction project. Many activities have to be carefully defined and given a time scale, and it is necessary not only to marshal and list the information but also to display it visually in terms of the contract's objectives and the calendar. The working sequences and the relationships between individual activities must be clearly conveyed in this visual presentation.

A construction programme is a 'statement of intended actions' which, when properly used, provides management with its plan of campaign. It should communicate unequivocally, providing the common reference for the timing of all activities related to the project. It is an important common reference and shows how the contractor has interpreted the detail of the contract documents and other information, and sets out the whole as a statement of intent for the building. As the key programme for the construction work its content is of the greatest significance to all the parties charged with handing over to the client a building fit for its intended use within the contract time and with optimum economy.

Programmes must provide the information necessary for management to carry out its functions in:

- Establishing the suitable timing of information requirements
- Forecasting and monitoring cash flow
- Forecasting labour and staff requirements
- Scheduling material supplies
- Coordinating the activities of subcontractors and statutory undertakers
- Measuring and controlling performance
- Assessing the effect of variations and change
- Reviewing assumptions
- Costing (and bonusing or performance-related pay).

Contracts or construction managers must ensure that information is disseminated to all parties using the programme. If contractors are not committed to its construction programmes, it is unlikely that any other function will obtain the benefits which they can provide. When a construction programme exists, realistic in its expectation, there is a basis for performance assessment and control. Indeed, the only basis for performance control can be a programme. Often secondary programmes, produced for specific purposes are used. They may depict overall short-term site work and/or specific trade activities.

The principles, which must be applied in producing a construction programme, are as follows:

The construction programme must be:

- Realistic
- Capable of achievement

- Unambiguous

- Based on available information

- Appropriate in degree of detail for the particular project or sections of the project

- Coordinated with any other programmes for the project.

The programme must show:

- All significant activities which should be clearly defined

- The work of specialists

- Consistent forms of visual expression for clarity and easy identification

- A unique reference number

- Ease of monitoring performance.

The programme must reflect:

- Sound construction methods

- Available and economic use of resources

- Constraints of all kinds, including health and safety and environmental influence

- Holidays and other calendar irregularities

- Seasonal influences.

As discussed earlier in the chapter, various graphic techniques are available to display a programme's intention. Bar charts have been used longest for construction programmes, and they are easy to understand. They concentrate on the duration of activities, their position on the timescale and the identification of broadly defined work sequences. The bar chart requires a formalized layout and an example is shown in Figure 9.10.

All parties have an interest in managing with the aid of programmes and the progress of projects should be reviewed at regular intervals. The intervals should be neither too frequent so that they needlessly waste effort, nor too infrequent so that remedial action is taken too late. Usually programmes are reviewed or monitored monthly or fortnightly. To undertake a review, a target or week commencing date represented on the programme is compared with actual progress on-site. Any differences between the target and the achievement are called a deviation. Each activity can either be behind, or ahead of programme.

Where deviations from programme are jointly studied and the responsibility for remedy is clearly identified, action plans must

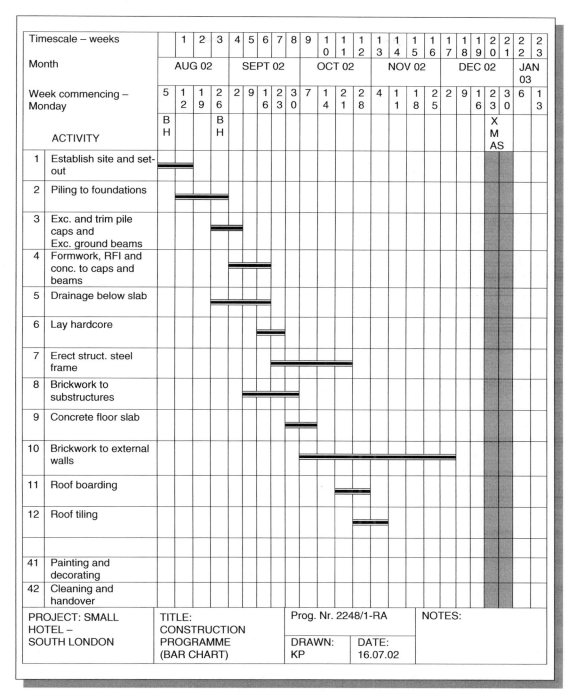

Figure 9.10
Construction programme bar chart

be formulated and agreed. Such plans may mean the simple re-deployment of site resources. Corrective action may, however, involve re-scheduling of working sequences. In view of its contractual significance, the decision to re-schedule the works must not be taken lightly in view of its far-reaching implications and attendant risks.

8 Contract review

Contract reviews are applied pre-contract, as a 'start-up' meeting, during the contract, as monthly or fortnightly progress meetings, and post-contract, as an 'end-of-contract de-brief' meeting. The following addresses progress meetings held during the contract. These meetings ensure that cost, progress and quality are reviewed at regular intervals (usually monthly, and sometimes fortnightly) and that reports and monitors are produced by the site team for review by senior management.

The contract review is all encompassing with a typical agenda, shown in Figure 9.11.

This thorough review will allow both the site team and senior management to assess planning and progress in all aspects of the project, time, quality and cost, together with actual and/or possible delays. Recovery plans where necessary can be discussed and approved quickly, detailing the effects of any decisions made or actions taken.

The contract review is a powerful tool, allowing the site team to report on project specific issues, with the senior management team being able to make decisions and take actions on a company wide basis.

Compliance

Compliance can be defined as:

> An affirmative indication or judgement that a product or service has met the requirements of the relevant specifications, contract or regulation. Also the state of meeting the requirements.

Within the construction industry it is recognized that an increasing amount of time is being spent in the preparation or examination of contractual claims. It has also become apparent that, for a variety of reasons, there is a diminishing return from such claims. A key to this is the increased sophistication of clients in applying the requirements of the standard forms of building contract. These contracts clearly place the burden of proof on the contractor. The task of providing this proof, often in the form of documentary evidence, is frequently complicated by a lack of pertinent records. A failure promptly to provide the required documents disturbs the

1 **Programme and progress**
  - XSite manager's report
  - Marked-up programme

2 **Information requirements**
  - Drawing and information required schedule
  - Drawing and bending schedule registers
  - RFI (request for information) index

3 **Variations**
  - CVI (confirmation of verbal instruction) index
  - Contract instructions (received from the client) index
  - Dayworks

4 **Procurement and hire**
  - Subcontractors procurement schedule
  - Materials schedule
  - Plant

5 **Performance/problems**
  - Subcontractors
  - Suppliers
  - Direct labour

6 **Health and safety**
  - Accidents
  - Audit Report(s) and non-conformity level
  - Health & Safety Executive visits
  - Problems

7 **Environmental**
  - Incidents
  - Risk assessment compliance/non-conformity level
  - Problems

8 **Quality/tidiness**
  - Inspection and test record
  - NCR (non-conformance report) registers
  - CAR (corrective action report) registers
  - Audit report(s)

9 **Temporary works**
  - Temporary works register
  - Works complete/pending

10 **Client Relationship and Future Opportunities**

11 **Site administration and management systems**

12 **Finance**
  - Financial report
  - CVR (cost, value, reconciliation)
  - Forecast
  - Payments

13 **Any other business**

Figure 9.11
Typical contract review meeting agenda

relationship between building contractor and client and/or more particularly appointed agents. Therefore to make things worse economic loss is often accompanied by loss of goodwill. In addition, when tracing the history of some of these disputes it becomes clear that the problems which form the basis of these claims, although frequently materializing at site level, regularly have had their root cause earlier in the management and even in the design process.

Examination of project records shows that questions have not been asked when they should have been, problems are not seen until after they have occurred. It is typically not the case that the individuals involved lack expertise or initiative. It is more often the case that they are pressed for time by other concerns resulting in them giving these issues scant attention. A further difficulty arises where an individual's lack of experience limits their personal horizon and dims their perspective of the problems ahead. Crises caused by poor quality have often overtaken projects that appeared to be proceeding successfully, with the resultant delay and cost undoing the supposed benefits that had been accrued. It is clear that as the cost of getting it wrong increases, regardless of which party is at fault, the cost of getting it right becomes the sensible economic objective.

One of the major problems encountered is an overemphasis by management on time and cost. These are indeed important factors, but are only two parts of what is in effect a three-sided triangle of time, cost and quality. Often, building contractors say, 'Good job, we finished on-time, to budget.' Similarly, clients might say, 'Good job, but they finished late and it cost me a fortune.' These factors must be in balance, as any neglect of one will have a corresponding detrimental effect upon the other two. Historically there has been an attempt to manage the construction process by controlling time and cost in progress, while quality tends to be managed in retrospect. This is understandable since most management control systems highlight time and cost and leave the responsibility for quality to others, such as subcontractors, suppliers, designers and even the client's agents.

Building contractors have always accepted a level of risk. The secret of success has been to keep the risk within confined and controllable limits. In the UK, the risks currently associated with the discovery of defective work are increasing in both the long and short term. The Latent Damage Act, 1986, places the burden of 15 years liability, with this period of liability running from the date of discovery. The Joint Contracts Tribunal (JCT) and other similar intermediate forms of contract have introduced new power for architects following the discovery of defects to establish, at no cost to the client, that no similar failure exists.

The building contractors share of risk is being expanded from a number of sources; legal decisions (duty of care) are providing a tendency toward consumer protection and this is likely to lead to an expansion of legal liability seen now in the UK's Construction

(Design and Management) Regulations: 1994. Standard contract amendments have provided that, not withstanding the architect's obligations, the contractor is fully responsible. Pressures on architects and all designers via their professional indemnity insurance will continue this trend. In the shorter term building contractors can expect to find increasing pressure for compliance with better drafted contracts and specifications, and government support is likely to expand this to many areas of public expenditure.

It is recognized that the cost of rectifying defects increases in relation to progress. The later the problem is found the more expensive it is to put right. The building contractor now needs to ensure compliance with ever increasing client's and legislative requirements, over the period of the project and long after it is complete. This chapter will look at, briefly; health and safety, environmental and the employer's requirements (the specification).

Health and safety

The construction industry in the UK accounts for a quarter of all deaths that occur at work, and for more than 4000 serious injuries each year. This worrying record has serious and far-reaching consequences for individuals and businesses alike, and contributes to the industry's and the builders' poor image. It is vital that this health and safety record improves. Such legislation, both in the UK and elsewhere, means that no one can relieve the building contractor of his or her duties. Under these provisions, building contractors, via their managers and supervisors, now need a thorough understanding of the following issues:

Possible dangers:

- Need for the effective supervision of employees, subcontractors and others

- Health and safety policy, organization and arrangements of the employer

- Why persons will adopt unsafe behaviour at times

- How accidents and ill health can be prevented on-site.

Avoiding danger:

- Planning and scheduling work so as to avoid hazards

- Carrying out a risk assessment

- Preparing a method statement

- Benefit of giving toolbox talks

- How to give clear and explicit health and safety instructions

- Actions to take in the event of imminent or perceived danger

- Actions to take when employees or subcontractors are seen working unsafely.

The above shows that the resultant knowledge requirements on individual managers and supervisors are vast and far-reaching. There are often heavy penalties for breaching this legislation. Accordingly, the concept of risk assessment has been introduced into the European industry by the provisions of the management of health and safety at work regulations, and a similar approach is used in respect of health risks. A 'risk assessment' is an examination of a work process, or assessment carried out by a competent person on behalf of an employer, which assesses the hazards inherent in an operation and the risks to workers and all others who may be affected by the work to be carried out. It involves identifying the risks present in a work operation, and evaluating these risks, taking into account whatever precautions are already in place. Once the risk has been identified, a work method (or method statement) can be developed. A method statement is a report prepared within the company detailing exactly how a work operation is to be carried out in a manner which is safe and without risk to health.

There is also the requirement under European law for the building contractor to publish a health and safety policy which addresses:

- Emergency procedures

- Key personnel with special safety duties

- Fire prevention plans

- Risk evaluation

- Details of arrangements to minimize risk

- Details of training of management and the workforce.

Environment

Environmental legislation is extensive, far-reaching and subject to on-going modification and addition. In the last 10–15 years the field of environmental law has witnessed a proliferation of new laws, regulations and directives, both at national and international level. A common theme can be traced to the four basic principles of European environmental policy:

- Prevention better than cure

- Polluter pays

- Proximity principle

- Precautionary principle.

In Europe there is legal enforcement of environmental problems by government agencies, covering pollution to air, land or water. The environment can be defined as any physical surroundings consisting of air, water and land. Damage to the environment, and therefore prosecution, may arise from most construction site activities, which may include any or all of the following pollutants:

Air

- Duct and radiation

- Exhaust emissions

- Gases or vapours

- Noise

- Smoke.

Land

- Chemicals

- Litter

- Oils and fuels

- Spillage of materials

- Waste materials.

Water courses and drainage systems

- Chemicals

- Contaminated water run-off

- Effluent

- Oils and fuels

- Hazardous solid matter

- Slurry.

In order to avoid penalties for environmental pollution, European building contractors are turning to BS EN ISO14001:1996 the environmental management standard, in order to develop policies, processes and guidelines, and to review site operations to assess their environmental impacts, and set objections and targets. It is these significant effects which are addressed and controlled via risk assessment and method statement, similar to, but far more complex and onerous than health and safety risk assessment. Environmental risk assessment may be required in the following areas:

- Waste management
- Asbestos
- Fuel/oil storage and distribution
- Bituminous/solvent materials – storage, distribution and application on-site
- Noise in construction
- Pollution of controlled waters
- Land contamination
- Air pollution
- Cementious products
- Use of pesticides
- Protecting animals, plants and their habitats.

Employer's requirements (the specification)

A specification is a written document prepared by the client and members of the team and provides fundamental information which, for various reasons, cannot be incorporated on the production drawings for a proposed project. It is and will form an integral part of the design process because it describes the quality of work which is considered necessary during construction. Information for a specification can evolve during the preparation of the production drawings, or in the case of design and build contracts, will be documented prior to the preparation of the design, and to which the design and subsequent construction will need to comply.

The employer's requirements and/or specification is usually issued in two main parts:

1 Preliminaries. Describes the legal contract through which the construction work is controlled, including insurances, facilities on site, details of access routes, roads and local restrictions, hours of working, generation of noise and dust.

2 Trade clauses. Documents the actual construction methods (materials and techniques) to be adopted and may be provided in the following ways:
   - Precisely describing the materials to be used and the work to be executed under each trade
   - Outlining the materials and work required for each separate part or element

- Giving a 'performance specification' (statement of requirements) which accurately details the quality of work expected in terms of performance criteria for each part involved, without describing a method of achieving it.

In order to ensure compliance with the specification, and to 'get it right first time,' nearly all medium- to large-sized building contractors are certificated by accredited bodies such as the British Standards Institute (BSI) to the new ISO9000:2000 Quality Management Systems family of standards, which is an all-encompassing series of standards that lays down requirements for incorporating the management of quality into the design, manufacture and delivery of products, services and software. This international standard has enabled contractors to document management systems, with the systems being proactive in setting down the procedures that must be followed to ensure quality, thus compliance. The contract management plan or quality plan is an integral part of the systems, and sets down the management structure at project level, the choice of structure and individual roles. The quality plan procedures involve the development of an inspection and testing plan which combined with the handling and storage procedures and the check on receipt ensure that at all stages of construction compliance is verified.

In order to understand the process of inspecting and testing, the key terminology is as follows:

- *Inspection*. Activities such as measuring, examining, testing, gauging one or more characteristics of a product or service and comparing these with specified requirements to determine conformity.

- *Test*. A critical trial or examination of one or more properties or characteristics of a material, product or set of observations.

- *Hold point*. A point beyond which work shall not proceed without the written authorization of a designated individual or organization.

Inspection and testing falls mainly under two headings:

1 Inspection and testing of materials

Inspections are carried out on materials received to ensure that they are:

- Identified and correspond with the procurement documents

- Accepted, or rejected, as per pre-determined instructions as described in the purchase order

- Identified as to their inspection status and are either held in a controlled storage area or used directly in the works.

Non-conforming items are controlled and identified until proper disposal, correction and/or acceptance is accomplished. Stored items are inspected regularly as to their condition and the adequacy of the storage area. Where materials are used before specified inspection and testing is completed, their location in the works will be ascertained from the indent/order, location drawing or similar record.

2 Inspection of works

Where formal inspections are required by the contract, these will be included in the Inspection and Test Plan, and where relevant, referenced to individual subcontractor inspection and test plans and/or documented trade (work) processes. Where a subcontractor is not certificated to ISO 9000, or cannot provide a suitable inspection and test plan, the site management team will produce a trade (work) process which will consist of the following:

- A method statement stating how the works are to be carried out
- An inspection sheet or check list which sets out and monitors the stages of the trade.

The site management team will agree the information to be prepared for (and to be contained in) the inspection sheet or check list with regard to the following:

- Contract/subcontract documents (including specifications, drawings and bills of quantities)
- British Standards, codes of practice and manufacturers' literature
- Specific method of construction (including preparation, access, safety and fixings)
- Setting out (including dimensional, alignment and plumb/level checks)
- Interface with other trades (including subsequent trades and protection)
- Samples, trials, inspection and testing (including cleanliness, uniformity appearance and test certificates).

The above will adequately define the 'hold points' where an inspection is to take place and where approval to proceed is required before the next operation in a sequence is to take place, e.g. inspection of block walls before plastering, inspection of plastering before painting. If a finished wall is subsequently found to be out of alignment or out of plumb/level, this will mean that the wall will have to be taken down and once again plastered and painted – a waste of time, money and resource.

Formats for inspection and test plans vary enormously, most will include samples and trials, and will contain some or all of the following requirements, usually set out in a table:

1 Item number

2 Description

3 Specification clause

4 Description of test and/or inspection

5 Acceptance/rejection criteria

6 Frequency or timing of test and/or inspection

7 Method of test and/or inspection

8 Action of those responsible for carrying out the test and/or inspection

9 Action when non-conforming

10 Inspection requirement – by the client or contractor under the following criteria:
   - H – Hold point, permission to proceed
   - R – Submit for information/record
   - A – Submit for approval

11 Type of record.

The 'type of record' will indicate the document or written record which verifies that the inspection and/or test has been carried out. Types of records will vary from laboratory test certificates to simple trade check lists or inspection sheets. All records will invariably require signatures and dates to verify who had carried out the inspection and/or test and when.

Most building contractors have now recognized that the relatively small cost employed in getting it right far outweighs the ever increasing cost of getting it wrong, and rectifying defects long after the project is completed.

Conclusion

This chapter has highlighted the structural changes in the construction industry, causing the major construction companies to change from being builders into providing construction management and design services dealing with the procurement and coordination of subcontractors and suppliers. With a decline in the skilled tradesmen available the industry has moved into using more pre-manufactured products, something that architects and designers need to consider more in applying their skills. The common negative perception of builders is equally being addressed by construction companies, and in order to satisfy clients' performance requirements for cost, time and quality, more focus is being placed on planning and programming. At the same time such issues as health and safety, environment and other matters are becoming more regulated and this demands that greater management skills are applied to the whole process of construction development. This chapter provides an insight into the process of construction from the viewpoint of the builder, thereby enabling those responsible for development better to manage this important part of the development process.

Review questions

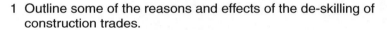

1 Outline some of the reasons and effects of the de-skilling of construction trades.

2 What is the public perception of builders, and suggest ways in which this might be addressed.

3 Give examples of possible environmental pollution scenarios.

PART 4

Operations

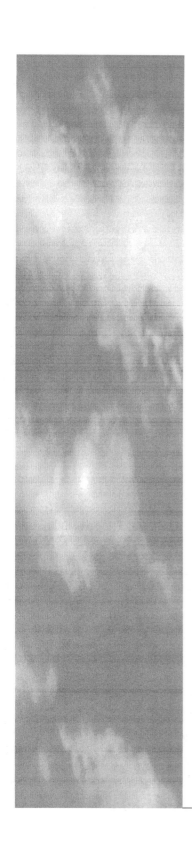

CHAPTER 10

Operational planning and relationships

Dick Penner

This chapter considers the operational planning relationships which influence the design of the hotel's public areas and discusses how they are different among the various types and classes of hotel.

The chapter is structured under the following headings:

- Definitions
- Characteristics
- Applications
- Best practice
- Future trends
- Conclusion.

The operational issues related to guestrooms and suites will be discussed in the next chapter and those influencing the back-of-house service areas in the succeeding one.

Hotels and related lodging properties must carefully balance a number of design and functional relationships to be successful. This balance varies depending on the type of hotel, resort, or inn: whether developed for the leisure or business or group market; whether urban, suburban, or more remote; whether traditional, contemporary, or strikingly *avant-garde*; whether chain operated or independent; and so forth. But whatever this mix of characteristics, the overall hotel, as well as each of its functional areas (lobby, food and beverage outlets, meeting areas, guestrooms and suites, and service areas, for example), must both exhibit a well conceived aesthetic design and be efficient and functional. A luxury resort or small urban boutique hotel, of course, will push this balance heavily toward the design and visual end, incorporating luscious and extravagant materials or utilizing very hip, cutting edge features and details. On the other hand, the roadside motel or economy-priced city hotel will tip the balance toward low-maintenance surfaces, simple design elements, and highly efficient space layouts.

Definitions

Operational planning is the concept of organizing the hotel[1] or another facility to meet the requirements of both the user (hotel guest) and operator, rather than principally along aesthetic or design themes. Given the competitive nature of the lodging business, establishing clear operational planning objectives is essential to a successful venture. The owner and design team must constantly balance the operational needs of the various stakeholders with 'good' design to create a cost-effective, safe, and marketable property.

Characteristics

Planning for effective operations needs to be considered throughout all areas of the hotel or resort, guestrooms, public areas, and service area, as well as in the siting of the building and the layout of the roadways and parking areas and beyond the details of the physical relationships, how the individual spaces and functional areas are organized. Equally important is the design brief, incorporating the facilities list and space programme (the amount of area (m^2) devoted to each function) along with operational and staffing requirements. For instance, operational planning requires that the owner or developer know whether the guestroom should be, say,

---

[1]Note: throughout this chapter the word 'hotel' is used for any type of lodging property: hotel, resort, inn, lodge, motel, conference centre, or whatever.

$30\,m^2$ or $34\,m^2$ or whether the restaurant needs to have $1.6\,m^2$ or $2.0\,m^2$ per seat in order to meet guest expectations, operational efficiencies, and financial objectives. In addition, the team needs to define a myriad of operational details: how is luggage handled? Or room service? Is there an in-house hotel laundry? What staff is needed to respond to guest-service calls? Each of these has implications for the physical planning and for guest satisfaction, as well as for setting staffing levels. The following discussion of operational planning will consider these disparate aspects:

- Design brief
- Site layout and arrival
- Lobby and public circulation
- Food and beverage outlets
- Function areas (meeting facilities)
- Recreational areas.

The succeeding chapters will cover related issues with respect to guest accommodation (Chapter 11) and service provision (Chapter 12).

Applications

Design brief

Among the first tasks of the development process is to establish the design brief or programme for the proposed hotel. This is a cooperative effort, based on the feasibility study (Chapter 4), with input from the owner, management company, architect, and numerous consultants.

Even at the earliest phase of a project it is valuable to know the approximate amount of space dedicated to the principal functions in a hotel, especially the approximate balance between guestrooms and public/support areas. This varies from over 90% guestroom space in budget properties and many motels, where there is limited or no food and beverage, meeting, or back-of-house functions, to less than 65% guestroom space in large convention and resort properties, where the public and support functions are essential to enabling the property to gain market share. Figure 10.1 illustrates these broad area allocation percentages for a range of lodging facilities.

For each type of hotel, developed at a particular location to meet the needs of a specific target market at a given price range, an experienced developer or management company can provide a tentative list of facilities and an early estimate of space requirements. Until a more detailed programme is established, this gross approximation

Percentage of total hotel area				
	Number of guestrooms	Guestrooms	Public areas	Service areas
Motel, economy hotel	<100	90	5	5
All-suite hotel	100–200	80	12	8
Urban business hotel	100–300+	75	14	11
Resort	100–500	70	16	14
Convention hotel	300–1 000+	65	20	15

Note: The number of guestrooms/hotel depends on local market conditions and shows a large variation from country to country. The area percentages remain largely the same worldwide.

Figure 10.1
Hotel space programme: Percentage in guestrooms, public, and service areas

	Guestroom area (m^2)		Total hotel gross area (m^2)
	Net	Gross	
Motel, economy hotel	28	35	39
All-suite hotel	40	55	70
Urban business hotel	32	45	60
Resort	36	50	72
Convention hotel	32	45	70

Figure 10.2
Hotel space programme: Floor area per guestroom

Figures are floor area (m^2) per guestroom. Guestroom net area is the usable area including bathroom and vestibule. Guestroom gross area includes walls, stairways, corridors, etc. on the guestroom floors (excludes public and service areas). Total hotel gross area is the entire hotel, excluding parking.

of project size is the critical basis for all cost estimates. Figure 10.2 represents fairly typical space allocation requirements per guestroom for different types of lodging properties.

The development of the design brief, especially the space programme, does not occur at one time nor does it result in a static document. Frequently, the team refines the initial brief, little more than a thumbnail set of requirements, during the schematic and design development phases, into a comprehensive set of operational and planning standards. This may be based, in part, on information conveyed by the management company in its design guide. That is, throughout the early design stages, the brief evolves as the team collaboratively develops an understanding of the building's design and its potential operational relationships.

Site layout and arrival

The first step in planning a hotel is to recognize the constraints and opportunities inherent in its site, and how these influence the organization of the building. Different types of lodging properties require sites with varying characteristics and different amounts of land. While a flat, treeless parcel may be the least expensive for construction, one with more interest may enhance the building design and guest experience, whether it offers a moderate slope, trees or other landscape, or even existing buildings which could be adapted creatively to particular hotel, conference, or resort uses. The architectural team needs to analyse the site characteristics before it can begin to develop the building form and organization. These include such factors as visibility and accessibility for arriving guests, surface and subsurface conditions, environmental constraints, available utilities, regulatory restrictions, and the potential to accommodate future expansion.

Once the architects understand the influence of the site on the building programme they can begin to formulate the concept. Sometimes this is most influenced by the surrounding buildings or natural terrain: a 15-storey glass-and-steel tower may fit an urban location while a cluster of heavily landscaped low-rise villas is more appropriate for a Mediterranean beachfront resort. But many hotel projects are not so clear-cut and in these the architect must create a unified image and building concept to meet the owner's objectives, the operator's functional requirements, and the future guest's expectations. Once the concept is formed, the architect must organize the hotel functions to meet clear operational goals, both from the guest and staff standpoints. In addition to designing the hotel building itself, the architect is responsible for coordinating the development of the site plan including vehicular circulation, landscaping, and outdoor sports areas. For most lodging properties parking is the most important of these, including the design of the approach, driveways, sidewalks, receiving area, and emergency access. Generally, the parking requirement is specified in the local zoning ordinance and may require, especially in smaller cities and suburban locations, more than one parking space per guestroom. In major urban areas, where a large number of guests arrive by cab, the final parking agreement may be negotiated between the developer and the city. Providing sufficient parking is critical if a hotel intends to attract banquet and dinner business and, therefore, the developer must carefully analyse and balance the real need for parking against its cost. Often, nearby garages are used to meet peak demand.

Even before the guests enter the lobby or are greeted by the staff they will have formed an impression based on the approach and arrival sequence: are the grounds landscaped? Is there adequate and convenient parking? Is there clear signage? Is the building illuminated? Is there a sufficient entrance canopy? Larger hotels may incorporate a number of different entrances. This is helpful to separate overnight guests from those using the ballroom, to reduce the amount of unnecessary traffic through the building, to establish a distinct identity for a restaurant or spa, or to provide increased security.

Among the most prominent entry features is the *porte cochère*, the entry canopy designed to protect guests from inclement weather and to provide visual emphasis to the entrance. The architect's design should incorporate lighting and signage and be of sufficient height for buses and emergency vehicles. The driveway beneath the *porte cochère* must be at least two lanes wide, preferably three lanes, or more in special situations, to facilitate peak numbers of arrivals and departures. The sidewalk needs to be wide enough for loading and unloading of baggage, including tour or airport buses, as well as to accommodate guests waiting for taxis. Thus, the design team needs to address a number of import-ant operational planning features on the site, before guests even arrive in the lobby, or incoming goods reach the receiving area.

Lobby and public circulation

The public areas in hotels have evolved, historically, to support the reasons people travelled and the needs of different social classes. In the eighteenth century, the largest hotels were at resort locations, such as at Bath and Brighton, or in Baden-Baden on the Continent. Even in the early nineteenth century it was rare to find a hotel lobby, travellers stayed in small coaching inns along the post roads between cities. But, eventually, visionary entrepreneurs introduced much needed amenities. Prominent examples on each side of the Atlantic were the Royal Hotel in Plymouth, UK (1819) and the Tremont House in Boston, USA (1828), both of which featured, among other innovations, an 'office' (today's lobby) and a series of formal lounges, dining, and banquet rooms. The lobby soon became the most prominent of the public spaces because it was where overnight guests, banquet attendees, conventioneers, diners, and others came together. Even today, it may create the single overriding image for the hotel, such as is the case with the atrium lobby in many Hyatt Hotels in the USA.

In addition to establishing the image of the hotel, the lobby serves many obvious functional requirements. It is the main circulation space, helping to orient guests and direct them to the front desk, elevators, food and beverage outlets, meeting and banquet facilities, recreational areas, and so forth. Therefore, one of the key planning objectives for hotels is literally to cluster these public functions, restaurants, lounges, meeting rooms, etc., around the lobby, helping assure that the hotel guests find the various facilities with a minimum of difficulty. As guests linger, it serves also as an informal gathering space. To management, it functions as a control point, with the staff able visually to oversee access into and through the building.

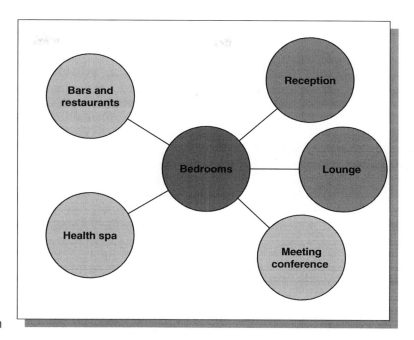

Figure 10.3
Hotel schematic bubble diagram

Based on the particular markets the hotel serves and its design concept, the development team must establish its own priorities for planning the lobby and circulation spaces. Typically, these operational planning criteria include:

- Circulation: provide clear paths to front desk, elevators, F&B outlets, function space, etc.
- Front desk: locate desk visible to the entering guest and the elevators; include sufficient queuing space; provide direct access to front office.
- Luggage: provide space for bellman, luggage storage, and other locked storage.
- Seating: provide seating near front desk and main entrance; provide more private seating nearby; consider use for lobby lounge.
- Support functions: locate retail outlet, concierge desk, public toilets, house and pay phones, coatrooms, etc. convenient to the lobby.
- Décor: establish hotel image with millwork, furnishings, artwork, lighting, signage, etc. appropriate to locale.

Food and beverage outlets

Hotel food service goes through frequent cycles of changing popularity with the public. Since the mid 1980s, with the increasing need to generate revenue from as much of the hotel as possible, hotel management has striven to create innovative dining rooms and bars. Operators realize that well-conceived food and beverage outlets increase the demand for guestrooms and meetings, attract the general public, especially at lunch and dinner, and generate additional profits. These outlets, however, vary so widely in quality and character that the programme and design of each outlet must be developed individually based on a survey of the local market and existing competition.

Occasionally, at luxury hotels or the boutique properties, the hotel restaurant or bar (rather than the exterior design or lobby) creates the overriding image for the property. For example, many upscale travellers seek out the top-rated Jean Georges in the Trump International Hotel and Towers in New York or animate the lounge in the St Martin's Lane or Sandersons hotels in London. More commonly, though, the hotel operator provides restaurants and lounges as a service to the guests, and, hopefully, to generate revenue.

Hotel food and beverage areas are developed differently depending on the quality and price-level of the hotel and on the management company. Franchise and many mid-price chains establish a prototype restaurant concept which they install in scores of properties regionally or nationwide. This may be a corner of the lobby outfitted for breakfast in a small economy motel or a three-meal restaurant in a mid-price highway property. The sameness provides an established quality level and satisfies a particular guest expectation, and can be developed again and again at a known cost.

On the other hand, upscale hotel management companies attempt to create individual and distinctive outlets in their larger first-class and luxury properties. Some operators carefully script the restaurant or lounge early in the development, describing the look of the space, the theme, menu, service style, table decoration, in short, writing full stage directions for the eventual production. Other operators provide relatively generic descriptions of the several outlets and, only when the architectural and interior design direction are established, provide the operational detail to bring the outlet to reality. The development and design team must determine consciously the most appropriate approach depending on the need for a distinctive outlet and the talents available. The feasibility study should identify the demand and supply characteristics of the market including competitive hotel restaurants and their salient characteristics, and recommend a mix of restaurant and bar outlets. However, it is necessary for the development team to confirm these recommendations and establish their own concepts for the F&B areas. As hotels increase in size developers usually provide additional outlets so that the scale of any one restaurant or lounge does not become overbearing. These include the three-meal restaurant, sometimes a 'café'

Illustration 10.1
Restaurant NH Hotels Brussels Airport (Courtesy Scott Brownrigg)

or given a signature identity, and a speciality restaurant, perhaps based on an ethnic (Italian, Chinese) or food (seafood) theme, or a specialty coffee outlet or casual deli. Each restaurant has its own image and, while attracting hotel guests, it also attempts to compete for different groups of outside diners.

As hotel operators strive to lower overheads and simplify their operations, many try to reduce the number of different operations and develop a single restaurant with several distinct moods appropriate to the different meal periods and their level of formality. One suburban Hyatt Regency in the USA features a hotel restaurant located in the central atrium space, in full view of other guests, with three clearly delineated zones: One is in the atrium, where diners are seated in a park-like setting, amid natural light and trees, and surrounded by the building. A second area is at the edge of the atrium, where fabric awnings partially shelter the patrons and provide a semi-private setting not unlike a sidewalk café. The third is further back from the atrium, under the upper floors of guestrooms, in a low-ceilinged interior space, much as though the diner had passed from outdoors into a small restaurant. The atrium area is treated most casually, with brick paving, trees, and tables with placemats or cloth runners. The intermediate zone is slightly more formal and the 'interior' section includes leather banquettes, table linen, darker lighting levels, and such additional accessories as artwork. The restaurant is highly successful because it offers different moods for breakfast or dinner, for family groups or couples, and for informal meals or special-occasion dinners.

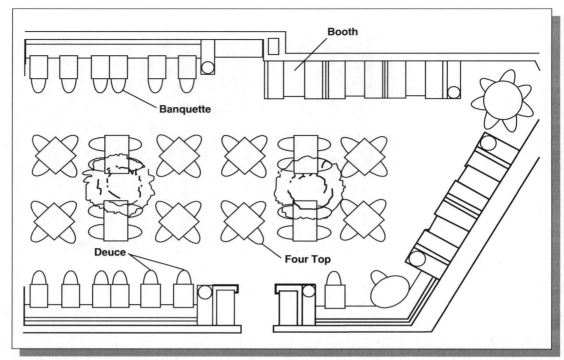

Figure 10.4
Restaurant plan

In a similar fashion, the hotel management company establishes the programme for the hotel bars and lounges, the architect prepares preliminary plans to accommodate these requirements, and the interior designer fully develops the concepts. In a small downtown hotel the primary beverage outlet may be a quiet and luxuriously furnished lobby lounge whereas in a convention or resort property, it may be an action-oriented sports bar. The lobby lounge grew in popularity in the 1970s and 1980s to create activity and excitement, first, in the open atrium space and, after its success as a revenue generator was proven, even in the more traditional lobby. Open to the lobby space, the lounge provides a small bar, limited food or tea service, occasional entertainment, and lounge seating which can be used flexibly to expand the capacity of the lobby.

A second beverage outlet often is a cocktail bar or entertainment room. This facility is completely enclosed, and features lower light levels and more tightly spaced seating. Depending on the theme, the lounge might have distinct sections, including a sit-down bar, an entertainment area with a stage and dance floor, a games area with billiards or backgammon, and quieter seating alcoves.

Restaurants and lounges, because they face such severe outside competition, create the greatest operational and design challenges.

Whatever the concept, the food and beverage designer must attempt to meet many generally accepted planning and operational objectives.

- Location: position the main three-meal restaurant convenient to the lobby; position the specialty restaurant with direct exterior access.

- Service: group all food outlets close to the kitchen or a satellite pantry; provide bars with service backup.

- Flexibility: design larger restaurants and bars so that sections can be closed during slow periods.

- Support areas: provide public toilets, coatrooms, and telephones nearby.

- Layout: provide host desk, multiple service stations, a flexible mix of table sizes; minimize or eliminate level changes to better accommodate handicapped guests.

Function areas

Perhaps the clearest distinguishing feature among the different types of lodging properties is the size and mix of their function space: the ballrooms, smaller meeting and banquet rooms, reception and exhibit spaces, and dedicated conference and board rooms. First introduced in the mid-nineteenth century to accommodate important civic and social gatherings, function space now is utilized more often for corporate and association meetings. The two create different demands: the corporate group requires a variety of relatively small but high-quality spaces for sales and management meetings, new product introductions, and continuing-education programmes for executives. The association market primarily needs facilities for large group meetings, smaller rooms for seminars and workshops, and extensive exhibition space. In addition, local organizations use hotel function space for a variety of meetings, banquets, and receptions.

Again, the design brief should expand on the mix of function space listed in the feasibility study, based on an analysis of the demand for different types of business and social uses. Or, before proceeding with a renovation, management confirms which types of rooms customers request most often and what features they require. Small mid-price properties generally offer a single multi-purpose ballroom, simply decorated and equipped to accommodate a full range of small meetings, civic lunches, wedding receptions, and local product displays. It only infrequently is used to attract group rooms business.

On the other hand, convention hotels include a major ballroom, for 1000 or more people, junior ballrooms, and dozens of smaller breakout rooms. The ballrooms are designed for major banquets

(i)

Illustration 10.2
Royal Garden Hotel,
London: function room
(Courtesy Royal Garden
Hotel)

(ii)

and social functions but include audio/visual and other systems for meetings. The secondary rooms, all essentially meeting rooms, can be combined in numerous configurations, and have few built-in features and only limited audio/visual systems installed.

Conference centres are different still, designed for smaller groups, no larger than, say, 100 to 200 people, and feature dedicated single-purpose banquet, meeting, conference, and boardrooms so that each customer has a specialized room for a particular need. They offer such amenities as extensive foyer and gathering areas, 24-hour use of meeting rooms, additional conference services, and full audio/visual systems, sometimes even including a recording studio.

Because of the differences among the many types of lodging properties and the markets they serve, and the highly competitive nature of the meetings business, the design team must review carefully the programming and design criteria. In smaller, less-sophisticated hotels the total function space may be as little as $2\,m^2$ per guestroom. However, in convention hotels and dedicated conference centres it may reach $6\,m^2$ or $10\,m^2$ per room, respectively. Considering the additional kitchen and back-of-house areas needed to support fully a first-class convention facility, the potential investment in the hotel function space is substantial. Therefore, most successful developers carefully consider the appropriate balance between large and small rooms, their décor, and equipment, analysing the initial cost versus customer demand versus staff and other operational costs. Just as with the restaurants, where consultants are included to deal with specific elements, the planning of the function space may require building code consultants, acoustic and audio/visual specialists, and lighting designers. For large properties the operator may assemble a focus group consisting of meeting planners to discuss which meeting room features are most critical to help assure their future business. These have led to a number of typical planning and design criteria for meeting and banquet space to assure a more efficient operation:

- Location: group all function areas together in a location easily accessible from the lobby; however, in major convention hotels consider creating two or more separate function zones to better accommodate multiple groups.

- Flexibility: provide moveable partitions in larger rooms; determine need for multi-purpose versus dedicated rooms; create multiple pre-function areas.

- Access: provide separate function entrance from street or parking; provide public and service access to every room and subdivision, and display access to ballroom and exhibit areas.

- Support areas: provide sufficient toilets, coatrooms, and telephones for the public; provide banquet pantry, furniture and audio/visual storage, service corridors, etc.

- Structure: provide column-free spaces; locate ballroom and larger meeting rooms independent of the guestroom tower to simplify structure.

- Ceiling height: determine need for projection booth; consider implications of high space on second floor.

- Windows: determine need for natural light in function and assembly areas.

For new projects, the architect early in the schematic design must address these planning issues because they have a major impact on the hotel's ability to attract group business, an essential requirement in the major convention markets. In existing hotels that do not meet many of these planning objectives, the owners must assess the scope of any potential renovation to make the meeting and banquet areas more functional, for both the public and operations. Although expensive to modify, an older hotel may need to undertake a major overhaul to remain competitive for the next decade.

Once the schematic design is accepted, the architect, interior designer, management staff, and other consultants need to focus on the operational details. For example, consider the placement of meeting registration desks or portable bars in the pre-function area and how guests move through the space. Or study alternative furniture layouts for each individual meeting or banquet

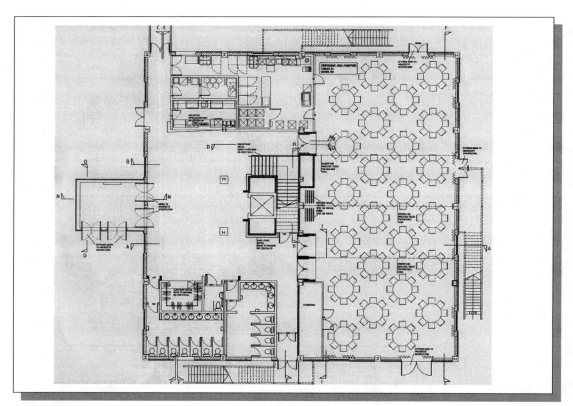

Figure 10.5
Function area plan

room; that is, test whether the room dimensions accommodate classroom, U-shaped, and banquet configurations efficiently. Such a step, relatively early in design, often shows that a minor adjustment to the planning will offer substantial improvement in flexibility or increased capacity. Experienced designers are familiar with many simple features which result in a better experience for the banquet guest or meeting attendee or which offer operational advantages. Most of these do not cost any more to implement if incorporated into the designs at an early stage. Consider the potential problems if banquet guests have unscreened views into the service corridor or kitchen, or if too few public toilets are installed, or inadequate directional and room signage is provided. Little design details can enhance the guest's experience or substantially improve operational efficiency. For example, experienced designers may specify a ballroom carpet with a pattern repeat of approximately 55 cm to help the housemen quickly set chairs in straight rows (both rows of stacking chairs and the aisles between them precisely align with the carpet pattern). A sample of such seemingly insignificant design issues, each of which improves guest satisfaction or reduces operational inefficiencies, are listed in the following checklist.

- Floors: select carpet pattern to aid in room setup; use portable dance floor for special functions.

- Walls: apply chair rail to protect wall finish; add fabric panels to improve acoustics and upgrade appearance.

- Ceiling: consider flexible lighting including decorative chandeliers, track, and fluorescent fixtures; provide fully dimmable lighting system; organize HVAC, sound system, fire protection, and other systems into a unified design.

- Windows: add full blackout capability.

- Furniture: select balance of rectangular classroom tables, round or oval banquet tables, stacking chairs, risers, lecterns, etc.; select high quality chairs for upgraded conference rooms.

- HVAC systems: separate the mechanical, electrical, and sound systems for each room division.

- Communications: include TV, telephone, recording, data lines in each function and control room.

Recreational areas

In the 1980s and early 1990s recreational amenities became a larger component in many hotels and resorts. The travelling public became more fitness conscious and many hotels added full health clubs, especially destination resorts and urban properties catering to a business clientele. A generation ago most lodging properties, whether it was a smaller roadside motel or convention hotel, had little more than a swimming pool, if that. Slowly, as part of the amenity-creep common in lodging, developers began to realize the competitive advantage gained by more expansive fitness facilities and added exercise equipment and limited health club facilities. Now it is common for a first-class or luxury hotel to include a full-size spa to complement its other business-oriented facilities; for a suburban hotel or small town motel to enclose its pool area to provide a swim and health club for the community; and for a conference centre to add extensive outdoor jogging, tennis, and golf facilities to its indoor pool and spa to attract high-level executive retreats.

The appropriate mix of recreation facilities must be based on an understanding of the market needs and a competitive analysis of other properties in the area. Consider, also, the possible revenue

Illustration 10.3
Bahamas hotel

that can be generated by local memberships, promoted in part to even-out usage during less busy periods. Among the planning guidelines are considerations for guest access to the facilities and the relative need to isolate them from other building elements. In upscale properties the architect should try to separate the pool area so that guests do not need to pass through the lobby, or other major public areas, in swimwear or robes. Where the health club is used by outside members they will need convenient access to the facility from the parking area.

Some of the recreational facilities create noise or other negative impacts and, as a result, need to be separated from public areas and, perhaps, guestrooms. For example, meeting rooms should be kept away from racquet courts or the swimming pool but the three-meal restaurant might benefit if it features views of the pool area. Unfortunately, the chlorine odour and high humidity usually require that the pool be fully enclosed and not share an interior room with non-recreational functions.

Best practice

Many of the larger international and domestic hotel-management chains emphasize operational planning in their new developments. They have strong marketing departments, many of which conduct regular research on customer preferences and use focus groups to understand what features of a proposed project are especially desirable to the users. For example, it is common to build a full-scale mock-up or model guestroom for any new hotel of more than about 200 rooms. This may be at the construction site or in a warehouse nearby. Each mock-up room, which might cost €30–40 000 to construct, is an exact duplicate of the future guestroom: complete interior finishes, all furniture and soft-goods, lighting and air conditioning, bathroom fixtures, and so forth. Only the bathroom fixtures are not plumbed. The finished model room is studied by the owner and members of the design team, often leading to a dozen or more changes, a few major, most insignificant. The operator tries to assure that the room will successfully meet the guest's practical needs, create a good visual impression, be easy to maintain, and cost-effective to construct. In addition, the room is photographed for pre-opening promotional materials and used as a marketing tool for prospective customers.

Many larger chains develop a proprietary, in-house *Design Guide*, carefully setting out the operational planning requirements for all spaces within the hotel. Again, from years of experience, these hotel chains attempt to create the best possible product at the lowest initial and operating costs.

As this chapter has emphasized, much of the effort is to balance often conflicting sets of objectives. First, the different users have a variety of demands: the overnight guest, the meeting attendee, the health club member, adults and children, all need and appreciate something different in the operational design. Other stakeholders, the owner, the management company, the administrative and hourly staff similarly have different needs. And there is always a budget to limit what is practical. Therefore, the development and design group must carefully (and constantly) balance differing values in making the planning and design decisions.

Future trends

The industry should continue to see increased segmentation, globalization, and technological innovation, all having an impact on the operational planning of hotels and resorts. Many of the largest international management companies have embraced segmentation, developing a series of different hotel products for different markets. Among the largest is Marriott, offering the luxury Ritz-Carlton, first-class Marriott and Renaissance, mid-price Courtyard, economy-level Fairfield Inn, extended-stay Residence Inn, all-suite SpringHill, as well as time-share, senior-living, and executive apartment concepts. Each 'product' has its own target markets, its own brand identity, and its own design brief and operational standards. This creates a new customization of the hotel product, which offers great opportunities for creative new approaches to design and operational solutions.

Developing countries offer an immense opportunity for these transnational firms, or for smaller regional and domestic companies, to target a particular market niche and gain competitive advantage. But this requires understanding very different local markets, then carefully tailoring the building design and crafting its operational design to meet the needs and price constraints of the locale.

Technological innovation continues to have an impact on hotel planning issues. Management attempts to reduce staff in order to squeeze more profitability from the hotel in an increasingly competitive environment. Computers and cell phones are everywhere; sensors monitor activity and can turn on/off practically any building system. A few chains are experimenting with self-check-in kiosks, eliminating front-desk staff, although generally garnering lukewarm approval from guests. Still, most travellers seek speed and efficiency and increasingly accept self-service systems such as bank ATMs. Recognizing this, most hotel operators continue to pursue sensible forms of automation.

Conclusion

This chapter has addressed the ways in which the development and design team approaches the operational planning of the hotel site and the building's public areas. Given increasing development, construction, and operating costs, not to mention the competitiveness of the operating environment, the successful developer must carefully assess operational planning to assure a successful project. Such efforts lead to a design that better meets guest and employee requirements, is more efficient and cost effective, and establishes itself in the business community.

References

Huffadine, M. (2000) *Resort Design: Planning, Architecture, and Interiors*. McGraw-Hill.

Lawson, F. R. (1995) *Hotels and Resorts, Planning Design and Refurbishment*. Butterworth Architecture.

McDonough, et al. (2001) *Building Type Basics for Hospitality Facilities*. John Wiley & Sons.

Penner, R. H. (1991) *Conference Center Planning and Design*. Whitney Library of Design.

Rutes, W. A., Penner, R. H. and Adams, L. (2001) *Hotel Design, Planning, and Development*. Architectural Press.

Review questions

1 Contrast the space allocation requirements for guestrooms in a motel, all-suite hotel and an urban business hotel.

2 What are the operational planning criteria for lobby and circulation spaces?

3 Outline some of the issues in managing the design of recreational facilities.

Case Study

Hotel developers solve the many operational planning relationships in different ways. In many resort properties, which tend to be spread out over a larger site, the public facilities often are on one floor, with the restaurants, lounges, meeting foyers, and so forth extending out on to terraces and gardens. City hotels, on the other hand, given smaller urban sites, tend to be more vertical, with public functions stacked on two or more floors. In this case, the design team must make a number of operational planning decisions which influence how the guest and staff react to the layout. For example, often the team will locate the food and beverage outlets on one floor and the function space on another floor. The team then adds a grand stair or escalator, or introduces additional elevators for the public; and the team must decide whether the main kitchen is better next to the restaurant or to the main banquet facility.

Consider the planning decisions which were made in the accompanying example of a recent city hotel.

Much of the planning solution successfully meets the operational relationships noted in the chapter. Guests arrive under cover, beneath the edge of the upper floors. They have alternative routes into the building, directly into the hotel lobby/reception area or into the zone of functions along the lower edge of the building: retail shop, lobby lounge, and three-meal restaurant. However, there is not a separate entrance for guests arriving to attend events in the function space (floors 2–4); these people must pass through the lobby or lobby lounge. Also worth noting: the front desk provides good visual control over activity in the lobby.

The main ballroom and some mid-sized meeting rooms are two levels above the ground floor, accessible by escalators and the lifts. (Additional meeting space is on the second and fourth floors.) The plan shows a large, two-storey-high, subdivisible ballroom ($930\,m^2$), with separate entrances for the public and for food service. The central pre-function space also serves several smaller meeting rooms ($60–100\,m^2$), and public rest rooms. The proposal also includes a fitness centre and pool on the roof of the ballroom, well isolated from public areas of the hotel, accessible from the lowest guestroom floor.

The architects, in collaboration with other members of the team, have created a compact design which meets most of the principal operational requirements. What additional positive and negative features can you observe in the plans of the two floors?

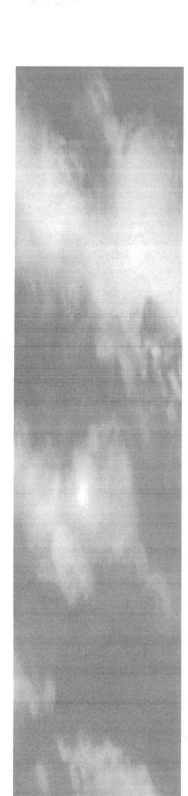

CHAPTER 11

Planning accommodation

Sue Davis

Planning accommodation, especially bedroom space, is an important activity for hotels, not least because this is normally the main source of revenue. When people stay away from home in hotels they spend at least one third of that time in the bedroom, and one of the prime 'satisfiers' for hotel guests is the room quality, as judged by subjective and objective factors such as convenience, aesthetics and design. This chapter considers some of the myriad factors in planning and designing hotel accommodation:

- Context
- Product segmentation
- Planning bedroom facilities
- Bedroom floor plates
- Amenities
- Form and function
- Future trends
- Conclusion.

Context

It is only in relatively recent times that design has been recognized as having the ability to add significant value to the hospitality product. Design has long been acknowledged in the worlds of fashion and car manufacturing for example. However, it is really only in the last 20–30 years that interior design has been one of the specialist skills that has played an integral part in creating or revitalizing the 'product'. Further, it is only in the last 10 years that research has been done which proves that good design can add significant value to the marketability and profitability of hotels. This in part is due to a greater public awareness and understanding of the impact of design, which creates a demand. Another reason is that the entrepreneurs of the hospitality industry are taking a more radical approach to hotel development and using design to differentiate their product from the corporate hotelier by offering individuality.

There is no such thing as the typical consumer any more when it comes to travel and leisure – customers are becoming ever more discerning and better educated. No longer are the masses uneducated. Compared to 50 years ago, the general public travel far more, and more widely, and therefore have a better understanding of the variety of value and quality on offer. Nevertheless, the market is generally driven by the courage and vision of the independent hotel developers.

The industry is at a new stage of growth in its maturity. Twenty years ago staying in even a mid-range hotel was a treat, as in-room TVs and en-suite bathrooms were still a luxury at home. Now they are far more commonplace in the home, therefore the industry looks to introduce new innovations to create the marketing unique selling points and the 'wow' factor. This has resulted in the increased understanding of the benefit that good design can bring. But design is not just about the 'wow' factor, nor is it just decorating the space. Good design has emotional impact as well as physical, and not only provides an experience for the guest, but also an efficient working space for the staff, as design is as much about the functionality as it is the style.

This chapter looks to explore the elements of design and their applications, and the differentiation this has created in the marketplace.

Product segmentation

As discussed in another chapter, the hotel industry has grown from its origins of the coaching inns to what we now identify as business or tourist hotels, with star ratings giving a clue to their quality or at least the facilities provided. More recently there has been a divergence, or segmentation of the markets, so that it is possible to classify these hotels in many different ways even within the quality bands. This ranges from city centre hotel or provincial conference venue, to airport hotel; all-inclusive resort to urban resort. Each requires a different personality: a different feel; a different experience. Gone are the days when 'one size fits all', and hoteliers are now providing choice through targeting specific market segments. A recent trend has been for 'lifestyle' hotels, a term which has been synonymous with hotels like the 'Sanderson' by Ian Schrager in London, designed to cater for the upwardly mobile with high disposable incomes. There is now though a growing understanding of the term 'lifestyle' as having a broader meaning and encompassing niche market products aimed at specific market sectors. There could be argument for a golfing hotel, for example, to be classed as a 'lifestyle' product.

The corporate hospitality chains meanwhile are targeting as broad a market appeal as possible, catering for the weekend leisure guest, and weekday business traveller. At the same time the demographics of the hotel guest are changing too, with a marked increase in women travellers, an ageing population, and single parent families for example. Other forces at work are legislation such as the DDA in the UK (Disability Discrimination Act) and others, driving the industry to acknowledge the needs of the disabled. There is also an increase in the requirement for environmentally responsible hospitality, although with both these issues it may be said that we are doing no more than is necessary at present. All these factors have some impact, or should at least be considered, when developing the hospitality product.

For example, there are now a number of hotel chains that specifically target the woman traveller, in acknowledgement of the market share they now provide. A number of factors are key here, especially security, real or perceived. Operators who are sensitive to the lone female traveller seldom check them in to ground floor rooms, for those reasons. Ideal female traveller rooms should also be close to the lift and a good distance from the fire exit. Not many women are confident of dining alone, so they should be seated somewhere discreet, preferably close to the reception desk or maître d' station, and the staff should be particularly conscious of them to give them overt reassurance. In terms of designing the room product, there should be adequate shelf/storage in the bathroom for toiletries. There is nothing more infuriating for a female traveller than having to leave their make-up bag balanced on the cistern! Suitable, appropriate lighting is a necessity by the vanity mirror – down lighters can be very unkind. A spyhole in the bedroom door for security is crucial. A good hairdryer with a sensible length of cable, positioned so it can be used right- or left-handed adjacent to a mirror, is still not guaranteed, and yet is a prerequisite for most men as well as women. In-room dining facilities should also be considered carefully, as many women prefer to use room service than the restaurant. Operations staff should therefore be consulted to ensure there is adequate table space for the style of service, whether by tray or trolley.

Planning bedroom facilities

The human's instinctive reaction to space is very strong. Even if people cannot vocalize why, they instinctively know immediately on entering a space whether they feel comfortable or not. Obvious examples of this are medieval homes with very low ceilings, which leave some people feeling oppressed and claustrophobic. Similarly an airport terminal is a vast inhuman space, and this makes some people feel small and vulnerable. In some cases these emotions are created deliberately, such as in a church, to convey a sense of awe and wonder.

In the same way, space creates impact and emotion in the hospitality product. For a large de luxe hotel a guest walking through the main entrance to be greeted by an atrium or a large sweeping staircase across the magnificent marble floored lobby, is going to make them feel important – like they have 'arrived'. As with the church, they are given that sense of awe and wonder. Meanwhile a guest arriving at the entrance to an exclusive niche market boutique hotel may well prefer a discreet understated entrance, and be less conspicuous.

How the designer approaches the planning of the bedroom depends upon the target market, staffing standards, operational requirements, and the average length of stay. Of course, much depends upon common sense. If the average length of stay is one or two nights, then the room will not need the same amount of wardrobe space as for an average two-week stay. If the hotel does not offer room service, then a breakfast table is not essential. If space is a premium, then a folding luggage rack may be preferable to a fixed one. However, if the hotel is a limited service/budget hotel with high volume, durability may be a greater consideration and therefore the fixed luggage rack would give better service. So the designer must fully appraise themselves of the operational and target market requirements before the planning process can begin.

Historically en-suite bathrooms were fairly small affairs. Currently, with many modern homes offering en-suites, and considering the amount of time we spend in the bathroom now, the hotel bathroom is given much greater consideration, and is as key to the 'offer' as the bedroom itself. There are now a number of examples in the 4 and 5 star sector where the bathroom and dressing area footprint is 50% of the overall room module. (Refer to case study.) Not only does this reflect more truly the time spent in each area for an average two-night stay, it also creates a differentiation. But whatever the space allocated, or quality standard, the bathroom must meet the same guest aspirations as the bedroom product, as it is as important in marketing terms. However, the more significant issue is that room design and planning overall is going through a new generation of change, with no real limitation on the designer's imagination. Obviously there are parameters of

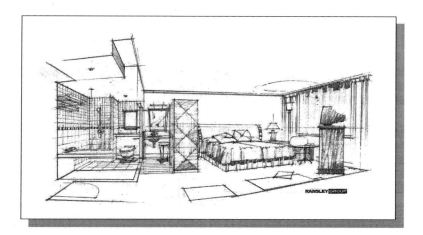

Illustration 11.1
NH Hoteles, Brussels:
sectional visual

cost and build efficiency, but these should be a natural part of the design process.

Planning is the first major stage of this process, and with the right space, and the right use of that space in layout terms, the rest of the design process falls in line relatively easily. This is where knowledge of the industry and preparation (briefing) is key in terms of providing functionality in the room product.

Bedroom modules range from $18\,\text{m}^2$ for the budget sector to, about $35\,\text{m}^2$ for the de luxe (this being a conservative figure, as land values are the only real limitation to size). Whatever size the room, there are a number of current prerequisite items required. These include:

- A bed
- Somewhere to sit: chair or couch
- A work surface (be it a desk or dressing table)
- Wardrobe
- Television
- Telephone
- Hair dryer.

There are bound to be some examples where not even all of these items are included, but these are the general market standards. Plus with the increase in 'lifestyle' hotels, at some point it could be established that a certain niche market would enjoy a TV-free room for example. However, these are the standard current expectations of the hotel guest. So it is the designer's role to come up with a new and interesting way of combining these elements into each room, whatever its size. The smaller the space the more challenging the design process, in order to maximize the sense of space and not allow the room to feel crowded. There is a similar challenge with the larger scale rooms too, as depending on budget parameters, it may not be feasible simply to fill the room with more incidental furniture, yet if there is too much empty space in the room it can make a person feel small. So balance and proportion again become critical.

Another key element of room planning and design is the housekeeping staff. What time are they allowed per room, and what is the quality of staff? If the hotel is in an area where good quality staff are hard to recruit, or staffing is low so they do not have long to turn the room around, the layout and design of the room should cater for this. For example, avoid beds on legs which are dust traps, and give adequate space between the bed and bedside units for vacuuming easily, and for making up the bed. With the right consideration given to the planning, not only does the guest feel comfortable in the room, the operational staff can enjoy working in an appropriate environment.

Bedroom floor plates

The key criteria in planning bedroom floor plates are maximizing the space for guestrooms and minimizing the area for circulation and service space. Separate but equally important are guestroom width to length and height per floor. All these factors relate directly to the overall cost of the building, therefore the greater the efficiency in planning bedroom floor plates the lower the overall cost of the building, as building costs relate directly to area and volume. Room width versus length is directly relevant as the wider the room the greater the length or size of site area required. Similarly, the front façade of the building is generally one of the most expensive elements. Therefore, the shorter the length of the façade, the lower the cost of building.

For these reasons the first step in the process should be establishing the most efficient room plan format. To illustrate the point, a building length of 60 m will facilitate in length 15×4 m wide room units or 16×3.75 m wide room units, therefore a building 60 m long with a double loaded corridor will accommodate 30 rooms, 7×4 m or 32 rooms 3.75×7.45 m, both being 28 m^2. While the façade length has not varied, the cost per room on each floor level is reduced by 9.6% (cost per floor level say £350 000/30 rooms = £11 666/room versus £350 000/32 = £10 938/room) or the façade length can be reduced by 3.75 m. A similar relationship exists in terms of room height whereby on a ten-storey building the difference between a floor to ceiling height of 2.6 m and 2.8 m increases the overall building height by 1.5 m which, on a building floor plate of 930 m^2, is an additional 1 395 m^2.

Having established the most efficient guestroom plan form, the next consideration relates to selecting the guestroom floor plate form. While this may be influenced by many different issues relative to the site plan, planning or building permit constraints, building orientation etc., from a space planning efficiency point of view a detailed analysis of a large number of plan layout variants identifies the more cost efficient solutions.

Figure 11.1 indicates the relative efficiency of different bedroom floor plates that can be measured by calculating the total floor area of the building allocated to guestrooms. As illustrated, this varies from 62% for an atrium plan to 72% for an offset slab plan form. The higher the percentage the lower the construction cost per room. In this regard, the main considerations in planning bedroom floor plate layouts are:

- Corridor loading: given site conditions are any single loaded rooms appropriate?

Configuration	Rooms per door	Dimension	Guestroom (percentage)	Corridor ft² (m²) per room	Comments
Single-loaded slab 	Varies 12−30+	32 ft (10 m) × any length	65%	80 ft² (7.5 m²)	Vertical core usually not affected by room module
Double-loaded slab 	Varies 16−40+	60 ft (18 m) × any length	70%	45 ft² (4.2 m²)	Economical length limited by egress stair placement to meet building code
Offset slab 	Varies 24−40+	80 ft (24 m) × any length	72%	50 ft² (4.6 m²)	Core is buried, creating less perimeter wall per room, more corridor because of elevator lobby
Rectangular tower 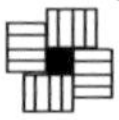	16−24	110 × 110 ft (34 × 34 m)	65%	60 ft² (5.6 m²)	Planning issues focus on access to corner rooms; fewer rooms per floor make core layout difficult
Circular tower 	16−24	90−130 ft diameter (27−40 m)	67%	45−65 ft² (4.2−6 m²)	High amounts of exterior wall per room; difficult to plan guest bathroom
Triangular tower 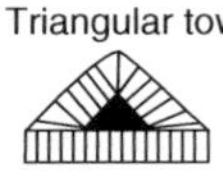	24−30	Varies	64%	65−85 ft² (5−7.9 m²)	Central core inefficient due to shape; corner rooms easier to plan than with square tower
Atrium 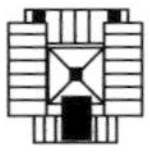	24+	90 ft + (27 m)	62%	95 ft² (8.8 m²)	Open volume creates spectacular space, open corridors, opportunity for glass elevators; requires careful engineering for HVAC and smoke evacuation

Each guestroom floor configuration has certain characteristics that affect its potential planning efficiency. The table shows the basic building dimensions, the usual percentage of floor area devoted to guestrooms, and the amount of area per room needed for corridors. For example, the table shows that the offset double-loaded slab is the most efficient in terms of guestroom area percentage and that the atrium configuration is the least economical, largely because of the high amount of corridor area required per room.

Figure 11.1
Guestroom floor analysis (Source: Rutes, Penner and Adams (2001; 259)

- Plan form: which particular shape (straight, offset, L, knuckle, courtyard or other configuration) best meets the site and building constraints?

- Circulation core location: should the public and the service cores be combined or separated, where in the plan form should they be positioned?

- Circulation core layout: what is the best way to organize public and service lifts, maids' service rooms and other support areas?

- Stair locations: which is the most efficient way to integrate fire escape and/or accommodation stairwells in the plan?

For rectangular bedroom floor plates, double loaded corridors with the circulation and stairwell cores partially or fully incorporated within the plan form, are generally the most efficient, especially when the service rooms areas are placed behind the lift covers. The limiting factor in most countries is the requirement to limit the maximum distance between fire escape stairwells (Europe max. travel distance/US in sprinkled building 300 ft (91 m)). In tower plan configurations the critical planning element proves to be keeping the vertical circulation core to minimum areas, as this also reduces the corridor area, the most efficient number of rooms per floor is between 16 and 24 rooms.

Atrium design plans, while aspirational, should only be utilized in statement buildings as they generally utilize single loaded corridors and are the least efficient in area and cost per room.

Amenities

The independent developer again often drives amenity creep. By giving their product differentiation by including, for example, a CD player in room, other operators start feeling obliged to follow suit. This is how the standard 'givens' of the TV, the en-suite, the iron, and the hairdryer all started out too.

There are changes afoot now though, as the market segments further, and certain products are very specifically targeted, some of these 'givens' may start disappearing in some situations, and new ones appear in certain types of products. The increase in women travellers has already been mentioned, and rooms specifically designed for them have generally dispensed with the trouser press, and solely provided an iron. Meanwhile 'toys' such as Playstations are now often to be found, especially where the target market is the 25–40-year-old business executive!

But in the mainstream hotels amenity creep is a natural progression reflecting the needs of the guest to make their stay as comfortable as possible. Hence data ports are already commonplace, in recognition of the level of business travellers requiring access to the Internet and e-mail. Research also shows that an alarming number of businessmen also take their laptop on holiday for fear of losing touch with the office when away – so even tourist resorts should perhaps provide such access, albeit in a more limited way. Toiletries provided in the bathroom have come a long way from their early introduction of a bar of soap, and maybe some shampoo. It is now commonplace to get a good selection of items such as shampoo, conditioner, body lotion, shoe cleaners, tissues and shower caps. Many operators choose to have branded products, or their own range, all to complement and strengthen the marketing, and offer, of the overall product to the guest. These small additions can provide a big impact on the guest, who on seeing a good selection of quality products available to them, not only feel well

(i)

Illustration 11.2
Radisson Edwardian Free
Trade Hall Hotel,
Manchester (Courtesy
Scott Brownrigg)   (ii)

Illustration 11.2
(*Continued*)   (iii)

looked after, but also find a certain thrill in having so many 'goodies' in their room.

Form and function

Design = Form + Function

This is an old formula that still holds today. 'Form' refers to the overall space, and its style, image, and experience. 'Function' has many layers and can refer to the physical function, comfort, durability, maintenance and psychological factors, in other words the product's general functionality. A good example of a product that demonstrates all these elements is the Dyson upright vacuum cleaner. Consider the impact this product had on a long established market with the brand 'Hoover' having been accepted as the generic name for the item. The Dyson product has demonstrably taken 50% of its market in a few short years. In terms of its 'form' this vacuum cleaner has a very distinctive style. It is bought by some purely because it is 'stylish', others because of its reputed performance. A win/win situation for the marketers. In terms of 'function' the product is lighter than most, so very comfortable to use. It has a number of attachments that are easily clipped on, and is very effective at its main task of vacuuming, therefore very 'functional'. The design has dispensed with dust bags, and is made of robust materials, making it easy to 'maintain and clean'. Lastly it has a clear drum, so you can see how much dirt you are lifting up as you work, which is a great motivator and gives job satisfaction – a great 'psychological feature'. So every aspect of good design has been considered which has led to its runaway success. So how do we translate these same elements into the hotel room designs?

The style and image are a subjective issue. We all have personal preferences and taste. However, the designer and, in fact, the operator/developer should put their personal preferences to one side, as the design must be appropriate for the guests intended to use the hotel. Design practices are all very different, each has its own personality and approach, some even have a set signature style, so it is important to ensure an appropriate design practice is commissioned that has the experience and approach to suit the project.

The style and image set the tone. Space can be dressed up, or down, just like clothes in creating the desired atmosphere – the experience. In this day and age there is more casual dressing compared to even 20 years ago. It is no longer necessary to dress up for the theatre. Even at 'black tie' events women can wear a cocktail length dress rather than the full-length evening gown. But dress a restaurant up, give it an elegant and groomed look, and people are instinctively encouraged to dress up themselves – or at least be hesitant to arrive in jeans and trainers. So whatever the style, be it traditional, contemporary or themed, it should set the appropriate tone for the target market.

As discussed, 'function' has many facets, first comfort. When selling a room night the underlying promise is of a comfortable night's sleep, and a clean bath/shower room. In a budget hotel this is delivered in a fairly basic way, with no frills or attached fashion, although the budget sector is now becoming more competitive, with operators vying for trade by gradually increasing the offer. However, the core offer is just the room product, and guests in provincial town budget hotels may feel that they are getting reasonable value. As the spend per night increases, so do the expectations. A guest paying a premium city centre rate wants to walk into the room and immediately see 'comfort'. They should not need to go and lean on the bed to test its comfort factor. Instead the room should ooze comfort. Whether achieved by lots of puffy cushions on the bed, and soft sumptuous fabrics swagged around the room, or by a clean uncluttered minimal scheme, with tactile fabrics and beautiful textures of a more modern scheme, comfort should be implied visually.

There are also other elements of comfort required. These are more physical. For example, a chair should be comfortable to sit in but it should also be comfortable to move. A chair too heavy to slide in and out of the dressing table is an irritant. Or a chair that is too low up against the table is uncomfortable. This also dovetails with functionality too. A room that is entirely comfortable, whether budget or luxury is one where everything does what it should, efficiently and effectively.

A desk, if in a business hotel targeted at the busy executive, should provide good, clear working space, easily accessible data ports and power sockets and not have the guest scrabbling around on the floor in danger of tripping over cables. Ease of use of the hairdryer has already been mentioned, but there is also a similar issue with the iron and ironing board where provided, which is often absolutely no use to someone who is left handed or traps the user in the bedroom lobby until the job is done. (What happens when room service arrives?)

Light switches should also receive careful consideration. They should be sited with a tired disorientated guest in mind, so they are easy to locate and the switching programmed logically. Two-way switching is a wonderful thing, unless you get into bed thinking you only have to throw the switch over the nightstand, to find you have to get out of bed again!

Durability requirements are generally set by the owner/operator, as the length of service of each element of the room will be dictated by their financial parameters. It is also influenced of course by the type of hotel product and by staffing standards. A high volume budget hotel is going to take some hard wear and staffing levels are generally low. Therefore all the elements of the room must be highly durable. It should be obvious therefore that a cream carpet would not be appropriate but less obvious is how the carpet fitting is detailed. Will it run under the skirting in traditional fashion or should it be wrapped up the wall and used as skirting. A cleaner in a hurry can cause painted softwood skirting a lot of damage over time. A table may be made of a durable material but are the legs stable enough to take a knocking.

Conversely, in the luxury end of the market, a cream coloured carpet may be acceptable for its impact (most average families of 2.4 children plus dog would not dare at home, so there is a big 'wow' factor) and because of higher staffing levels they are prepared for the time and maintenance it may require and possibly justify a higher spend if more regular replacement is required.

The normal or acceptable lifecycle of the room product is 3–5 years for the soft furnishings and 7–10 years for the whole product. However, there are many variants to this and it is generally dictated by the individual investor/operator. There are sadly many examples of hotel rooms that are seriously overdue refurbishment, having given 15–20 years service yet obviously not designed to do so.

Of course, there are also opposite extremes. For example one timeshare resort undertakes soft refurbishments every year. This is first because the budgets set for the capital expenditure are too low and because what money they do spend they do so unwisely, buying for example, domestic fabric that cannot take the wear and tear of a commercial environment. This also creates the problem that instead of capital expenditure they are spending money on the staff managing this annual refurbishment and should factor in the loss of room stock each year.

The issue of cleaning has in part already been covered. Consideration should be given though in the planning process for ease of cleaning and vacuuming. Dusting and polishing are made a slow process by a multitude of open shelves and awkward corners, or fielded panels on doors. Full height mirrors are arguably a must for the guest, but have housekeeping staff good access to the mirror for cleaning? If it is a floor to ceiling mirror, will they need a ladder to do the job? For certain hotels this will be entirely acceptable but the wise designer will always get the head of housekeeping to buy into the idea first. It is of course paramount that the bathroom design allows for a high standard of cleanliness, as no guest in any quality of hotel will forgive a dirty bathroom.

With maintenance in, say, the budget sector, it will either be contracted out, or regionalized. Hence the need for the designer to have provided a durable and maintenance free product as far as possible. As the quality of the hotel product increases so do the maintenance requirements and so an in-house maintenance person or small team becomes more normal. They look after broken furniture, touching up the paintwork, replacing light bulbs etc. as well as more general maintenance of plant and equipment. However, the designers should be aiming to minimize their workload where possible. Light bulbs are a good example. While a variety of lighting in a room is essential (such as ambient lighting and task lighting) a wide range of light fittings can lead to an unnecessarily burdensome variety of light bulbs that need to be kept on standby. Again, if there is a maintenance team and plenty of back of house storage this could be acceptable, but this needs to be agreed and understood at the design stage.

The psychological issues in terms of space and comfort have already been discussed, but as with the Dyson vacuum cleaners, there can also be psychological 'features' in a design. Sometimes this is just to add to the experience or to create an illusion. One classic example would be in a room with a disproportionately

Illustration 11.3
Radisson SAS Hotel, Manchester Airport (Courtesy Ransley Group)

high ceiling, where using a darker colour on the ceiling than the walls, gives the optical illusion of lowering the ceiling. At other times a psychological feature will be used to direct guests or temper their behaviour. For example, at the Radisson SAS Manchester Airport, the reception area lies off the main Terminal Skylink. Because of the openness of the architecture and the size of the spaces concerned, a ceiling feature, resembling an inverted runway, runs from the main entrance to the reception desk. This gives a subliminal message of direction to the guest, in support of the directional signage. In another example, a busy conference hotel which has large numbers of guests checking in at the same time, would have many guests vying for the attention of the desk staff at the same time if a traditional single long counter had been used. Instead reception comprises of a number of individual desks at which the staff stand so having direct eye contact with guest. Also by being individual desks a crowd automatically dissipates into smaller groups. The final, clever, design feature, is that in front of each desk, about a metre back from the counter are motifs in the floor finish. At first glance these are purely decorative, but they have a psychological impact on the guests who again are subliminally led to queue from these points in the floor, also providing a comfortable distance from the guest already talking to the reception staff, therefore giving them a sense of some privacy.

Future trends

It is impossible to foretell exactly what will happen in the future of the hotel product. If current trends continue, segmentation will further develop as new niche markets are identified, and continuing analysis of the demographics of the traveller gives clues to their specific requirements. The growth in recent years of the budget sector is now seeing this market mature and develop, and the amenity creep factor in to current developments, as each brand vies for market share.

Demographic changes and the ageing population have yet to have any major impact on the mainstream hotels in the business market. However, with the over-80s age group believed to set to double in the next 10 years or so, and pension provisions being currently eroded, there may be a much higher proportion of older business travellers before too long. This would create a number of issues for room design. Bed height becomes important – a low slung bed is not going to offer much comfort if the guest cannot easily lower themselves down on it. The casegoods should offer access to storage a good height from the ground. Floor finishes will need a good texture to offer grip when walking, not least to avoid costly litigation. The bathroom will need to provide plenty of grab rails and non-slip surfaces, with showers being more predominant. This is not for disabled guests, but for the average 65-year-old, with a normal level of aches and pains that they experience.

However, if a hotel has a high proportion of older guests then the room design must cater for them accordingly.

Hopefully the next decade will see innovations in design and facility that will cater more widely for the needs of the disabled, not just wheelchair users, but the disabled in the broader sense, with disabilities such as sight impairments and hearing difficulties. With technology advancing at its current rate there should be many innovations that, along with sensitive design, will enable the hotel room product to cater for this demographic more generally within the standard hotel room.

Also environmental issues are becoming more prominent, and will continue to do so if the strength of feeling of many current students is maintained into their professional life. It is now more commonplace to find eco-friendly developments in developing countries and areas with fragile eco-systems. As products and technology are tested and proven in these areas it will give strength to the argument to use them in urban areas too.

There are already positive examples of such developments in the western world. William McDonough, an American based architect, is responsible for a number of major developments where great consideration has been given to energy efficiency, and an environmentally friendly environment. These properties are proving that while the initial capital outlay is higher than a traditional approach, the ongoing operational costs are much reduced, and payback is achieved within a few years. These are fine examples of the possibilities, which will undoubtedly filter through to the hospitality product.

An external factor that also may have a major impact would be the introduction of aviation fuel tax, which is currently under discussion by the UK government at least. At an industry event early in 2003 Lord Thurso (MP for Caithness, Sutherland and Easter Ross, – previously MD of Champneys, and also General Manager of Cliveden) spoke of this, and the fact that this is the only form of fuel that is currently not taxed. He believes if this were to proceed, it is inevitable that flight costs would increase, possibly most affecting the long haul traveller, leading to, for instance, American and Japanese travellers visiting the UK less often, but staying for longer. If this were to be the case this could have a major impact on room design. For the mainstream business hotel the average stay is two room nights. However, if a hotel enjoys a high ratio of long haul guest, this may change to two or more weeks, requiring not only extra storage space, more commonly provided in the leisure/tourist product, it would also require a higher degree of personalization to their taste in order to attain loyalty.

As stated, corporate hotel chains generally go for a broad market appeal, which is possible as most people will put up with certain small inconveniences for a couple of nights. If the guest is now more commonly staying a significant length of time small inconveniences can become major irritations. For example, some American industry standards have changed recently in acknowledgement of the nations increased average stature, so bar stools have increased in diameter to reflect this. Would the European hotelier therefore need to apply American standards to make the long-stay American guest feel comfortable?

The Scandinavians are generally taller in stature than most of their European counterparts, (a fact that was acknowledged by Scandic Hotels whose beds were generally 2.3 metres long), and who may also appreciate taller doorframes. A product catering for these markets might be wise to accommodate such requirements, if the average stay increases to that extent. These are specific examples, but at least give an idea of the issues. How would these issues be resolved for an hotelier catering for long-haul and domestic guests?

Conclusion

The design process for the hotel bedroom therefore, is first one of planning and research. It is crucial that the designer has a sound understanding not only of the profile of the guest, but also of the operational style and requirements of the operator. The designer should also be keenly aware of the budgetary parameters established for the project, and respect them. The success and ongoing profitability of any hotel is dependent on a number of factors, first that the development has been realized to the budget, which should have been set to an appropriate level for the type of product, giving the investors the opportunity to get the planned return on investment. Secondly, that the operator can easily and efficiently manage the hotel, with the design supporting and assisting them, and not working against them. Thirdly, but just as important, that the product should have such an appeal that the guest has a positive experience. The designer therefore has at least three clients for any project, the investor, the operator, and the guest.

Design alone rarely holds the key to success. A room may be stunning, but if the guest receives poor service they are unlikely to return. However, there are a number of examples of tired old hotels which have been starved of ongoing investment, who still enjoy relative profitability because of the quality of service. But quality of service is one of the most difficult elements to achieve and maintain. However, good planning and design can assist the operator, give the hotel marketing strength, and give the guest a feel good factor.

Reference

Rutes, A. W., Penner, H. R. and Adams, L. (2001) *Hotel Design: planning and development*, WW Norton, New York.

Review questions

1 Outline ways in which the travelling public's attitudes have affected designing accommodation.

2 What are the prerequisite items for inclusion in a typical hotel bedroom?

3 Explain what is meant by 'Design = Form + Function.'

Service provision

David Pantin and Josef Ransley

One of the key objectives of developing a hospitality property is to provide a level of service in the future which will attract customers and permit smooth operations. This chapter considers some of the key issues to be addressed in the countdown to opening or re-opening a hotel:

- Introduction
- Service and design planning integration
- Operational philosophy briefing document
- Pre-opening operational finance
- Pre-opening sales and marketing
- Management and staff recruitment
- Establishing departmental procedures
- Staff training
- Operating supplies and equipment (OS & E)
- Managing on a building site pre-opening
- Conclusion.

Introduction

This chapter looks at project development from the point of view of the hotel unit manager who will not necessarily be involved in the early concept or design development stages of the process, as these are often dealt with by head office staff, or are part of established brand standards. Whether the unit manager is involved in the early stages or not, it does not alter the fact that he or she becomes responsible for establishing the operational service provision of the unit hotel upon completion of the construction. This key step is at the interface between concept, planning, building and maintenance (as shown in Figure 12.1), when the development is 'operationalized' into a living unit.

Establishing the operation will entail either starting from scratch or with selective support from the larger organization, usually some six to nine months prior to the planned opening date.

The initial steps in the process that occurs at the outset when the concept is initiated, which relate to the interaction between the service and design, are reviewed so that the whole process from the manager's perspective is clarified. An example of the access timescales needed by the operational team before completion is shown in Figure 12.2.

While construction or development is taking place, the operational team need staggered access to key areas in the hotel, and an example is given in Figure 12.2. In the example, sales and marketing might construct a hut on the site in order to begin to take bookings and create interest in the property between 16 and

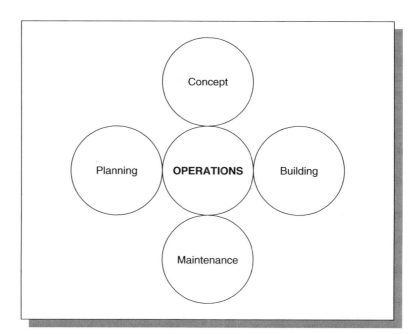

Figure 12.1
The centrality of operations in the development process

Area	Period before completion
Sales and marketing	16 to 25 weeks
Guest room sample	6 to 8 weeks
Kitchens	4 weeks
Stores (part)	2 to 4 weeks
Bedroom floor	2 weeks
Bar and restaurant	2 weeks
Reception and administration	2 weeks
Office/stores	2 weeks
Forecourt and car park	1 week

Figure 12.2
A typical operational access –
countdown to completion

Illustration 12.1
A de luxe bedroom at the Lowry
Hotel, Manchester (Courtesy of
Rocco Forte Hotels)

25 weeks before opening. The team would want to see a sample room (usually a single) 6–8 weeks before the handover date.

Imagine arriving at a building site that is nine months away from completion and that is the time available to you to recruit, train and staff an operational hotel, as well as deal with the many other aspects that are involved in turning a physical property into a functioning machine. This chapter aims to identify and guide those who will be involved in the process and hopefully increase awareness of the various aspects, thereby making the task less challenging.

Service and design planning integration

Every service concept relies on integrating the physical property with the service requirements. The greater the efficiency in the planning of these two aspects, at the design and planning stage, the lower the capital cost of the development and greater the potential to enhance the unit's potential operational profit. It has been shown that the designer will base the plan layout proposals on the area schedule provided in the design brief. Equally important to the size allocated to each area is its relationship to another, for instance, the kitchens in a conference hotel must be planned to provide easy and direct access to the restaurant and conference/events facility. Figure 12.3 illustrates a typical hotel relationship plan, normally provided to the designer, to indicate the relationships and movement of guests and staff between different areas. It is the task of the operator to analyse the plan layouts proposed to ensure that such relationships, guest and staff movement and distances meet the optimal operational performance.

Equally, as the designer will be considering the constraints of the site and building form, it is important that the two parties give due consideration to their respective constraints and collaborate to achieve the most efficient solution to satisfy their respective aspirations. The best results are normally achieved by the two parties participating in a workshop wherein they can interact with their respective expertise to develop a preliminary sketch layout plans. The designer can then develop these in detail and amendment until both parties are satisfied the optimum solution has been attained.

Having established the general arrangement layout plans, this process should be repeated for the more detailed planning of kitchen equipment, bar service counters, restaurant table layouts, etc. Some designers who have specialized in hospitality design will be able to address this stage with a better understanding of the operational requirements. However, it should be remembered that their knowledge will be based on previous experience with other projects and clients. This can be beneficial or negative, depending on the nature of the product one is seeking to realize, and their knowledge will never be equal to that of the experienced operator. Similarly the designer is foremost responsible for form, the operator for function, hence the interaction between the two is essential.

In conjunction with the layout planning stage, the designers will also have developed the concept scheme design clarifying the style, image and, importantly, the cost of the planned project. It is at this stage that the client has to decide on whether to approve the designer's proposals or not. Contractually if the designer has satisfied the requirements of the client's brief, the client has to accept the proposals. If the client wishes to change the requirements, there is a requirement to pay for additional design services,

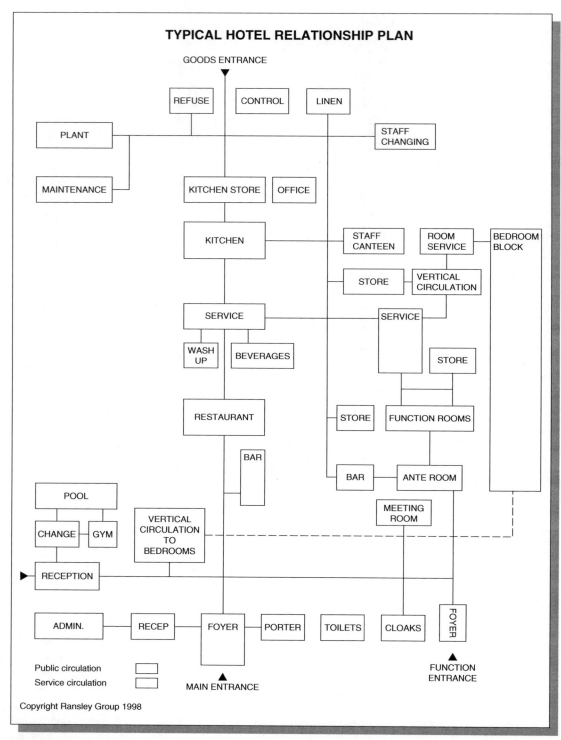

Figure 12.3
Typical hotel relationship plan

Illustration 12.2
Tides Bar at the St David's
Hotel & Spa, Cardiff

hence another reason why the design brief is such an important document. The decision on style is more subjective; nevertheless, if it reflects the design brief and the client does not like it, the designer has still fulfilled the contractual obligations. On the positive side, the design brief can be viewed as part of the business plan of the concept's development, and if all decisions in its development are made with reference to the original business plan, there is greater certainty of the concept being realized as planned.

Operational philosophy briefing document

The other essential document in the development of a new concept or project is the operational philosophy brief. As with the design brief, this document sets out the proposed methods and systems planned to be utilized in operating the unit and, combined, the two documents cover the requirements for the physical and operational aspects for the proposed product.

The operational philosophy briefing document needs to emanate from the developer who has initiated a commercial development, usually supported by an independent feasibility study, used to assist in the financing of the project and to obtain a suitable operator. The operator is likely to be chosen from a short list that matches the financial and service delivery aspirations of the hotel development in question.

Pre-opening operational finance

Modern technology dictates that detailed research is undertaken into the most relevant up-to-date back office systems. Consideration should be given as to how these will interface with front of house point of sales and to the corporate office. It is again essential that a detailed activity schedule be undertaken with integrated dates of completion.

Decisions should be taken on areas of authority for the hotel financial controller. Dependent on the scale of the hotel, the role could encompass purchasing and IT, so pre-opening critical paths should reflect this. If the operation is a stand-alone development, an accounting manual should be produced, detailing policies and procedures, job tasks and standards of performance. A payroll system will need to be implemented and this can on many occasions be out-sourced to a specialist support company, often providing a more cost-effective solution. Cash control and credit policies should be established, ensuring secure money handling. Credit card commissions, supplier accounts, insurance, contract schedules, credit search policies, guest ledger review systems, stock control systems, order, delivery and invoice note controls, stock control and banking procedures are all important items to be established during pre-opening.

One of the most important elements to the long-term success of the business is the preparation and delivery of first class management information in a pre-opening. This means evaluating all specialist software support, ensuring its appropriate integration into other systems with specific regard to accounting. A suitable management reporting format should be compiled, supplemented by the creation of key performance indicators (KPIs). These KPIs include such items as breakfast sleeper ratios, departmental labour and productivity analysis, cost indicators often on a per room or per square metre calculation. The production of a daily report detailing the previous day's trading should be undertaken, and this document should convey detailed departmental trading analysis to budget and forecast in the initial year, and then subsequently including prior years. A weekly detailed trading summary should also reflect the aforementioned. A monthly report should detail the departmental profit and loss supplemented by relevant KPIs, and should include detailed sales and costs analyses. A verbal narrative can be used to supplement the financial reports.

Pre-opening sales and marketing

One of the most essential components of the pre-opening of any new hotel is the planning associated with the development of revenue streams. A pre-opening marketing budget should be established, integrating and phasing its key elements.

Core aspects of the pre-opening sales and marketing budget should include the following:

- *Advertising*. Consider advertising in relevant directories, magazines and newspapers to include short break visits, special events, food and beverage promotions, and conferences.

- *Public relations*. Should look at local, national and international support, often from different agencies with different strengths.

- *Representation*. There is a need to take into account international sales support if the hotel is independent, often from companies such as Leading Hotels of the World. These companies can provide sales representation, but also critically GDS code to enable agents worldwide to book the property.

- *Promotion*. This budget category should include sales teams' attendance at key trade shows relevant to the property, such as EIBTM in Geneva, ITME in Chicago, WTM in London, MIT in Hamburg, or Confex in London. Support or active participation in local or national tourist boards should be considered, as well as promotions through local chambers of commerce. This budget nominal should also include 'hard hat' and gala openings, as well as client gifts.

- *Print and design*. This needs to cover costs of preparation, copy, artwork and print for production of in-house and external collateral, as well as advertising in the aforementioned directories, magazines, and newspapers. Consideration should be given to a pre-opening brochure and a 'rack stuffer', as well as specialist productions for weekend or special interest packages, weddings, festive seasons and conferences. This budget nominal should also include hotel photography.

- *Travel and entertainment*. Travel for the general manager, sales team and any other personnel used in the pre-opening sales should be included in this. Entertainment of clients both domestically and internationally should also be included.

- *HR and administration costs*. Sales and marketing payroll should be included in this, together with any membership dues, postage and mailings related to sales and marketing and direct mail promotions. Automobiles, office supplies and sales staff events should also be included.

The execution of the pre-opening sales and marketing activity plan will commence initially with the appointment of a director of sales and marketing and production of a relevant critical path. The plan will ensure coverage of all areas contained within the above budget, and it is important that time-lines are met. Critical elements of the pre-opening activity must include establishing the updated competitor evaluation of both product and rate.

These issues are likely to have been originally addressed in the feasibility study carried out on behalf of the developers and funders. Interviewing of candidates for sales and marketing roles should be commenced against an agreed staffing time-line. The marketing plan should be commenced clarifying target market segments, agreeing room tiering and classification, and relevant rates. A key accounts list needs to be prepared with relevant sales action planning, allotment requirements and contracts for these clients should be prepared. A pre-opening flyer, together with other collateral needs, must be created to ensure direct mail programmes are fulfilled, and that the sales team has appropriate brochures to use.

A request for proposal (RFP) should be undertaken for the above-mentioned public relations, sales representation and advertising to ensure a competitive and well-evaluated support service. Sales and marketing staff need to be hired against an agreed departmental structure, which will reflect activity needed in specific markets. A range of familiarization visits should be undertaken for key potential clients, and sales visits on behalf of the hotel to domestic and international markets must be planned and executed. A website with booking engine should be created with relevant links established to local tourist bodies.

Management and staff recruitment

Clearly it is essential to support detailed departmental procedures and corporate objectives with the recruitment of first class management and staff. A budget needs to be undertaken detailing the number of staff required during pre-opening and over what period. It is again crucial to plan interviewing and commencement dates in a detailed and integrated manner, in order to be cost-effective within the constraints of the budget, and to coincide with previously developed training schedules. One of the dangers of a haphazard, poorly planned opening is the unpreparedness of new staff who will be unfamiliar with the logistics of a new hotel. Depending on the location of the new hotel, such staff may also have been recruited from outside the hospitality sector, and will therefore possess no other experience on which to fall back.

In considering the recruitment process for staff, due consideration must be given to the culture of the company, the type of product, and the destination involved. The usual process of recruitment would involve the appointment of the pre-opening general manager as the first employee. He or she will then determine the relevant structure of the management team and the difficulties in recruitment of those specialists when determining hiring time-lines. An example would be where the hotel project is on an island, there may be lengthy immigration procedures involved and there may also be different priorities placed upon the importance of certain positions, such as purchasing manager.

Once a general manager has established the priorities, he or she should recruit an HR manager to help oversee the development of a departmental critical path, relevant organization chart, staffing plan and hiring timetable. A budget for this area can then be prepared.

The most effective recruitment procedure would be the creation of assessment centres, supported by competency frameworks for each position that is being recruited. These frameworks are based upon technical and behavioural traits and will have been created by the HR manager in consultation with the general manager. These will first be applied to the key management positions and linked into the relevant job descriptions. These job descriptions can be prepared within the hotel or corporate office, or alternatively can be obtained through specialist companies such as the Freeman Group.

An assessment centre is organized by creating the suitable test means for demonstrating those key competencies. Tests would include behavioural, technical and personality profiles. The assessment centre would take place in an area where the majority of potential candidates are located, if possible, and would be administered by the HR manager or senior trained designee. This is a preferable method of recruitment as it is objective and measurable. It will scientifically take into account the culture of the company, and appropriately marry together the styles of employer and subordinate.

Once the appropriate staffing schedule and recruitment process has been coordinated, a number of other key elements are required from the HR team. It is necessary for the department to create salary structure and appropriate reward schemes. Appropriate terms and conditions of employment must reflect the prevailing legislation within the country of the development. The creation of appraisal formats should be undertaken, as well as grievance handling, disciplinary procedures and related HR forms. A general policies and procedures manual should be prepared and a mission statement conveyed to all staff. Basic employee benefits should be integrated into the development, such as lockers, staff restaurant and access breaks. A benefits plan should be completed. There should be consideration of a computer-integrated labour management system that monitors attendance, scheduling, and productivity. Dependent on the location, a strategy for the liaison with staff unions needs to be developed. A staff consultative committee should be established irrespective of unionization of the hotel. This will act as a forum for employer/employee communication and dispute solution.

Establishing departmental procedures

The success of any hotel is dependent upon well-defined and maintained policies and procedures. This is even more acute in a new hotel development.

ROCCO FORTE
HOTELS

In Room Dining

Waiter

Task 23: Open Champagne Bottles

PROCEDURE	STANDARD

• Check that the label and vintage is correct before approaching the table.
• Present to host for approval
• Steps to open:
  1 Keep bottle in ice bucket.
  2 Remove foil and place in bucket.
  3 Place left hand around neck of bottle and thumb over the cork.
  4 Point away from guests.
  5 Remove the wire guard while thumb on the cork.
  6 Cover cork with a napkin.
  7 Holding the cork, slowly turn the bottle allowing the cork to come out (avoid the pop).
  8 Present the cork to the host.
	• Host approves selected bottle before it is opened.
	• Always point bottle away from guests.
	• Cork is held securely while opening bottle to avoid any potential accidents.
	• No popping sound.
	• Always present cork to host.

Figure 12.4
Example of a standard of performance

It is essential to create a job task for each role within the hotel. These are then supplemented by the standards of performance manuals. Consideration in the creation of these standards has to be given to the desired standards of profitability of the hotel and to the matching guest expectations. An example of such a standard of performance for staff is shown in Figure 12.4.

These departmental procedures will be required to be trained to all new employees and incorporated into their subsequent appraisal system.

Staff training

The amount of money necessary in a new hotel development will be determined inter alia by the scarcity of skilled labour within the local environment. Where that development is in either a remote location or an area of low unemployment, it will be necessary to often recruit from the non-hospitality sector and/or individuals who are not experienced in the roles for which they are hired.

It is essential when recruiting that the culture and attitude fit of the employee is married to the aspirations of the company.

Technical training can then be undertaken either by full-time trainers employed by the company, or obtained from an external training company. A training plan should be initiated for all departments to integrate with the recruitment schedule and opening time-lines. Not all outlets may open simultaneously and so it is vital that these time-lines are adhered to, both for budgeting and standards. The trainers will use relevant job descriptions and standards of performance manuals in the execution of their work. In addition to technical training, it is often useful to employ a company specializing in cultural and motivational training, and it may also be necessary to undertake a range of courses designed to comply with local legislation, i.e. health and safety, employment law, non-discriminatory policies.

Consideration of course needs to be undertaken regarding the location of the pre-opening training as the physical site may not allow activities. It is often useful to seek funding from local governmental organizations, which may extend the hotel's training budget further. Specific general training initiatives can include the creation of 'Train the Trainer' courses and craft trainers. This however will all have been identified within the Training Needs Analysis matrix.

Consideration should be given to a series of team building exercises to engender a motivated workforce. Strong specialist IT training is required in a modern hotel environment – some of this is provided by a contract support agreement from software suppliers, but additionally some in-house specialist support may be required.

Operating supplies and equipment (OS & E)

Dependent on the level of support obtained from the corporate office, the purchasing manager can be one of the most important appointments in the pre-opening of a new hotel. That individual will need to coordinate a significant programme for the acquisition of diverse items. Much of this work can also be undertaken by a third party specialist company. In a particularly large development with a complex location, such as the Lucaya Resort on Grand Bahama Island, a 1400 room, US$450 m development was on a small island, part of the Bahamas archipelago. A purchasing manager supervised a company based in Miami, Florida, who specialized in the purchasing of all operating suppliers and equipment for the hotels. It ensured that a complex programme of bid and tender was undertaken by a group of people with established supplier links and skilled internal manpower that specialized in specific areas of OS & E. This type of company has significant historic data on exactly on what items are required, what new market innovations exist, and updated pricing to fit the relevant commodity in question.

Key areas that will require identifying expenses are restaurant supplies such as crockery, cutlery, linen, bar supplies including glassware, coffee machines, blenders, ice machines, conference and banqueting items, room service items, guest supplies, maintenance supplies, etc. An example of a particularly departmental pre-opening list is shown in the case study.

Managing on a building site pre-opening

It can be a challenging task to integrate the needs of the operational team alongside the demands of the building site workforce. It is almost entirely the case that the pre-opening operational team will require offices away from the building site. This presents challenges closer to the opening of the property where segments of the building are being handed back from the developer to the operator. While it is always desirable to finish a project on time, it is often the case that specific time-lines of construction are not met, delaying the entry for the operator. This can pose the following difficulties:

- Unfulfilled training

- Unfinished snagging

- Lack of awareness by the employees of the logistics of the building and whereabouts of the tools with which to do their jobs

- Poor guest satisfaction, leading to low employee morale and start-up.

The developer usually controls access to the site due principally for health and safety legislation and to ensure uninterrupted work to the building site from specialists who are set deadlines for completion of their respective areas. It is helpful for the operator and the senior team to have a sound working relationship with the developer and the constructor, and the two parties should ensure a full communication schedule is established at the beginning of the project. This will allow for the immediate problems that arise during the construction of the building to be resolved with the operator's input.

Once the building has opened, there will be a period during which construction defects need to be resolved by the developer. The operator is at that stage in control of the site and the construction workforce will need to complete their snagging to an approved schedule that ensures minimal guest disturbance and guest dissatisfaction.

Conclusion

In summary, experiences suggest that it is essential to open a hotel with the following in place:

- *Operator critical path.* This outlines the tasks to be done by the operating team throughout the pre-opening of the hotel.

These should be done by departments with strict time-lines and accountability to specific individuals.

- *Communication plan.* A strong internal communications plan should exist, ensuring that senior management meet regularly to update progress, and to review any slippage to critical path, ensuring immediate remedial action.

- *Cooperation between developer and operator.* It is particularly advantageous for there to be a strong cooperative relationship between the developer and the operator. The operator should be fully included in all aspects of the design and planning stage of the hotel development, in order to ensure smooth operation, good logistics, and a customer-focused experience.

The dangers of either poor preparation or poor execution of a plan are as follows:

- Overspend on budget

- Book-outs of reservations taken for commencement of hotel operations

- Customer dissatisfaction at incomplete product

- Long-term damage through poor public relations in local market

- Long-term damage with intermediary clients, such as travel agents.

A hotel is a commercial undertaking, usually comprised of a mix of debt and equity, and required to achieve certain financial objectives. A poor start through any of the above is likely to result in decreased financial performance, thereby putting the pressure on the operator to achieve financial objectives, with resultant obvious possible occurrences such as labour cut-backs, scaling down of product and eventual possible liquidation.

Review questions

1 Review the main milestones in the countdown to completion.

2 What are the key aspects of pre-opening finance?

3 Outline the issues in an effective pre-opening procedure.

Case Study

The Lowry Hotel, Manchester

The Lowry Hotel was the sixth major international hotel whose pre-opening I had overseen either as general manager or as corporate officer responsible for the hotel.

My first initiative has always been to ensure the creation of a critical path integrating all pre-opening activities to defined timelines and with specifically identified personnel being held accountable for the execution of each item. The critical path at the Lowry Hotel had in excess of 1000 key tasks to be undertaken during a 10-month period prior to opening. An example of this is shown in Figure 12.5.

With specific regard to the Lowry Hotel, Sir Rocco Forte decided to undertake a design and build programme where every element of that programme had been detailed, clarified and agreed prior to commencement of building. This meant that a budget had been agreed for the entire project and guarantees obtained from the builder. It also meant that my colleagues and I had to be very detailed about our operational requirements at an extremely early stage. The tremendous advantage of the design and build programme was reflected in the fact that our hotel came in on budget, thereby preventing one of the most concerning elements of any new hotel development, specifically, budget overruns. This did not mean that we made no changes throughout the build-out of the hotel, but it ensured that we were held to a discipline whereby each and every work order had to be approved right the way up the line to our chairman, and that we had to seek corresponding reductions in other areas that had not commenced. Fortunately very few

Illustration 12.3
Lowry Hotel, Manchester by night (Courtesy of Rocco Forte Hotels)

changes occurred. This particular approach was in direct contrast to the operational pre-opening of a major international resort I had previously overseen, where the owners amended their vision of their end result too frequently, with numerous additional specifications contributing to significant cost over-runs and delaying the operator's ability to take control of the hotel on the date of initial reservations.

ROOMS DIVISION	Mar-01				Apr-01					Comments	By Who
	5	12	19	26	2	9	16	23	30		
Establish message and paging procedures										Completed	PV/TJ
Set up pre-opening reservation system										Completed	MP/YB/NT
Determine in-room amenities										Completed	MC/JB
Determine the safety procedures for luggage room										Completed	NT/JB
Establish car park procedure										Completed	JB/NT
Establish Business Centre charges										Completed	
Familiarize teams with Business Centre design										In progress	
Telephone operator (supervisor) on board										Completed	MP/PC
Confirm assignment of phone extension numbers										Completed	MP/JB
Establish dry run schedule										Completed	MP
Coordinate with Telecom on installation of phone lines										Completed	TJ
Compile guest reference/material Concierge Desk										Completed	TJ
Set up arrangements to use car parks in the vicinity										Completed	
Establish weekly rooms forecast										Completed	
Establish check in/out procedures										Completed	
Establish VIP check in/out procedures										Completed	
Front office operations manuals completed										Completed	MP/YB/NT
Review key processes of check in/out messages										Completed	
Determine VIP guests amenities programme										In progress	MP/YB/NT
Establish minimum quality standards										Completed	MP/YB/NT
Develop guest recognition/history programme										Completed	MP/YB
Establish front office set up procedures										Completed	PV/TJ
Establish incoming fax/mail/message procedures										Completed	PV/TJ
Set up IDD call accounting procedures										In progress	MP/YB
Set up telephone system										In progress	MP

Figure 12.5 An example of the rooms division key tasks for the opening of the Lowry Hotel, Manchester

The pre-opening critical path at the Lowry Hotel, coupled with strong corporate communication from Rocco Forte Hotels with the constructor, Jarvis plc, ensured that there was minimal slippage in the readiness of most operational areas of the hotel. The only difficulty became the delivery of the restaurant on time, which was handed over on the date of opening, rather than as planned, two weeks earlier. This resulted in some difficulties being encountered through lack of staff awareness of the logistics of that departmental operation and some training inadequacies. The hotel quickly, however, came up to its desired standard of operation and has subsequently received numerous industry awards and accolades.

Developing a hotel in Manchester is, however, often less complicated than attempting the same in either a developing country or a remote part of a large country, or indeed on an island. It is essential in those circumstances to consider the distances involved for both supply lines and staff recruitment, and there are often nuances of local cultures that need to be considered. Indeed, one of the more difficult aspects of developing the aforementioned resort was the immigration laws of that country and unionization of the construction force. No two projects can therefore be the same and an element of luck is also necessary in getting everything right. However, downsides can be negated and challenges more easily withstood by very detailed planning, and my personal approach has always been to use a detailed critical path. It is one of the most satisfying challenges in the industry, and when it all comes together, one of the most rewarding.

Asset management

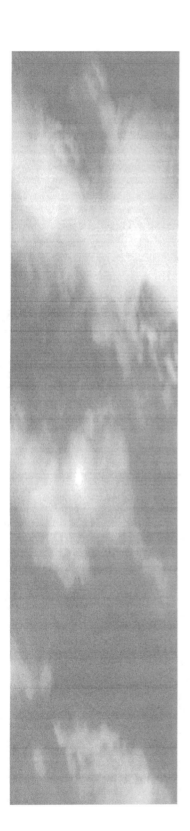

Asset management

David Bridge and Arthur de Haast

This chapter seeks to define asset management as an activity, by examining the current role of the asset manager and how the role has developed following changes in ownership within the hotel industry and the advent of more experienced debt providers. There is a description of the types of organization employing asset managers ranging from owners of single assets to portfolio owners and to branded hotel operators and an assessment of the different skills required by these different organizations. Subsequently, the chapter looks at the significance of the asset manager's role and how that role can benefit the operation and development of the hotel. This includes the importance of strategic planning and product benchmarking to secure the continued competitiveness of a hotel and hence its financial robustness from an owner's standpoint, a robustness that will often need to survive the life of the operating agreement.

The chapter also covers the different types of organization supplying asset management services and how these have been impacted by the change in ownership patterns as well as changes in lease and management contracts, which have made asset management more relevant to a larger investor population. Further consideration is given of current best practice within the industry and includes case studies. Finally current trends are reviewed and in particular the advent of the financial investor and the impact that this has already had and is likely to have in the coming years. This has to a large extent been driven by the current fall in returns from the world's equity markets and to some extent by an overheating in certain property sectors, which no doubt will adjust, but the widening of the investor population and the continued globalization of hotel operators will have a continuing and interesting impact on the role of the asset manager in coming years. In the conclusion to this chapter, there is a discussion of the role played by the asset manager in the book's development model.

The structure is as follows:

- Historical perspective
- Current perspective
- Defining asset management
- The significance of asset management
- Hotel departments
- Service and operating standards
- Financial supervision
- Who are the asset managers?
- Relevance to the development model
- Future trends.

Historical perspective

Historically, asset managers have been recruited from the ranks of hotel operators where they have been employed as general managers or operational vice presidents. As such, they acquired their skills in operating environments controlled in many cases by brands, which often did not require them to possess or develop financial and strategic skills. Their primary focus was to maintain the service and product standards set by the brand at corporate level. In addition, their attention as operators would have been directed to short-term operational performance rather then long-term value enhancement, which was deemed to be the domain of the owner.

The training and experience of asset managers was also influenced by the type of owners, many of whose hotel property investments were limited to one or two assets and who therefore did not have the critical mass to employ or to train asset managers internally and thus were obliged to rely on hotel professionals trained by the major chains. Due to this disparate ownership, the hotel operators tended to exercise stronger control over the properties and this coloured many asset managers' view of what was acceptable and what could be challenged.

The asset manager's background and training often led them to regard as normal a style of operating agreement, peculiar to the hotel industry, which stressed the rights of the hotel operator to manage the property peacefully according to their own internal standards, but was, in many cases, more silent on the services to be provided by the hotel operator. In addition, although the basic fee structures were clearly set out, recharges for expenses such as marketing were often not quantifiable from the contract. The historical asset manager therefore found himself in a form of 'self-policing' role rather than in an independent role, due to background and training.

As a result of the above, asset management was perceived as being focused on the following areas:

- Review of operating standards

- Review of maintenance standards

- Review of marketing strategy

- Budget negotiation

- Quarterly operating reviews

- Operating agreement and lease agreement compliance

- Verification of management fees and other recharges

- FF&E reserve usage monitoring

- Review of capital expenditure programmes

- Operating agreement reviews and renegotiations on expiry.

Asset managers were often only employed after the investor had made the acquisition and therefore the asset manager had little ability to influence any aspects of the acquisition or to assist the buyer in benefiting from any opportunities presented by the acquisition.

Current perspective

So what has led to the change in the role of the asset manager and what are the new services expected of him or her? First, the nature of the typical hotel owner has changed. Owners are now more likely to hold a larger number of hotels than in previous years. Second, the role has also been affected by the economic downturns of the late 1980s and early 1990s that affected the hotel industry, with arguably the international financing banks being among the first to recognize the merits of strong independent asset management due to a relatively greater exposure to the hotel sector than most owners.

In the late 1990s, several financial investment funds teamed up with hotel operating partners, with the investment funds taking the major equity risk, but with the hotel partner having a significant share in any upside in the value of the hotel portfolio created by them. These funds had professional business plans with clearly defined financial hurdles, which were written into the deal structure with the hotel's operating partners. This marriage of industry knowledge and strategic planning created a new brand of asset manager. Many of these hotel investment funds had a hold period of some three to five years and saw a significant proportion of the return coming from a successful divestment. Thus, the hotel partner, who was essentially the asset manager for these funds, was focused not only on short-term operating results but also on medium-term value.

As the hotel assets were now being acquired with a view to a future sale either as a single asset or as part of a portfolio, further skills were required of the asset manager. It was no longer enough just to look at the hotel operator's annual budget, as the new owners wanted to ensure that they could create a positive divestment story and for this they needed a strategic plan that covered their projected hold period, which would result in a capital gain on exit. As many of the current hotel operators are not contractually required to produce such a strategic document, it fell to the asset managers to produce such plans and to try to ensure that the strategic goals set under the plan were achieved through negotiation of the annual budgets and monitoring of the actual performance with the hotel operating companies.

As owners were beginning to own portfolios rather than a collection of single assets, it became important for asset managers to deal with questions such as portfolio fit and risk assessment. As these portfolios became more diverse, the asset manager was obliged to look at geographical, product and hotel operator spread to ensure that the value of the whole portfolio could be maximized in order to ensure a successful divestment at the end of the hold period. In addition, many of the funds sought high debt leverage and it was important that the debt providers had confidence in the asset manager and the ability to achieve the strategic objectives. The asset manager had therefore to be conversant with debt financing and to be able to maintain a good relationship with those providers through supplying appropriate financial information to the financing banks and by keeping them abreast of developments within both the operating and investment markets as well as reporting on the progress made in achieving the strategic goals. This sometimes meant that the asset manager had to act as intermediary between the hotel operators and the financing banks.

Many hotel operators have now set up their own in-house asset management groups to manage their own hotels rather than make the asset management part of the duties of the hotel operators themselves. This demonstrates most effectively the difference in goals between the operators with their short-term operating goals, on which most of their earnings are based, and the goals of the asset management, with its focus on sustainable earnings and value. With their growing familiarity with the hotel industry, some of these financial investors have also become involved in development projects, demanding the involvement of the asset manager in the hotel developments as well. Thus, the asset manger is now expected to be involved in the complete cycle as a key member of the owner's professional team.

Defining asset management

So what is asset management? In essence, it is the safeguarding of a hotel's or group of hotels' earnings, earnings capacity and value through correct product and service definition, selection of the appropriate operator, setting of strategic and operational goals and monitoring and adjusting those goals in the light of changes in both the operating, debt and investment markets.

The significance of asset management

The areas where an asset manager can have most impact are the following:

- Product definition
- Service and operating standards
- Financial supervision.

In preparing the strategic plan, a consensus needs to be reached between owner and operator. Both have to agree on the hotel positioning and the volume of capital expenditure to maintain that position. Second, the strategic plan has to take into account opportunities in the hotel or facilities that will need to be amended or added in order for the hotel to maintain or improve its market penetration and respond to the growing needs of its current and future guests. The starting point for most strategic plans is a SWOT (strengths, weaknesses, opportunities and threats) analysis of the existing hotel, segment by segment, comparing the hotel against its competitive set. A complete inspection of the property and visits to competitive hotels is a prerequisite for this analysis. The asset manager can facilitate this process by bringing objective experience to bear on the potentially different points of view of owner and operator.

The asset manager often provides a fresh pair of eyes with which to view the property. For example, the asset manager might find areas such as storerooms, staff accommodation or empty spaces that might be adapted to revenue-producing areas such as bedrooms or small meeting rooms. In addition, certain of the facilities might have lost their original allure and require remodelling in the light of changes in consumer demand. This review and analysis will result in a wish list that then needs to be prioritized so that both owner and operator can ensure that their visions are met and that any FF&E reserve spending and owner's capital spending are used effectively to fund the agreed strategic plan.

The strategic plan will also help with the programming of the works and hopefully avoid abortive costs. Unlike many local authorities, it is far from desirable to shut down the same facilities on different occasions in order to carry out different projects. The cost in terms of business interruption, increased cost of working and the danger of losing clientele due to gaining a reputation of constantly being subjected to disturbance can be high. It is therefore important that all activities are phased and coordinated and here again the asset manager may play a significant role in persuading the owner to invest more in the infrastructure initially in order to facilitate future changes, rather than limiting current expenditure and bearing an increased but perhaps hidden cost later.

Hotel departments

In order to review the potential areas of conflict, each typical hotel department will be examined, from rooms to food and beverage, to meeting and other facilities.

Rooms

As Chapter 11 shows, many changes have taken place in hotel bedroom design over the last decade. The room stock obviously needs to accommodate the various clients from the business mix attracted by the hotel and to take into account any new business targeted by owner and operator. Many chains carry out detailed market research on their new rooms concepts, but these do not always get communicated to the owner. Again the asset manager can facilitate communication in this area. The room design is often based on a corporate model, which often needs to be adapted to cater for local, regional, national and international tastes. Again the asset manager can be instrumental to achieving this realignment.

Another conflict that arises in the design of new rooms is the different views of the interior design teams and the operators. These designers might be either employed by the owner or the operator. The design team are trying to create a design that will be noticed as being original. They might thus seek to introduce new fabrics and materials. The operator, although also keen to create an impact, is also motivated to ensure that the rooms can be cleaned and maintained as efficiently as possible and that none of the design features will create additional operating costs. Again, the asset manager needs to be sensitive to these issues, as the hotel operations team might not wish to enter into conflict with their own interior design team.

Food and beverage

This is often a source of dispute between owner and operator, with the operator wishing to maintain their brand standards with fine dining facilities, which often do not appear to make a financial return, but are required according to the operator to attract the higher paying guests. The mix of facilities is often critical to a hotel's success as a food and beverage venue and can help drive both meetings and rooms business. Again the important factor here is to balance demand with supply and to try to ensure that capital investment is made in an appropriate manner. It also has to be recognized that fashion now changes rapidly in this area, and that therefore the cycle for such facilities is shorter, which means that the facility either has to achieve a higher return or investment has to be scaled at a commensurate level. The location of the hotel and local eating habits are also important. If the hotel is situated in the heart of a major city, it is often difficult to retain in-house guests for more than one night. However, it may be possible to win outside guests, but the restaurant style will need to suit local taste and be easily accessible to such outside guests.

Meeting facilities

One of the most important drivers for many hotels is the provision of meeting and convention facilities. Again the balance between the meeting facilities themselves, the rooms, the food and beverage outlets and the other supporting facilities need to be optimized. However, in order to achieve optimization, data have to be constantly collated, not only as to the average size of groups accommodated, but also as to the nature of business lost to other hotels or lost due to other reasons, such as a lack of breakout rooms or leisure facilities. The asset manager should investigate these areas and request the operator to set up a system to collate the information. It is often possible through such studies to determine niche opportunities, which might be grasped through conversion of existing facilities or better use of redundant space. However, before committing such capital expenditure, it is important that the asset manager obtains the necessary data from the operator.

Other facilities

Again a balance needs to be created in the type of supporting facility made available. Does the hotel require a leisure centre? Can the leisure centre accommodate an outside membership as well as meeting the hotel residents' needs? Can a resort hotel have outside members for its golf and other facilities and offer inducements such as exclusive tee times to the detriment of the hotel guest. Again, it is important for an asset manager with local knowledge to study these matters and look for ways of reconciling all users

257

Illustration 13.1
Paramount Hotel, Oxford:
meeting pod, let by the hour
(Courtesy Scott Brownrigg)

to the benefit of the financial results and reputation of the property. The operator may be sensitive to bringing in such additional business due to the impact it may have on the hotel operator's corporate client and loyalty club members. Again, the asset manager will need to reconcile the interest of owner and operator.

Summary

In essence, what the asset manager is trying to achieve is a balance between the needs of current and future guests, the standards of the operator and the volume of investment required to be made by the owner. It often requires vision to create the right balance and the asset manager can facilitate the discussions between the parties and bring an objective view to bear on the issues. In addition, a balance has to be struck between rigid brand standard adherence and local, regional and national diversity, particularly as many of the reservations for the hotel will be generated in a radius close to the hotel. This aspect has become more important due to brand globalization, with the loss of some local and national brands.

Service and operating standards

The key questions for most hotel owners, once the product definition has been ascertained, is how to maximize the sustainable cash flow from all facilities provided, while at the same time maintaining the quality and character of the hotel. The hotel operator would probably change the order of the foregoing, due to the desire to promote brand and increase distribution and with a substantial part of compensation based on turnover.

It is clear that the operator will have extensive marketing experience and with its brand, sales network and loyalty programme will be able to attract a diverse client base, which protects the hotel from swings in the individual local, regional and national markets. This marketing reach may have a significant positive impact on the value of the hotel. However, this expert knowledge with regard to accommodation services may not be replicated in the area of food and beverage and other supporting facilities. Here there may be other operators, who will attract the same form of loyalty as the hotel operators do from their devotees. This may mean that by employing such specialist operators the owner is able to generate a higher level of profit, than if all facilities were demised to the hotel operator. Again the asset manager, with local knowledge and experience, may be able to source more appropriate operators for these facilities.

However, with the diversification in operators, the problem arises as to who is responsible for setting and maintaining the service and operating standards. These need to be consistent throughout all the hotel, and the hotel operator, as the person most clearly associated with the product, will be most sensitive to these questions. Again the asset manager will need to ensure that a balance is found.

Subcontracting and leasing can bring its own problems. First and foremost, the needs of the hotel guest must be addressed and all operators need to have this as a first priority. Services such as the provision of breakfast are often not attractive to most restaurant operators as they do not see the breakfast period as a key meal period for revenue or profit generation, but it is obviously a very important component of a guest's stay, which may impact on guest retention.

The service and operating standards are also important from a cost perspective. Again the questions arise as to what is the most cost effective way to service the rooms, provide catering services, carry out the maintenance etc. Again, the owner is looking first at the cost, while attempting to maintain the standard. The operator might however prefer to accept a higher cost rather than jeopardize

(i)

(ii)

Illustration 13.2
Poor maintenance = high
repair costs

brand standards. This might have a significant impact on the cost base for the hotel, with outside contractors willing to charge on the basis of rooms cleaned, which will maximize productivity, while the direct employment of staff, although permitting greater control over training and on-going standards will result in higher labour costs, and a cost that cannot be altered without considerable cost and effort, particularly in certain European jurisdictions.

Other areas of potential conflict are the maintenance standards. Again it is important that there is a clearly defined and phased strategic plan. It is important that basic standards are maintained, but expenditure needs to be restricted for areas which are due for a major refurbishment. Equally, at the end of an operating contract, the property still needs to be maintained to the brand standard, and every effort needs to be taken to ensure that standards are not reduced, so as to maximize fees. Again the asset manager needs to be aware of these issues and supervise the property in an appropriate manner.

Summary

Given the various areas for conflict, the asset manager needs to act as the intermediary between owner and operator in order to protect both parties' legitimate interests. The major duty of the asset manager is both to challenge and support the operator to ensure that the most appropriate service and operating standards are set that support the value of the hotel and its operating performance. Some deviations may be required from brand standards in order to customize the global brand standard to a more local and customized standard. However, the essential element is as stated above to have a clearly defined strategy that is shared by both owner and operator, so that conflicts of this nature are minimized.

Financial supervision

This aspect is perhaps the most understood area of asset management. The annual cycle starts with the negotiation of the annual budget, which would include both the projected operating results as well as the intended capital expenditure programme. This might then be followed by regular monthly/quarterly trading reviews with the asset manager presenting written reports to the owners reporting on the achievement of the budget.

As stated previously, most hotel operators are not contractually obliged to present strategic plans to the owner, although some do present capital expenditure plans for future years but based on their own case goods or soft goods replacement standards. It is therefore the responsibility of the asset manager to maintain the strategic plan, and update it on an annual basis in the light of the budget presented by the hotel operator.

The level of asset management is to some extent dictated by the terms of the contractual operating agreements between the parties, but hotel operators will rarely refer to the operating agreement when discussing the annual budget or operating results, as they have now begun to view the asset manager as a useful mediator rather than as a policeman. Although the asset manager still continues to monitor the charging of fees and other costs from the operator and challenges other operating costs, the focus is on ensuring that an achievable budget is negotiated, which can then be issued to the debt provider with the intention of avoiding surprises. This does not mean that the asset manager will not push the hotel operator in certain aspects of revenue generation or cost control, or try to persuade the owner that some of the profit aspirations are not realistic, but the overall aim is to negotiate a budget that is challenging but achievable.

The budget negotiation and some of the operating reviews will be attended by corporate staff from the hotel operator. This will allow both owner and operator to question the level of support given by the operator through regional and global sales and marketing and other operational support areas as well as to question the hotel operator on their marketing and other strategies going forward. It is important to ensure that local management are being given the necessary support, particularly if the local market changes and new initiatives have to be taken, that involve the deployment of new resources within the hotel operator's organization. It is also important to ensure that the owner's property is given reasonable prominence in the operator's booking systems and marketing collateral, particularly if the hotel operator manages, leases or owns other hotels in the same catchment area. Thus, it is important to carry out test calls to the hotel operator's reservation offices and to carry out searches on the hotel operator's websites to ensure appropriate treatment.

Many hotel operators use the asset manager to get an initial reaction to proposals they wish to make to owners to determine the likely response or to couch the proposal in more acceptable terms. The hotel operator will normally have an impressive marketing network staffed by well-trained professional staff, with many years of experience in penetrating new markets. However, they might not have direct experience of a market where they are new entrants and here again the asset manager can be of assistance as a sounding board for the proposals of the operator and a source of knowledge of the local market.

Summary

The above financial monitoring responsibilities are important to ensure that the owner's strategy is being implemented and that the operator's performance is being monitored in an appropriate manner. However, most reporting is looking at history. It is also important that the asset manager looks at the underlying trends, new hotel supply, changes in the cost base as well as business that the hotel has been unable to accept. All these elements will have an effect on the hotel going forward and help the asset manager assist both owner and operator to adjust the strategic plans to meet these new trends.

Who are the asset managers?

Two types of organization have historically provided asset management services. The first group includes property specialists such as chartered surveyors. This group benefited from specialist property knowledge and had dealings with owners of various asset classes including hotels. Initially, these property specialists provided valuation and divestment services. This group was also experienced in negotiating lease contracts and development contracts for other property classes, but again used the recruitment of hotel specialist to extend their expertise to cover the negotiation of operating agreements and franchise agreements. The advent of overseas investors presented this group with the opportunity to add asset management to their range of services. This group was also interested in generating annuity income to smooth out their transaction income, which was substantial but by its nature sporadic. The second group comprises other professionals who provided services to hotel owners, such as accountants, independent valuers and other similar consultants. This group also saw the opportunity of earning annuity income.

Recently, these historical groups have been supplemented by new arrivals. These have included private owners and operators, who had strong operating capabilities, but who did not have a strong brand and whose ability to expand as owner/operators was limited by this lack of brand and their consequent inability to raise substantial finance. These groups have partnered with private equity companies to combine their operational experience with the financial strength of the private equity players to create a powerful partnership. However, the partnerships are founded on a relatively short-term hold profile and it will be interesting to see what happens when the private equity companies want to divest.

A growing number of companies are seeking to provide asset management services, attracted by three major factors. The first is the large number of financial investors seeking to enter the sector, with little direct hotel experience. They are attracted by the speed with which hotels can recover from a downturn and the relative security provided by a strong brand with an international reach. The second factor is the number of investors who are now willing to accept some turnover element to their leases, which therefore requires a closer monitoring of the underlying operation rather than a financial review of the lessee's covenant. The third factor is the difficult trading conditions in countries such as Germany where structural change has not been possible, but the banks have not been willing to initiate bankruptcy proceedings against defaulting hotel loans for fear of destroying value even further. It would appear that all these factors would increase the demand for asset management services for some time.

Relevance to the development model

Due to the varying nature of the tasks currently expected of them, asset managers are able to contribute to all aspects of the development cycle. We have a slightly different view of the development cycle, in that we believe that asset management is not a stage in the development cycle, but rather that asset management forms a continuous inner ring to the cycle. With their knowledge of product, operators, competition and market, asset managers are well placed to assist in all aspects of the cycle from concept, operator search and selection, contract negotiation and, based on this knowledge, assistance with seeking finance, coordination between owner, operator and project manager during construction and between owner, operator, financier and owner's professional team on opening. We all look forward to this potentially very interesting and rewarding development in asset management.

Future trends

As has been shown, there has been a move from independent asset managers acting as consultants to asset managers forming part of a joint venture team with equity providers. New entrants to the market with little direct hotel experience have brought about this change.

Given the further consolidation of international hotel brands, the balance of power between owner and operator will change significantly, but the growing power of the operators will be offset by the influence exercised by the private equity players. The major areas of play will be the length of operating agreements, where the private equity players will want to introduce break clauses on divestment and the hotel operators wishing to maintain their 20-year contracts with unilateral extension periods.

What does this mean for the asset manager? Obviously those asset managers wishing to make some form of equity contribution to align their interests with the private equity funds will continue to flourish, although, by having such a close association with a fund, their independence in other areas might be subject to challenge. It may well be that separate asset management companies will be formed to ensure that any close relationships with purchasers does not impact on other clients using other services of the groups. We have already seen auditors divesting themselves of consultancy groups as a result of being obliged to maintain some form of independence from their audit clients. It would not be difficult to imagine a similar scenario with asset management.

In addition, how will the independent owners react to the consolidation of the brands and the consolidation in ownership of some of their competitors? It is likely that they will seek strong independent asset management to ensure that they receive the same level of focus as the private equity and other financial investors. This may mean the formation of active owners' pressure groups to ensure equal treatment of all owners. This will no doubt alter the balance between operator and owner and perhaps lead to more balanced operating agreements, where the duties of the operator are much more clearly defined.

Review questions

1 Summarize the historical role of the asset manager.

2 Explain how financial supervisions applied to asset management.

3 State briefly the relevance of asset management to the revised development model shown in the Introduction (Figure I.2).

Product development and brand management

Josef Ransley

This chapter aspires to address some of the issues relative to a product that is constantly evolving within a physical property not designed to accommodate major change. Further, the value of the product rests in its financial performance, derived from its service, property standards, location and profile. We define 'profile' as an established international brand or brand name.

- Context
- Market demand and capital constraints
- Branding
- Market segmentation
- Planned growth
- Product development
- Refresh or reposition
- New product
- Mixed use developments
- Conclusion.

Context

For many centuries hospitality properties have been developed and built for the purpose of providing accommodation and ancillary facilities in every part of the world. As with the materials and methods in construction, the nature and systems in hospitality have evolved over time. Consequently there are examples of buildings constructed over four hundred years ago as coaching inns that are still in use today as hotels. Such properties have been altered, adapted or extended at different times to suit, so far as possible, the prevalent requirements or standards of the industry. The great railway hotels built around the world, some hundred years ago, are today generally either large premier or luxury hotels having been subject to much change over the years. Similarly, many of today's classic luxury or premier city centre hotels were built in the early part of the last century. Examples abound, including the Ritz hotels in many of Europe's capital cities, and the Plaza and St Regis in New York; often these buildings will have been classified as monuments or listed buildings, ensuring that their original features are preserved to varying degrees for future generations. For an industry that continues to evolve and is subject to changing consumer tastes and aspirations, the financial fundamentals of preservation and change can be challenging. Equally when the building is an integral part of the product and the value of the property is based on its financial performance these issues are critical. The life cycle of a building and the life of a particular product may be very different. For example, the old classic hotels had their accommodation designed to suit customers travelling with their servants. The rooms built on the building frontage would generally be large in size, whereas the rear or attic rooms would be much smaller to provide accommodation for the servants. Standardizing such anomalies in room sizes within the constraints of structural grids on an economically viable basis is not easily accomplished. Multiply this example by a factor of ten to fifty and it is possible to conceive how difficult it can be to adapt existing buildings. This is especially the case considering the introduction of modern building services, including air conditioning. Each building constructed over the last hundred years (with the exception of some of the hotels built by the chains such as Sheraton and Hilton in the 1970s and the more recent budget hotels, which were developed on a standardized basis) was of individual design, layout and construction. It has been shown in previous chapters that fire and other building regulations in different countries, while sharing a certain commonality, will have meaningful differences which impact on a building's design and construction.

Market demand and capital constraints

In Chapter 4, Paul Slattery demonstrates the latent and growing demand globally for hospitality accommodation. Similarly he argues for the major hospitality companies to address the raising of capital funds on a grander scale, if they are to grow sufficiently fast enough internationally, and be in a position to satisfy the projected global demand with adequate supply. The solution to the supply and demand equation therefore appears to be vested in the large internationally-based branded groups whom he considers are the only entities that credibly have any opportunity of delivering and managing such volume of product. This argument does, however, rely on two criteria, namely that the product, branded or otherwise, is suitable for such rapid expansion and equally can be operated and managed on such a global scale.

Branding

Branding is an established format of product identity and recognition, utilized to facilitate growth of sales volume, with the benefit of clear management systems and controls, economies of scale or volume and enhanced marketing and distribution systems. Brands require consistency in the delivery of product, providing consumers with the reassurance at the point of purchase that price is relative to the quality irrespective of its point of delivery. For hospitality products, which are rarely purchased at the point of delivery, an established brand therefore can have enormous value, and is a powerful tool to deliver volume and manage price. Market expansion is simplified as established brands attain greater market penetration by virtue of their ability to attract home market customers into their different international locations. American brands therefore have proved particularly successful in international expansion, as they can draw from a large and high volume home market. Brands having attained a certain critical mass and, if managed correctly to convert new markets into an enlarged 'home' market, become self-perpetuating, giving rise to the concept of globalization or establishment of a global brand. Currently, global brands exist in a number of industries such as, Coca-Cola in soft drinks, Nestlé in chocolate, HSBC in banking and CNN in TV media. In the service sector, McDonald's are probably the most readily recognized global brand. Interestingly, brands that are globally successful are low cost, high volume products which are relatively simple to manage and can readily be produced and delivered to a consistent standard utilizing clear management systems and controls, particularly in the cost of production and delivery. Not surprisingly in terms of hospitality brand development the branded budget or limited ser-vice hotel products have attained the greater growth within the sector, whereas the full service products' growth rates have only benefited in a more marginal way. This is marginal in the sense that full service brands such as Marriott, Hilton, Holiday Inn have added meaningful volume in terms of improvement in profit, profit and performance, but not necessarily growth.

The reason for this anomaly is readily apparent in the difference in the complexity of the product content. Whereas a limited service product focuses solely on the delivery of the physical content of the hospitality product, a comparatively simple element to manage, a full service product is required to deliver a consistent standard in both physical and service standards, the latter refers to the historical recognition of hospitality being a 'people' industry. People are more complex to manage, especially where the quality of service delivery is judged on the interaction between individuals, the service provider and customer.

The earlier example of McDonald's is useful. The McDonald's product, like a full service hotel, combines both the physical and service elements of a product, the significant difference is that in a McDonald's unit there is only one interaction between server and customer. In a full service hotel, the interaction is multiple and often of a more complex or subjective nature. The impact of this on managing consistent quality is therefore dramatic, as the more complex and emotive the interaction, the more empowered the server inherently has to be. Empowerment entails high skill levels in process and people management across a wide range of tasks, involving cultural diversity of staff and customer alike. Historically, these issues have been addressed by way of fragmenting tasks and standardizing processes. This manifests itself in strict limitations imposed on staff, trained to function in a similar manner to those working on a motor manufacturing production line. Staff are trained to perform a specific and limited task in a specified manner or format, 'a fragmentation'. Fragmenting interactive tasks in this manner therefore replicates the McDonald's principle by limiting the skill level and automating the individual's task. The effect of this system of human automation on staff has been externally recognized as possibly de-motivating. While in the car production line the limited task and skill was applied to an inert entity, when applied to another person it can be not only de-motivating, but also degrading and, in an ever more classless society, counter productive from the customer's point of view.

The challenge for the full service sector in its expansion of branded products is in its ability to recruit, train, retain and develop its staff on an international basis, while increasingly acknowledging the resurgence of regional cultures. Similarly, its product must be suitable to provide for adaptation to suit local variations, both in character and physical property terms. For management, this involves establishing structures that facilitate more regional governance, invest more in staff development and retention, and focus on the development of products that enable regional variance, while retaining core brand values and communicating the essence of the brand.

Market segmentation

Market segmentation goes some way to rationalizing such issues, because the variance in mid-market full service physical product is not great, but is more visible through service standards. Generally, the lower the perceived quality standard and price, the lower the customer's aspirations. In an industry where volume or higher occupancy is noted in repeat business, matching or exceeding customer's aspirations is essential. Establishing a clear definition of product segmentation is therefore a central issue, as is maintaining this during highs or lows in inevitable market cycles. Consistency across a brand's portfolio in service standard is, arguably, more important than that of the physical product. Not surprisingly, when the unit delivers better quality standards rather than the defined standard, this can be as harmful to a brand's reputation. The reason is that this raises customers' aspirations above the medium standard deliverable across the brand portfolio. Establishing and monitoring clear and defined service standards, where the differentiation is evident to the consumer, is as essential in the mid-market sector as in the luxury sector.

Historically, the star rating system lacked clarity due to its subjective criteria and, while understood by the industry, it was never clearly understood by the consumer. The advent of branding as a more powerful marketing, sales and distribution system equally lacked clarity in differentiation. The industry's lack of ability to resolve these issues at a time when information technology was rapidly expanding and becoming more accessible to the consumer, has resulted in consumer purchase decisions being based more on an individual unit's profile and price rather than any form of brand loyalty. Similarly, corporate purchases are, arguably, influenced by location, facilities, price and incentive rather than brand loyalty. Currently, brand value in monetary terms has not attained the benefits comparable to those of other industries. Effective product development and brand management in the hospitality industry should be rooted in communication between consumer and supplier. The core product or brand value should be clearly defined in the mind of both, in order to enable the brand to grow in terms of recognition, market and value.

Planned growth

Where the product's constituent parts consist of a physical property and service delivery, it is essential that the standard for both are compatible, definable and recognizable. Strategically they should be suited to facilitate growth at a defined level of capital expenditure and operational cost in targeted locations of established or anticipated demand. For the product to develop into a brand, it needs to achieve a geographical coverage or critical mass, maintain consistency in service and property standards, have effective distribution channels, develop a requisite public profile, and articulate an appropriate pricing policy.

In order to achieve rapid expansion, the requirements of both the physical and service standards must be deliverable in a wide geographical area in which there are diverse attributes of cost, labour and other resources on a consistent basis. The rate of expansion needs to be realistically targeted at the outset, as this will define the required resources, both financial and human, but also the characteristics of the physical and service elements of the product. For example, if the brand to be developed requires the physical property to be consistent, then it will generally be new built. This means that its rate of expansion will be limited to the time taken for land acquisition, period for design, obtaining relevant permissions and permits, the procurement and construction stages, as well as operational commissioning period. For the average mid-market hotel product, this is likely to be a 2–3-year development programme per unit, consequently, a company developing 10 units per year would only complete 50 units in seven to eight years.

For this reason, rapid and numerically meaningful expansion of a new limited service hotel brand (such as Express by Holiday Inn who have developed over 300 units in the space of eight years, after two years' development of the product for the European market) has only attained such a rapid rate of development in Europe, by way of franchising the branded product. Even then, such growth was only viable because the product was fully standardized, the construction industrialized and systemized and service standards of a minimal level. This allowed the company to franchise the development, management and operation of the product by third party owners, knowing that they, as franchisers, could monitor, control and enforce adherence to the brand standards. Beneficially, the development of such units was focused in secondary locations that benefited from low land costs and construction on greenfield sites. These factors, together with planned volume, ensured that reliable and realistic cost parameters were sustainable and, with latent demand evident for a low-cost high-volume product in the market place, capital returns were of sufficient quality to attract the required investment finance. Using the UK as an example in Europe, Table 14.1 illustrates the rapid growth attained by a limited number of companies that have concentrated on this market.

While the limited service product has been the consistent success story in the sector for the last decade, a period that has conversely witnessed spells of high returns and extreme lows in the full service sector, it is notable that development of the limited service sector is now slowing down in the UK. The slowdown in growth is not relative to any change in demand but more related to the fact that the appropriate sites are no longer available and that expansion into the city centre locations is prohibited by

Operator	Brand	Hotels	Rooms	Average rooms	Growth (2002) %	Growth (2001) %
Whitbread	Travel Inn	292	16 602	57	4.7	4.9
Permira*	Travelodge	231	12 596	55	7.9	2.9
Scottish & Newcastle Retail**	Premier Lodge	131	8 130	62	5.6	13.8
InterContinental Hotels	Express by Holiday Inn	71	6 700	94	7.6	42.9
Mitchells & Butler	Innkeepers Lodge	65	1 713	26	30.0	42.9
Accor	Ibis	39	4 055	104	8.3	9.1
CHE Group	Comfort Inns	33	2 195	67	6.5	0.0
Cendant	Days Inn	19	1 476	78	26.7	25.0
Group Envergure	Campanile	15	1 110	74	0.0	0.0
Accor	Formule 1	10	746	75	0.0	11.1
CHE Group	Sleep Inn	4	308	77	33.3	200.0
Cendant	Howard Johnson	3	375	125	0.0	−25.0
Accor	Etap	2	150	75	100.0	0.0
Golden Tulip UK	Tulip Inn	2	235	118	100.0	0.0
Somerston Hotels	Ramada Encore	1	104	104	n/a	n/a
Others	Various	15	527	36.4	n/a	n/a
Total		933	57 022	61	8.6	8.2

* Permira acquired Travelodge from Compass in February 2003
** Scottish & Newcastle Retail is in the process of being acquired by Spirit Amber

Source: Deloitte and Touche

Table 14.1
Limited service hotel growth in the UK

virtue of the higher land values in such locations. Equally relevant is the fact that the franchise system imposes restrictions on the development of the same branded unit within a specific geographical area to protect the dilution of the initial investment of the first unit developed in a specific location. As the number of established brands in the UK is limited, especially those operating a franchise system, the delivery of further product into the market will have to await further competitors or new product that facilitates entry into the city centre locations on a financially viable basis.

Examples of fully serviced branded products have been shown in previous chapters. Their expansion is much more limited because the product is more complex in terms of service standards, facilities and size, and not suitable except in a new build format for standardization. For companies managing full service products, expansion has, therefore, focused on a mix of acquisition and new build. The problem with acquisition has proved to be brand integrity. Marriott Hotels, for example, (who place great reliance on the standardization of the physical property aspects of their brand product) have found that acquisition has generally not proved financially viable when the costs of compliance works have been added to the purchase costs. In turn, the Hilton Group based in the UK (who have been prepared to accept a wide diversity in the physical product) have grown their portfolio in the UK and Scandinavia through acquisition, but at the expense of accepting a wide range of quality and service standards within their product portfolio.

Product development

Product development in the industry has historically been concerned with copying, or producing a similar product to the competition. Individual entrepreneurs who, having established themselves in the marketplace, have then been bought out by the large chains who have the resources to expand the product quickly, have generally introduced new innovations to the marketplace. Examples of this are extensive in the bar and restaurant market, for example, Café Rouge and All Bar One, as well as new hotel concepts such as Malmaison.

Illustration 14.1
Malmaison Hotels: one of the first lifestyle hotel brands (Courtesy Malmaison Hotels)

At the time of writing, there is evidence that the major branded limited service hotel groups in Europe are venturing into planning and implementing research and development programmes to refresh their existing brands. The latter are driven by a desire to maintain brand share and acceptability to the customer, whose aspirations have risen as competitive supply has grown. However, new product development originated by the major companies is still not part of the industry's agenda. Unlike many other industries, they are still in reactive mode rather then proactive. The advent of asset management has given rise to individual properties' performance being constantly reviewed, which has accelerated the process of existing products being 'refreshed' or capacity increased. Similarly, other properties are being refurbished to reposition them into a new market sector. The latter is increasingly undertaken as part of the current industry consolidation.

While the steps in undertaking a refresh, reposition or new product development are not very different, it is surprising to note that companies still resist developing their own new concepts or products. The usual defensive argument utilized is the large investment and financial risk. However, if an analysis were made of the value of entrepreneurial ventures bought over the last ten years and their subsequent failure rate after the new management systems had been applied, this would make interesting reading.

Refresh or reposition?

The implications of not adapting the hospitality product can be in decline. Good operators know instinctively that the process is an iterative one and that it will be costly, inconvenient and often plain messy. Nevertheless, the implications of delay can be incremental, as shown in Figure 14.1.

Figure 14.1 shows that, when the property, or some of its profit centres (such as bar, restaurant or spa) becomes overdue for refreshment, some of the less loyal customers will look at alternatives.

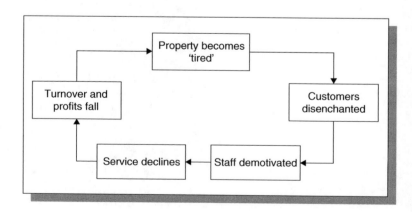

Figure 14.1
The vicious circle of hospitality property decline

Similarly, staff will be sensitive to customer opinion and perhaps will wish for better working conditions themselves. The result is that morale, turnover and profits will decline, so that there is less residual profit or financial and market credibility to ensure that the refurbishment occurs. The best operators are aware that the time to think about improving the product is when business is good and profits are high. At such times, it is easier to source funds for capital investment and to attract good quality staff and management to ensure that standards remain high.

As demonstrated in Figure 14.2, the virtuous circle requires timely development of the property or some of its features. This leads to satisfied customers and motivated staff, who provide a service that is appropriate to the target market. Consequently, the hospitality property makes profits which can be re-invested as capital projects to ensure its future prosperity. This type of iterative change is the essence of hospitality development.

The prime objective of a renovation to refresh or to reposition an existing product is to maintain market share or improve the property's financial performance. The process usually consists of growth followed by a stabilized period of income and then gradual decline as the product ages. If demand in the locality is still strong, then a refreshment renovation programme can be implemented. This can consist of a soft refurbishment or a hard refurbishment or any level between the two:

- Soft refurbishment: usually consists of replacement of soft furnishings, furniture elements and minor redecoration but excludes any major building works.

- Hard refurbishment: normally includes all aspects of a soft refurbishment but also entails major building works such as replacement of bathrooms and public area fit-out.

However, the capital costs for refurbishment are usually lower than those associated with a repositioning exercise. Soft refurbishments are usually planned as part of the normal trading

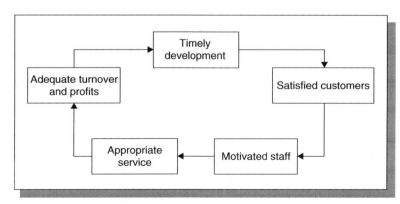

Figure 14.2
The virtuous circle of hospitality property development

(i)

Illustration 14.2
De Vere Hotel, Daresbury:
before and after refurbishment
(Courtesy Ransley Group)   (ii)

(iii)

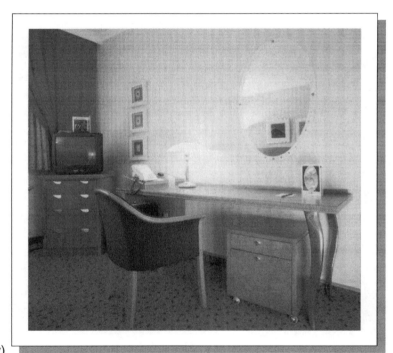

Illustration 14.2
(*Continued*)

(iv)

requirement of a hotel and, as such, a capital reserve account is established as a normal part of the hotel's trading accounts. Annual contributions normally consist of 3–4% of the property's earnings, although recent research indicates that the requirement over an 8/9-year cycle more realistically requires 8–10%. A repositioning programme is usually triggered by a change in local market demand or an opportunity to leverage the property into a

Illustration 14.2
(*Continued*)

(v)

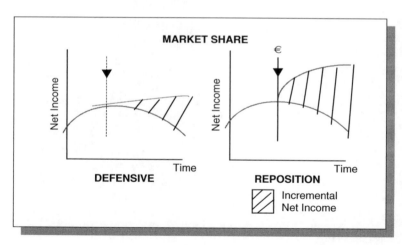

Figure 14.3
Capital cost differentiation in
refurbishment projects

higher or, in some areas, lower market segment. This provides the
opportunity to enhance returns and increase capital values. Repositioning normally involves major remodelling of the property
and normally incorporates opportunities to expand the property
or increase the number of lettable units.

As the diagram in Figure 14.3 shows, the capital investment
required for repositioning a property is greater and the property
will also need to be launched into a new market segment, increasing cost and risk. This means that staffing, operational systems and

the sales and marketing of the product will be new and reformatted to suit. The increasing lack of sites or property available in high demand locations (such as capital or gateway cities) means that this type of activity has become commonplace in the developed countries. Similarly, market consolidation has resulted in the large groups, operating a stable of brands, being regularly involved in this process after completing a major group transaction that requires them to rationalize and integrate the new product supply purchased.

The hospitality industry may be said to be obsessed with valuations being quoted on a cost per room, value calculated on earnings per available room less costs multiplied by the relevant multiple. It is often overlooked that a 230-bedroom hotel may not always be more valuable than a 200-bedroom hotel. If the mix of the first is, say, 80 single rooms and 150-double/twin rooms, and the second has 200 double/twin rooms, the latter may generate a higher revenue and profit. More detailed analysis, such as that used in the retail sector, demonstrates that yield per available m^2/sq ft, linked for instance, to GOPPAR (gross operating profit per available room), can demonstrate that reliance on REVPAR (revenue per available room) less costs, alone is not necessarily the best way of calculating a building's value.

New product

New product development is concerned with identifying products, goods or services that will appeal to the consumer and satisfy changes in their lifestyle, or respond to changing demographics or other trends. Classic examples are, an ageing population, Internet shopping, health foods and lifestyle products. It is a common dictum change is the only constant in modern life, and that the great opportunity for companies that seek to succeed. Declining industries are characterized by companies that do not innovate or constantly undertake some form of creative modelling. The argument that product development requires large investments at high risk was sustainable 30–40 years ago, but the advent of computer modelling and other methods have drastically reduced the cost and time. For example, to develop a new car model with the aid of computer modelling now takes far less time and costs much less than 20–30 years ago; similarly, computer-modelling programs can model virtual tours through buildings. This can be undertaken in the design stage and the resultant imagery could be used in market testing programmes to access consumer response to the physical aspects of a new concept. Financial modelling daily becomes more sophisticated, providing new tools to reduce the cost and risk of new product development.

With the marketplace continuing to become increasingly more vibrant, product information and direct purchasing methods more accessible, consumers will become even more discerning, powerful and transcend from price to value as the prime purchase motivator. Value will be determined in many different ways reflecting the diversity of the individual. Inevitably this will create a more segmented marketplace, one where the aspiration of a global brand will be realized by those companies that develop a brand profile in hospitality similar to that of Unilever in food and household wares. A hypothetical global hospitality company would manage an extensive range of individual branded hotel products. Such individual branded hotels establish themselves by focusing on identifying consumer trends and developing suitable products. This does not require 'reinvention of the wheel', because the basic mechanics of a motorcar have changed little in the last decade but, nevertheless, the range of models available has exploded. Similarly, the basics of hospitality facilities are not likely to change in a meaningful way. However, the experience and packaging will become much more diverse to reflect consumers' regional, cultural, economical and aspirational preferences. This hypothetical globally branded company would be recognized for its ability to manage a diverse range of branded products, suited to different regions and markets, but all delivering recognized and appropriate standards of service and facilities to suit the guest's aspirational experience. In order to reach global presence objectives, the challenge for the industry will be to grasp the mantle of developing the skills of product development and managing a diverse stable of different branded products that can deliver the sort of trading results that attract the long-term investors in property and stocks. In simple terms, the industry needs to accept that it is no different to any other industry, developing and selling products into a consumers' market, and that its management skills have to be the same. Acceptance of that simple fact will create an understanding that, as its product is property based and it cannot afford to be in property ownership and expand as it needs to, hotel operators need to be equally skilled in property development management.

This view of product development illustrates that the steps in managing the process are progressive. The difference between the existing practice of refreshment, repositioning and new is primarily the introduction of modelling and market testing. Computerized systems allow for 3D-modelling of the exterior and interiors of buildings, providing a virtual tour of the product. Modelling of such quality can facilitate market testing without a brick being laid.

Given that the ownership of property and management continues to be controlled by separate entities, the building owner will have to be encouraged to deliver a more flexible shell. With the advent of more systemized construction systems, this is currently viable. The operator, in turn, will be able to churn his product life cycle given that capital costs will be greatly reduced. Unquestionably, the building owner will incur a higher capital cost to deliver flexibility, but such buildings would attract a higher rental value and need not necessarily be a single use property. This is a current limitation of a hotel construction.

The first stage of product development, as illustrated in Figure 14.4, can essentially be a desktop exercise. In such an exercise, the market appraisal identifies the profile of the product which, translated into a brief with a schedule of areas, allows preliminary costings to be established, but utilizing benchmark costs for construction. The latter provides a capital cost which, combined with projected revenues and costs sourced from the market research and operational benchmark costs, provide the required information to run a financial feasibility programme to forecast planned returns on investment.

The processes illustrated in Figure 14.5, if based in an appropriate building shell, would provide for the continuous recycling of hospitality-based products located in an area of established demand. The skills to manage each of the different formats will be the same and, if the requirement to respond to changing consumer demand was incorporated as a value objective in the initial development, it would provide for a long-term utilization of the property.

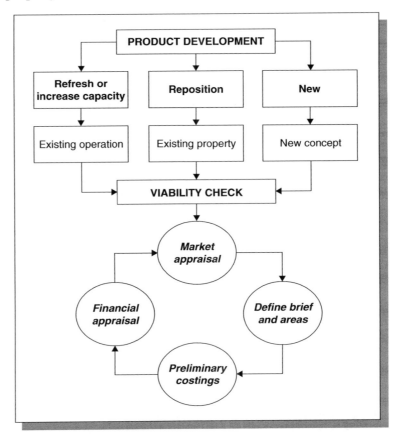

Figure 14.4
The product development matrix I

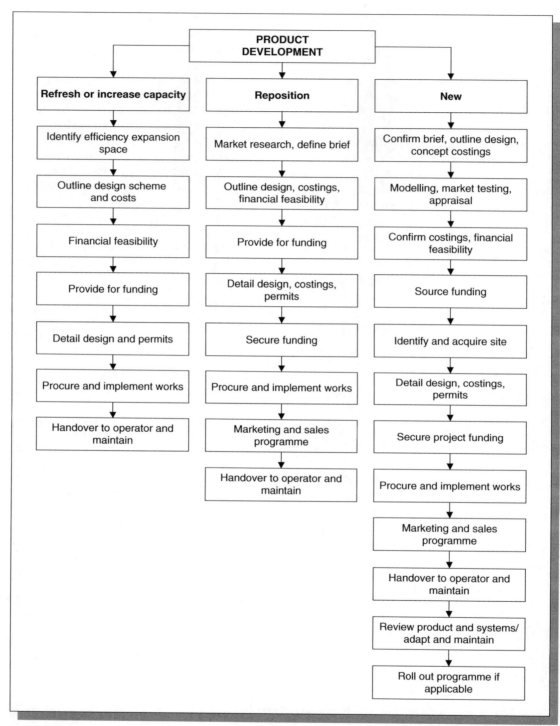

Figure 14.5
The product development matrix II

Illustration 14.3
Stuttgart International Centre: comprising theatre, offices, apartments, bars, restaurants, cinema, health spa and two hotels (Courtesy Ransley Group)

Mixed use developments

Mixed use developments incorporating retail, entertainment, bars and restaurants, residential and hotel accommodation are increasing in number and scale. In many, the property owners are utilizing facilities management companies to manage such properties. Each tenant operates their business independently and contributes to the overall common maintenance requirements of the complex managed by the facilities company on behalf of the owner. The hotel will inevitably manage its facility, including restaurant and bars, in competition with the other outlets in the complex, as it will duplicate some of the management of the facilities company in maintaining its own product.

Mixed-use developments therefore offer another opportunity for hospitality companies to expand their services product range. All the skills to manage and provide facility services for a mixed-use development are the very skills that a hospitality operator exercises each day. Hospitality operations entail the provision of services such as security, cleaning, maintenance, marketing and letting of space. By extending the range of facilities for which such skills are utilized both investor, owner and operator can benefit. This mixed use development is shown in Figure 14.6.

Further, such multi-use developments provide an opportunity for the hotel operator to address the provision and operation of food and beverage in a different manner. The hotel operator would manage food and beverages but have access to a larger catchments group, or have the food and beverages provided by an independent bar or restaurant owner in the complex, or a mix of the two. Considering the increased separation of ownership

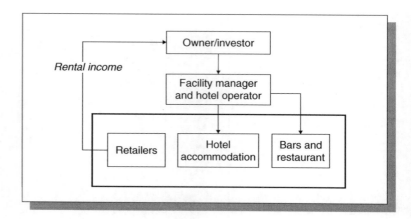

Figure 14.6
Mixed use developments

and management in the hotel industry and the increase in ownership by investment funds whose property folios cover all types of property like retail, office, leisure and hotels, such an extension in utilization of the hotelier's skills would seem natural.

Conclusion

This chapter attempts to challenge owners and operators to look beyond the traditional methods of development. The first few years of the 21st century have seen a dynamic change in the relationship of ownership and operations, driven by a desire to establish global brands. While branding is arguably a powerful tool in attaining growth and enhancing profits, it is to be questioned if the hospitality industry really understands the essence of a brand and brand management. Separately, this chapter reviews the process of product development and challenges the industry's ability to ignore innovations and new product development in the future. To develop, after all can mean to expand, realize potentialities or bring gradually to a fuller, greater or better state. In our view the industry is entering a challenging period and it will have to develop in the fullest sense of the word. Hopefully, this chapter will encourage innovation or at the very least a little inspiration.

Review questions

1 Suggest some of the attributes of global brands, and which hospitality brands might emulate them.

2 Outline traditional development methods, and ways in which they might be challenged.

3 What are the main implications of the three development methods: refresh, reposition or new?

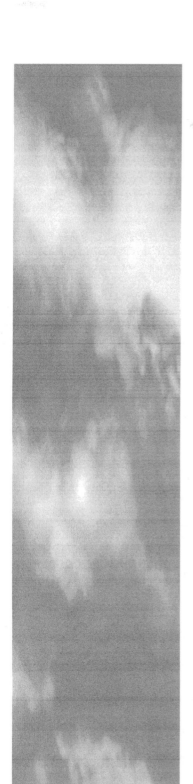

CHAPTER 15

International and cultural issues

Josef Ransley

As the hospitality industry is a truly international one, it follows that property development takes place in varied locations around the world. To cover these comprehensively would require a separate book. However, this chapter aims to generalize some aspects of the international development dimension using the conceptual framework shown from concept, through planning, building and operations to maintenance. First, however, some aspects of context and culture are explored in international development, using some examples from the hospitality industry. The aim is to provide the reader with a taste of the challenges, frustrations and exhilaration that such projects can occasion. The complexity of the development process is always affected by the conditions and context, and this chapter considers some of these, including:

- Background
- Culture
- Concepts
- Planning
- Building
- Operations
- Maintenance
- Conclusion
- Case study.

Background

Development is the inherent attribute of improved financial performance and growth for any company or product, whether it manifests itself in the refinement or improvement of a particular element or elements of the production, service, sales or financial management or by way of growth in the marketplace. The hospitality industry, as any other industry, is constantly striving to improve the former and driven to geographical expansion by the latter. In areas where demand exceeds supply, enhanced financial performance is easily attained by increasing price, but most countries control or more commonly restrict non-competitive or cartel practices, as such this generally establishes an equilibrium between demand and supply. Similarly, for an industry based on the mobility of its consumer, inevitably market supply and demand is of a cyclical nature with highs and lows in trading subject to numerous elements outside of its control and in most cases its ability to influence. Recent examples nationally include the foot and mouth outbreak in the UK, the impact on international travel occasioned by the terrorist attack in New York on 11 September 2001, the Gulf wars and the SARS scare of 2002.

The oil crises of the 1970s may be largely forgotten, but a similar event, in an age when air travel is so well established, would demonstrate the industry's dependence on consumers' mobility to have an equally dramatic impact. International geographical expansion, however, imposes numerous challenges of a more subtle nature, initially in the development stages and less evident in the longer term. When the investment in a single product unit can readily be £20 ($30) million plus, both the immediate and medium-term challenges and longer-term issues that impact on the investment returns warrant review. This chapter endeavours to look at some of the issues that recognizably affect international development and highlights some of the issues which affect development abroad. Relevant in this respect is the current vogue in the industry of the separation of ownership and management and who may be most exposed to risk.

The hospitality industry has been slow to adapt to change and is currently trying to come to terms with managing the process. In the future it will have to respond quickly and effectively. It is vital, therefore, that those involved in the development process gain a clear understanding of the complex issues that need to be integrated in any form of hospitality development. Most important is the need for operational and development staff to be able to understand and respond to each other's needs and challenges. Unless the main actors (often protagonists) in the hotel development process (the operational and development management teams) learn to work in unison and with a mutual understanding of their individual disciplines, they will continue to fail to provide the rest of the team involved in the development process with a clear, concise and unified brief. This will perpetuate the industry's inefficiencies in its capital development expenditure and consequentially its operational profitability. It is these working inefficiencies that have suppressed innovation and the industry's ability to service changing markets, nationally and internationally. This situation has failed consistently to attract institutional investment and certainly will not be sustainable in the next period of opportunity and potential growth.

Culture

The word 'culture' is defined as,

> The totality of socially transmitted behaviour patterns, arts, beliefs, institutions, and all other products of human work and thought characteristic of a community or population.
> *Readers Digest Universal Dictionary* (1986:382)

Inherent in the desire to travel is the need for diversity. Travellers may seek culture, climate, landscape or the more recent trend of those living in large conurbations, just to be elsewhere, including the experience of a fantasy world as epitomized, for instance, by Disneyland in Paris. The government of France has openly sought to protect the use of the French language, customs and other cultural attributes, proclaiming their opposition to US globalization. The USA is generally perceived as the world's most rich and powerful nation and, coincidentally, the home market of many of the world's major hotel companies. Perversely, France, like the UK and other European nations, has a relatively recent imperial history evidenced in the make-up of their present multi-cultural society. As the focus of French, and worldwide mistrust, the USA is in itself a nation with one of the greatest blends of cultures in the world, yet perceived as having the least tolerance of cultural diversity. Inevitably, cultural issues are confusing, primarily because they are often seen as indivisible from nationality, a fairly recent term in the context of cultural history. National borders are, after all, an illusion caused by artificial boundary lines that have historically been constantly redrawn on political maps. My own country of birth, Belgium, where I have never been a citizen, is widely recognized for its Flemish and Walloon, respectively Dutch and French, speaking regions. Divided into nine provinces, including one containing a German-speaking minority, it is a poignant example of a nation being artificially carved out without regard to any cultural considerations. This small nation of nine million people that is fiercely proud of its provincial heritage, local dialects and cultural diversity has become the political and executive centre for the expanding European Community. The European Community itself evolved to prevent future repetition of the worst manifestations of nationalism, epitomized by the tragedies of two world wars in the last century. Assuming that the political programme of the European Community, or more controversial United Europe, is successfully concluded, what implications would this have on the cultural diversity of Europe or indeed similar experiments in the other parts of the world? Will the perception of a European be as singular as our perception of an American or African, or will we all more readily learn to recognize and acknowledge more regionally and culturally based groupings? If this proves to be the case in the immediate future, the effects on hospitality development and operations will be significant.

Concepts

Since the Second World War, hospitality concepts have generally migrated from west to east. This does not necessarily mean that Americans are more skilled in the quality delivery of hospitality services, rather that they were more empowered to internationalize the industry at the time. With few exceptions, the American corporations were the main exponents of replicating their national products in different parts of the world. This was a strategy that led to the evolution of international branding, standards, operations, management structures and global reservations systems, among other aspects of current practice. At the same time, methods of financing and ownership in their different forms, such as franchising, sale and leaseback, management contracts, joint ventures, and other variants related to investment requirements, were evolved. These methods and standards have subsequently been adopted by other non-American based businesses in their international hospitality expansion strategies. The evolution of concepts, as has been identified earlier, did not occur until the last quarter of the nineteenth century, and then only as an adaptation of the basic form related to quality standards – economy, mid-market and luxury hotels. Some examples of these products are US brand names, like Ritz Carlton, Hyatt, Hilton International, Sheraton and Holiday Inn Inc. At the end of the twentieth century, European companies such as the Ritz Group, Trust House Forte, Grand Metropolitan, Steigenberger and Wagon Lits were effectively still national, rather than international chains. The 1980s saw the development of new hospitality concepts in the form of low-service hotels, for example, Days Inn and Holiday Inn Express. Other examples are Travelodge in the UK and the French group Accor equivalent, Formula 1. These were closely followed by aparthotels, conference hotels, townhouse and club hotels, and a range of niche products such as the Paramount in New York, One The Aldwych, London and the Bleibtrau Hotel, Berlin. The latter examples are traditional full-service hotel products that have established a specific product image through interior design styling. Their contribution to the industry has been to demonstrate that style solutions provide an alternative to market segmentation

(i)

Illustration 15.1
Number One Aldwych,
London (Courtesy Number
One Aldwych)

(ii)

or price. The main attribute of this variant, importantly, is to remind the hotel industry that their product is in part competing in the same marketplace as other consumable products. The industry must understand that the customer, in allocating disposable income, may be choosing between a new dress, golf club or night away from home. This imperative reinforces the importance of ensuring that the product appeals to the customer, and to remind the industry of the diversity of its competition. If product appeal is relegated to secondary importance, and assumptions are made that customers are happy with the existing product, the result can be an out-of-date, new hotel, opening two years later.

Planning

There are many factors that influence the planning and design of hospitality properties internationally, these include:

- Local regulations on fire, safety, building standards, health and safety and hygiene
- Location, development and infrastructure
- Staff costs and operational methods
- Climate and environment
- Building techniques, methods, costs and resources
- Accessibility and lifestyle
- Type of facility.

The most important factor, however, is one that is most often ignored – communication. The most common communication errors are based in the tacit assumptions made between the internal and external members of the development team. Whether written or spoken, the oft-quoted phrase, 'America and England, two nations separated by a common language' best illustrates this point. It is all too frequently assumed, when dealing with another nationality, that usage of a common language automatically guarantees understanding. This situation is normally compounded by a natural desire to avoid embarrassment or cause offence, either by appearing to be patronizing or misinformed. The golden rule should therefore always be to ask the same questions or describe a requirement in a number of different ways. It is far better (and usually less expensive) to be considered slow-witted but to achieve the objective. It is the author's view that the basic principles of construction are universal and transnational, and that it is in the detail that the variance is meaningful. If a local engineer in a Third World country were asked if the electrical supply is reliable, he is most likely to answer in the affirmative. There is no point in feeling aggrieved to discover that the electrical supply fails once a week, after all, locally this may mean a good standard of reliability.

Local standards, therefore, may be satisfactory but at the same time unacceptable to international operators. This analogy will generally also apply to local regulations for fire safety, building standards, health and hygiene, and other regulatory requirements. For international hospitality groups, this is of particular importance, as the international customer will expect to enjoy the same level of safety precautions in the hotel, irrespective of the country. Consumer protection law in some Western countries is such that, when booked before departure, the customer is entitled to such expectations. The sensible international operators will therefore define their own minimum requirements and ensure that these are implemented, even if they are of a higher standard than local requirements. Space standards will vary subject to location. The most common factors that impact on space standards are:

- Financial – cost of land or construction

- Storage – are deliveries made daily, weekly or even monthly?

- Site constraints – high or low rise, singular or multiple accommodation blocks

- Climate – including internal and external circulation, leisure facilities, balconies, water storage, capacity

- Culture and lifestyle – such as dining contexts (al fresco), personal hygiene and consumer preferences.

The effect of these factors will vary according to location. For example land availability in Hong Kong is not compatible with the Mid West in the USA. The availability and storage requirements for food and beverage provisions in Banjul, Gambia, are very different to those in Paris. Similarly, there would be no reason to provide an in-house laundry in Frankfurt or consider external corridors and courtyards in Helsinki, which, like restaurants and bars, are a standard option in St Lucia. Many Japanese visitors will shower before soaking in a full bathtub, while no one in Nairobi would sleep without a mosquito net. These examples illustrate the need to review local conditions prior to formalizing the briefing requirements and planning of an international hotel. In developing countries, where staff costs are low and it is a political requisite to create jobs, modern technology equipment to reduce staffing levels may not be desirable or economical. These, as well as other factors need to be considered at the early stages of planning and design for an international project. Irrespective of how fixed corporate standards may be, they will require adjustment to suit local conditions.

Building

As has been shown, context and culture will increasingly exert more influence on hospitality development internationally. These, and

(i)

Illustration 15.2
A traditional and a new
hotel in Zanzibar
(ii)

other factors, will entail hospitality designers resolving more complex conflicting needs.

Undoubtedly, the common sense of considering the use of historical building methods (whether for construction or services) will gain prominence, or at least influence new technology. The example from Zanzibar, for instance, utilized the latest, green technology that works with systems such as air displacement and other methods. Equally important in the method of local construction is the availability of utilities and materials as well as their maintenance. Hotels located in humid areas, especially with low season occupancy, do not lend themselves to the use of wool carpeting, which tends to rot in such conditions. Similarly, Cuba, for instance, is severely restricted in what it can import, so it is not unusual to find electrical wiring with more different colour coding

> **Electricity in Zanzibar**
> Zanzibar Town gets frequent cuts in the electrical supply. To overcome this, most of the hotels have generators, but some of the small ones do not, which means no lights or fans. If the lights go out, kerosene lamps may be provided but it is best to have a torch or candles handy just in case. When the fans stop working there is not much you can do, and inside rooms can get unbearable during Zanzibar's hot season. Bear this in mind when choosing a place to stay. Hotels that have been built recently rely on a constant electrical supply to work the fans or air-conditioning. Older hotels have been built to withstand the hot weather using designs that date from before the invention of electricity. If you cannot find a genuine old hotel, look for one built in traditional style – with large windows, thick walls, high ceilings, court-yards, wide verandas and even a double roof, not just a pseudo-oriental façade. If all the new hotels were built using genuine traditional designs, fans and air-conditioning would be unnecessary, Zanzibar would not need to burn so much imported oil, and tourists would be more comfortable during the power cuts.
>
> Else (1998)

than a painter's palette, somewhat disconcerting when trying to differentiate live from neutral electrical terminals.

Operations

Operating hotels internationally is not only different from operating nationally, but it can also be demanding for senior and local management. The one area that both levels of management might agree to be very different is that international operations are more time-consuming, mainly in respect of staff and employment issues. This can mean more time is devoted to managing the operation and less time is available to develop the business both locally and strategically.

Although somewhat dated, Table 15.1 shows comparisons between employee statistics in hotels in London and Hong Kong. Interestingly, in 1992 (at the time the survey was compiled), staff costs for a four-star hotel in London were double (HB) and treble (LB) those of Hong Kong. At the same time the Hong Kong hotels employed 59% (HB) and 86% (LB) more staff. However, the overall earnings per employee in London compared to Hong Kong were not very different as shown in Table 15.2. These figures show that the financial efficiency of using more staff in Hong Kong compared with London was not very different, but the management time to manage nearly double the number of staff in a Hong Kong (LB) hotel must be much greater.

While social costs in other European Union countries are generally higher, labour in these countries is also more unionized and personal taxation is higher, which can result in higher-paid, but less flexible staff. This can affect management's ability to maximize efficiency in an environment of complex employment

	London		Hong Kong	
	HB	**LB**	**HB**	**LB**
Employees per available room				
5-star hotel	1.36	1.22	1.43	1.27
4-star hotel	0.83	0.70	1.32	1.31
Sales per employee (US$)				
5-star hotel	88 058	91 551	51 505	46 155
4-star hotel	90 713	92 712	45 985	47 024
Cost per employee (US$)				
5-star hotel	25 059	27 477	16 612	12 253
4-star hotel	26 241	30 097	13 894	11 981

Note: HB = High profile corporate branded hotel (international); LB = Lower profile hotel operator (national).
Source: Howarth Consulting (1993).

Table 15.1
Comparative employee statistics in London and Hong Kong

4-star hotel	**HB**	**LB**
London	28.90	33.22
Hong Kong	30.21	25.44
Variance	+1.31	−7.78

Source: Howarth Consulting (1993).

Table 15.2
Percentage costs per employee to sales in London and Hong Kong

legislation and union dominance. Conversely, in the economically emerging countries, management time may not be as demanding in terms of legislation or dealing with unions. However, in these countries, the effort and time expended on training and politics is normally much greater. Some other aspects that are different operationally include:

- Minimal availability of support services

- High rates of inflation requiring regular salary reviews

- Two-tier room rate structures, government-fixed local rates and floating international rates

- Isolation from head office – little support for local sales and marketing

- Difference in investment criteria – conflict between prestige and rates of return

- International brand loyalty – high with international travellers, but national customers loyal to their own national brands

- Language skills

- Distance learning and training

- Work permit problems for skilled ex-patriot management staff.

In developing countries, local management often finds that, in addition to the above, the hotel's status usually means it is the epicentre of society in the community. The hotel general manager's role has a much higher social profile, with frequent exposure to national politicians. This means the time and attention paid to national politics is much greater, and in some cases, it is an everyday task. This can be even more demanding as, normally in these countries, politicians and/or governments may be part owners in the hotel property. Certainly, in such locations forward planning is essential, and hotel managers have to become familiar with importing supplies and goods direct. They have to be able to deal with such issues as import duties and letters of credit, as it can take up to three or four months to deal with large currency transfers. At the same time, regular business with airlines and tour operators for instance, tends to be negotiated locally, as are the conditions of contract. All these factors, including working in a different culture where living standards are much lower than the operational environment, place a high demand on managerial time. Obviously, the upside for managerial staff locally usually is the weather, status and lifestyle when the time is available to enjoy them. For senior management profitability and property value growth, especially, can be rewarding.

Maintenance

In most developed countries, the issue of maintenance is similar to that in the UK or USA, however, utility costs generally will be higher and this certainly will be the case in such areas as the West Indies and Africa. Electricity costs in the Caribbean, where every room is air-conditioned, for instance, can be 15% of total sales compared with 3–4% in the UK. Most hotels will have their own water desalination plant and sewage treatment units. In some ways, therefore, the hotel or resort property functions are similar to those of a small town in the UK. The big difference, of course, being that in the UK and other developed countries there is easy access to skilled tradespeople and spares. Replacing spares in less developed countries means importing direct or, sometimes even worse, through local agents. As in operations, it is imperative to plan well ahead. These issues should be considered at the development stage when equipment and systems that rely on imports can be minimized. For example, the logistics of importing 200 air-conditioning filters at the development stage may not have been a complex issue. However, for maintenance purposes, one or twenty replacements in practice can take four months to obtain. Developers should consider at the outset the maintenance strategy, stockholding, stock costs, as well as the storage and security of spares. Tasks that may be simple for a trained engineer in the UK can be more complex in a country where such engineers are not available. Multiply this one element by the hundreds or thousands of components needed in a fully serviced hotel, with limited skilled staff available, and maintenance can take on a different perspective. Equally, different climates and habitats provide some interesting maintenance and safety requirements. It is common procedure in West Africa to train security staff in the use of long poles to catch the occasional snake that may choose to sunbathe with guests by the poolside. Also, the prevalence of the disease Aids in many African countries casts the provision and maintenance of medical and first aid services in a different light. Security and guest relations staff must be sensitive to dealing with local cultural issues that can range from dealing with local population sensitivities to being photographed, to appeasing the local witch doctor. Similarly, hospitality staff in many Caribbean countries need to wear overcoats when using the freezer stores. On the other hand, in Sweden and Finland, keeping the service yard or access drive clear requires overcoats to deal with a different climate problem. Examples of the differences abound, most of which can be addressed with a little common sense, at least for those that enjoy a different challenge. Nevertheless, it is imperative that issues of health and safety, for guests and employees alike, together with regular and long-term maintenance issues, are considered at the outset.

Conclusion

This chapter has briefly outlined some of the issues that relate to international hospitality development. All the aspects of hospitality development covered in this book are applicable internationally; the chapter has therefore sought to highlight some of the issues that make international developments different. This is in no way intended to be comprehensive; rather the chapter seeks to set the subject in both historical and current contexts so that the reader can reflect on the cultural diversity inherent in the process. As the industry continuous to grow globally, more people involved in the sector will inevitably work in foreign places. It can be expected that there will be an emerging need for those developing hospitality services to give more consideration to local people, culture and custom in the future. As the world continues to become a smaller place, the hospitality industry's economic future will depend on preserving these resources, while at the same time providing the customer with the opportunity to enjoy and take pleasure in cultural diversity.

Review questions

1 Briefly describe the main cultural issues that affect international hospitality development.

2 What are the main factors that influence the planning and nature of hospitality concepts internationally? Briefly describe how these will affect major international brands in the next decade.

3 Write a critical comment on the impact of hospitality development and mass tourism in economically emerging countries.

Case Study

This case study describes some examples of the factors that can require consideration when planning development of hospitality properties in different parts of the world. Drawn from the experience of different individuals who have been involved with projects internationally, the author would particularly like to thank Anthony J. Horst, Robert Caston, Paal Borressen and Jesse Ransley for their contributions. There can be few more exotic foreign destinations than Bali. However, tourists visiting Kuta on the southern coast of Bali soon discover that, in order to see any aspect of Balinese culture, they need to join organized group tours to Ubuo in central Bali, where indigenous Balinese dancing, arts, crafts and fine dining can still be experienced. The impact of mass tourism on the island, dating from 1969, has had many long-term implications on the indigenous peoples and environment. The most conspicuous recent growth has been around Nusa Dua – traditional landholders have been displaced, land speculation is rampant, new coastal roads are planned and the signs of more construction are evident. If rapid growth continues, water may have to be piped in from Java. Around Nusa Dua, village wells dried up because the big hotels dug theirs much deeper, lowering the water table. The loss of

palm trees has detracted from the appearance of many areas. Coral reefs have been mined for building material, both ground down to make lime and cut as whole building blocks. The removal of coral destroys the marine environment, and the unprotected beaches can quickly disappear, as has happened at Candidsa. You can see whole stretches of coral reef turned into walls at the Bali Hyatt at Samur, the Bali Oberoi at Seminyak and Poppies Cottage at Kuta (Bali and Lombok, 1997). For those managing the operation of hotels in exotic locations, the impact of local culture and environment can also be imposing.

Alex Lesueur's (1998) book, *Running a Hotel on the Roof of the World*, illustrates an unusual management structure. Lesueur worked in Tibet at the Holiday Inn, Lhasa, for five years during the 1980s, and politics were integral to every working issue. He describes two strands of management, A and B, so that every department had a Holiday Inn appointed head and his 'shadow' from the Chinese authorities. The two groups had totally different agendas and methods (which were equally unlike those of the Tibetans working in the hotel). Alongside these internal complexities, there were also the added pressures of the larger political situation, intermittent civil unrest, the importance of being the first and only international operator allowed in by the Chinese, lack of food supplies, and the very high altitude (with its concomitant altitude sickness). The central heating was ruled by occupancy levels and, at one point, there were hundreds of rats decomposing in the ductwork. Some other interesting aspects to building properties internationally include:

1 The prevalence of rodents in certain locations is such that the use of PVC pipework and electrical conduit is not advisable as these are quickly eaten away.

2 In establishing the capital cost of construction in Chad, West Africa, it is advisable, owing to the local soil conditions, to allow for the deep piling of foundations, which can be up to 24 metres deep. In contrast, in Dubai every high-rise hotel almost certainly needs to provide its own helipad and be hurricane-proof.

3 Architects considering the external finish of their building design in climates where insects are prevalent should remember to avoid porous materials or textured surfaces, as these are attractive for insects to nest in or on. Similarly, iron or metal balustrading requires special non-corrosive treatment prior to painting if early oxidization and erosion is to be avoided.

4 While extreme low humidity is normally associated with some hot countries, it may come as a surprise that such conditions exist in winter conditions in Hanover, Germany. In this circumstance, a number of building elements require special attention, such as anti-static fibres woven into carpets, for example.

5 The use of concrete as a self-finishing material, common practice in many countries, can be problematic in areas where sandstorms occur, where the design of window frames also has to be suitable to prevent penetration of the sand.

6 Mildew, a bacterial growth, can be a problem in locations having regular high humidity, requiring all soft furnishing fabrics to be specially treated. The less natural the fabric material the greater the likelihood of a problem occurring.

7 The widespread use of glues in the current manufacturing methods of furniture means the designer has to consider the environmental conditions as glues perform differently in some climates.

These examples illustrate the issues that can be encountered when working in international locations. In an industry that is dominated by location and people, they are everyday problems. For those who believe there are no problems, only challenges, hospitality management can provide a most exhilarating career.

References

American Economics Group Inc. (1998) *The 1998 Worldwide Resort Timeshare Industry*. AEG.

Bali and Lombok (1997) 6th edn. Lonely Planet Publications.

Else, D. (1998) *Guide to Zanzibar*. Bradt Publications.

Horwath Consulting (1993) *The Case for Management Contracts*. Howarth Consulting.

Leseur, A. (1998) *Running a Hotel on the Roof of the World*. Summersdale.

Reader's Digest Universal Dictionary (1986) Lexical Databases, Houghton Mifflin, Boston.

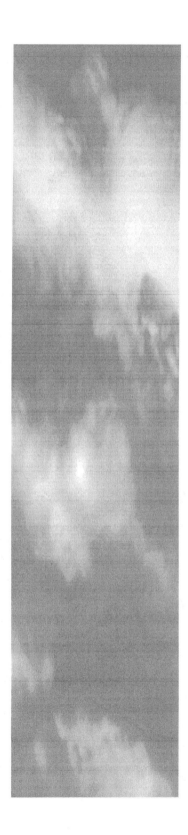

Conclusions

Josef Ransley and Hadyn Ingram

As with our 2000 edition, the preceding chapters have tried to show that hospitality development is a process, and it is in the interests of all concerned that they understand it as well as possible. It is not really necessary for operators to understand all the technicalities, although the acronyms and terms in the Glossary will help to communicate with, and to comprehend the words and documents of specialists. Rather, it is more important that all concerned understand the issues which might arise in planning and implementing a hospitality development.

The editors believe that hospitality development is characterized by the following:

- *Importance*. It is becoming ever more important to renew or refresh existing hospitality properties. For example managed public houses in the UK are regularly refurbished because there is a strong business case for linking a 'refreshed' pub with greater turnover and profits.

- *Complexity*. Since we wrote in 2000, the issues and pitfalls in development have become even more complex, especially as legislation and accountability proliferates. Complexity must be countered by understanding, as found in external research and suitable specialists who understand the area. The advice of such specialists may appear expensive, but may save the developer both cost and difficulty.

- *Management*. These chapters have shown that much can go wrong in a hospitality development, which can affect, for example, the quality of the final development, handover dates (and turnover) and the efficient operation of the completed work. All of these factors can be managed if the development team continually monitor the work and are aware of the potential pitfalls.

- *Communication*. There is a need to plan and articulate what is required (especially in the brief) and communicate this by means of plans, reports and specifications to others. Coordination in such complex and interconnected projects is vital to success.

Looking ahead

This section will review some issues on past developments in hospitality and comment on current development, in preparation for an assessment of future trends.

Past developments

As with other industries, the hospitality industry has evolved slowly over the centuries, affected by developments in transport technology, such as railways in the nineteenth century and motor cars in the twentieth century. For example, the availability of the motor vehicle for all has been the single most important factor in the emergence of motor hotels in the US lodging industry. Similarly, the growth in air transport has driven the internationalization of the hotel and tourist industry in the latter part of the twentieth century. However, the nineteenth and most of the twentieth centuries have been characterized by comparative stable market conditions, in which business decisions could be made with some certainty. There was largely stability of social conditions too, and low disposable income for many. Since the Second World War, however, technology has ensured that goods can be produced and supplied to market needs, and that the service sector has emerged as the primary activity in developed countries. Further, the pace of change and innovation in technology is affecting every walk of life.

New techniques of evaluating and managing assets developed in other industry sectors have been adopted by the hospitality industry. Airlines, for example, have led the way with technology to manage reservations and yield, and retailers have focused upon techniques to evaluate financial performance and space planning.

Current developments

The industry structure has changed from ownership in wholly autonomous units to the emergence of powerful groups of operators that can derive competitive advantage from economies of scale, bulk purchasing and marketing muscle. Such groups are increasingly becoming service providers and management operators rather than property owners. Similarly, senior management is devolving from operational managers to corporate managers as the focus continues to switch from hospitality to profits. The latter is being driven by greater institutional investment in the sector and the emergence of asset management and yield technology. Branding has become the current success story. Multi-unit hotel, restaurant and pub companies invariably arrange their units into categories and aim them at specific market segments. Examples include limited service (Holiday Inn Express and Travelodge), mid-service (Holiday Inn, Marriott and Accor), premier service brands (Intercontinental and RitzCarlton). These are being augmented by life-style products that focus on image and service levels (Malmaison and One Aldwych). Similarly, many properties deliver a specific product that is dependent upon their location, such as conference hotels at airport or motorway junctions, luxury hotels in capital cities.

There is a discernable blurring as branded hotel products emerge in the twenty-first century. For example, the UK-based Hotel du Vin Group has put food and beverage at the centre of their offering, while Malmaison aims for low cost and high rates. Hilton and Le Méridien are current powerful and well-known brands, but what exactly is their product and how does it differ from others? Perhaps the Express by Holiday Inn is the ideal hotel brand because it is distinguished by 'hard' differentiators of specification, with limited service provision.

Social trends – consumerism, increases in travel, discretionary spending and greater awareness – have given rise to a more discerning customer. Similarly, levels of income and leisure time continue to rise in developed countries enhancing demand in both developed and emerging markets. These factors, as well as improved levels of education and communication have influenced the nature of the service provider and customer alike. The customer has become more discerning and the service provider more sophisticated.

The future

The core message of this book is that greater professionalism and continued improvement in performance will be demanded of hospitality practitioners in the future. Operations may well still be the central activity of hospitality managers, but product and service offerings will need to be adapted more frequently if units are to retain or improve market share. As information becomes more widely available and technology breaks new boundaries, there will be greater choice for all. Consolidation within the industry, with the benefits for brand globalization and corporate profits, will continue to be driven by international groups and institutional investors. Similarly, the growing confidence of the discerning customer will create more opportunities for the niche operator. Increasing customer focus on image and entertainment together with increased pressure on land use and value, may see further evolution in the form of 'limited life-cycle building product' as well as more 'multi-use hospitality and entertainment properties'.

A 'limited life-cycle building product' could be defined as a building designed to provide a single function, presented in a given form and style for a specified time period. For example, if a limited service hospitality unit is expected to have a product life of twenty-five years, is there any benefit in designing the building fabric and services to last more than thirty years? If not, can the building be realized for a lower capital cost, thereby enhancing profitability? It could justifiably be argued that many buildings that are totally refurbished with increased building services such as air-conditioning, would be cheaper to realize by demolishing the existing building fabric and developing a new unit. Even if this process might mean a marginal increase in capital costs, the efficiency gains in operation and reduced running and maintenance costs would offset these costs. Equally, the ability to control the product image, content and style rather than adapt these to suit the existing building structure would be beneficial. While not advocating demolition of buildings of historical merit, consideration of building value in the context of site or land value and operational profitability rather than bricks and mortar, will likely influence future refurbishment or rebuilding.

Location and trading historically has been the main driver in hospitality properties' values. It can be argued that the land area and its location has an inherent value, whereas the building, if we consider it a 'product', has a value relative only to its financial performance. While one cannot easily predict the nature of the future change on this location or any other, one can be confident change will be of similar import over the next fifteen to twenty years. Consolidation and a greater synergy in service product provision by global hospitality and tour groups, from product sales, travel and accommodation provision and customer loyalty programmes, will generate change in the tourist sector and product. Change in this sector will be driven by environmental and sustainability issues, as well as demand generated by the change in age demographics. Many states and governments are realizing that stewardship of the planet and the environment must be more responsible and proactive, because it may denigrate irretrievably. The hospitality developer, too, must realize that they have a major part to play in this stewardship, if not for ethical reasons, then certainly for sound business reasons.

All these factors, and especially the ever-increasing level of information available to consumers and developers alike, can lead to confusion rather than clarity. This means more than ever that the operational manager and development team need to be aware of key issues and to work in a structured manner utilizing well-founded advice. We trust that this amended guide to the hospitality property development process will further assist those future practitioners involved in the ever challenging, exciting and rewarding process of creating social environments for work, rest and play and, above all, financial reward.

Case study 1:

Rosehill Enterprises

Arun Shaw scratched his head. 'How the heck', he thought, 'am I going to get this new hotel in Croatia built?' He remembered with a wry smile all the problems that he experienced with the Bannock Hotel, a 75-bedroom conversion in Scotland which was his pride and joy. He loved golf, and having the opportunity to develop a hotel in Scotland was a dream come true. He appointed a firm of architects in Edinburgh whom he later discovered had no experience of anything but residential development, and the builders, Arun's company, Rosehill Enterprises was still reeling from the budget overspend on the Bannock, and the problems they had experienced in removing all the asbestos from the nineteenth century building! In addition, trade back in the Rosehill Hotel was suffering too, thanks to the effects of terrorism and overseas wars. Even people in America were thinking carefully about spending money on golfing holidays, and this affected group profits. What to do?

His mind cast back to that day in 1969 when he had stepped off the boat in New York. He had seen films of the immigrants of the 1920s cheering as they sighted the Statue of Liberty, and had experienced the same feeling of elation. He was of Anglo-Indian background, one of the many entrepreneurial Asians who had been expelled from Uganda by Idi Amin. Like some of his fellow passengers, he was homeless, but, because of an American uncle, had managed to procure a work permit for the USA. Back in Uganda he had prospered in his father's clothes factories, but he had been expelled with little money and few prospects. Just after the explosion, he had visited his sole remaining relative, a maiden aunt who

lived in a small cottage in Devon, and she had given him money for the New York passage. Arun was grateful and realized that his future lay in his own hands.

That first night in the USA, he stayed in a YMCA hostel in Brooklyn, wandering the streets and marvelling at the skyscrapers which towered above him. He wandered the crowded streets of Manhattan, past apartment blocks, shops and hotels, resolving to return the next day to find work. In the morning, he strolled through the lobby of the downtown Surrey Hotel and asked the receptionist for work. He was directed to the back door, where a wary doorman directed him to the personnel office. He was lucky, the personnel office told him, because they had just fired the kitchen porter for being drunk on duty, and could he start straight away? He stammered a grateful 'yes', and was taken down to the basement area and the pot wash which was to be his work for the next three months. He hated the work, but it got him on his feet, with a small rented room in Yonkers and some new clothes. While cleaning the seemingly endless pile of dirty pots and pans, his mind was desperately trying to find a way out of this drudgery. One October morning, he happened to see a job advertised in the 'want ads' for a machinist in a clothes factory in the Bronx. He applied, and started a week later, in the Goldman factory. It did not take Si Goldman long to see that Arun was not a run of the mill machinist, but also knew how the complicated machines functioned. This was proved when Arun managed to fix the machine when the Puerto Rican engineer had failed. Goldman soon promoted Arun to supervisor and, over the next few years, came to respect Arun's business acumen and foresight. The truth was that Goldman Textiles was in bad shape and the owner, at 74, was tired and fed up.

In the fall of 1974, Goldman called Arun to the untidy office and offered him a partnership in the firm. Arun agreed gladly, because he could see that fashion rather than quality was the way forward for the garment industry. Events proved Arun correct because the fortunes of Goldman Textiles increased through the late 1970s; in 1980 Si Goldman died from a stroke. His wife Ruth had pre-deceased him and, as their marriage was childless, Si looked upon Arun as a son, leaving the business to him in his will. Arun's fortunes flourished and he bought himself a house in New Jersey, developing a taste for golf in his precious spare time. He met Janice, a girl from Utah in 1981 and married her in 1982.

Although Goldman Textiles was doing well, Arun recognized that cheap imports from the East would eventually scupper the garment trade, so he decided that he would branch out. What better to combine his pleasures with work and open a golfing hotel? After a short search he found the perfect location in Maryland, where the Rosehill Hotel and Golf Complex was for sale. Admittedly, the building needed lots of work, but the golf course was beautifully laid out and the Rosehill went from strength to strength in the prosperous 1980s.

Purchasing the Bannock Hotel in 1985 was a natural extension of Arun's business. He now had a core of US golf enthusiasts who would just love to visit Scotland and have the opportunity to shoot and fish as well. Arun had few contacts outside the USA but came across John Templemann on a reconnoitring visit to Edinburgh, appointing him general manager six months before the sale date. Templemann certainly had good credentials: trainee at the Savoy Hotel in London and experience in Switzerland, Canada and Singapore. Still, with all this hospitality operational experience, Templemann had never opened a new hotel and seemed out of his depth in handling the problems that beset the development.

Arun came across and personally supervised the handover, kicking himself that he had not had a more thorough survey done of the rambling Glenside property. From then, every day seemed to uncover new problems for Arun and John. They had set an opening date six months hence and were determined to make sure that the world knew about the Bannock Hotel. Twelve months later, the Bannock still had not opened and Arun was close to desperation. His builders, a local firm, were finding it difficult to keep up with the work, and to source the right trades in the remote location. Marble which Arun had ordered from Italy had been delayed and special tartan hangings for the reception walls needed to be returned to the manufacturers.

It was not until the spring of 1987 that the Bannock opened for business. By this time John Templemann and Arun Shaw had learned some harsh lessons about opening a new hotel in a foreign land. The Bannock had slowly turned the corner but Arun knew that he could not stand still – he had to be ahead of the game. When the wars in the Balkans subsided, peace made tourism possible again, and Arun became interested in development in Croatia. On a trip there in 1998 the beauty of the Dalmatian coast and its warm climate stunned him. He could see that property prices in France were rising fast and that Eastern Europe would follow next. He determined that he would look to open a luxury resort hotel which would attract those who were looking for a new holiday destination, with added value. Arun appointed Bloom Brothers of London to conduct some research for him and their conclusions were that:

- Croatia was an up-and-coming area, especially for trendsetting holidaymakers and the Dalmatian coast offered opportunities for water-related resorts.

- There was still the possibility of internal problems, but this should improve over time. The Croatian workforce was generally well educated and capable in service situations, and the government were open to internal tourism investment.

- There was a trend for holidaymakers to look for resorts which could offer a wide variety of activities: sports, leisure, cultural tourism and 'pampering'.

On the basis of this intelligence and conversations with John Templemann and Janice (now both directors of Rosehill Enterprises),

Arun decided that he would combine his love of golf in a resort which would also offer health and beauty treatments. He would open a 500-room four/five star hotel with a golf course and extensive treatments centre. This had not been done in Croatia before, so, based on his experiences with the Bannock Hotel, decided to look more deeply at the issues, and last week sent this e-mail:

From:	Arun Shaw [Arun@rosehillenterprises.com]
To:	John Templemann
Cc:	Janice
Subject:	Our dilemma

Dear John,

Janice has bought me a copy of *Developing Hospitality Properties and Facilities* and I am blown away at the complexity and interrelationship of all the issues. I like the model of hospitality development in the book and would like you to prepare me a strategic report which addresses the following questions:

- Is the project feasible? How to find out?
- What should be the key sequence of actions to research this opportunity and to implement it?
- What should the brief contain?
- Who should be included in the development team? How should they be sourced?
- What planning issues might arise?
- How should the construction be managed?
- How should the operational team prepare for opening?
- What international and cultural issues should be considered?
- How should the asset be managed?

Kind regards

Arun

Arun Shaw
Managing Director
Rosehill Enterprises

Case study 2:

Fortuna Inc.

Al Fortunatello's real estate empire had its beginnings in the 1980s when the juggernaut of Real Estate Investment Trusts (REITs) had started to roll. In the early 1980s, the boom in US office construction and favourable taxation legislation had enabled investing taxpayers to offset losses on property against tax. Booming profits provided Al with a war chest to acquire a range of properties in 22 US states, ranging from office developments, shopping malls, hotels and condominiums. As the US economy flourished in the 1990s, so Fortuna's profits continued to soar, reaching a peak of $267 million in 1998. This was a great source of satisfaction for Al, who hankered after expanding back to Europe, where his immigrant family had originated. One autumn day in 1999, he decided that he would send his trusted lieutenant and chief vice president, Karl Neilssen, to look at a possible acquisition in England: Verdant Holdings Ltd.

Verdant Holdings was developed by Frank and Tatiana Green, whose pub tenancy in the 1970s had led to their purchasing the White Swan Hotel in the Cotswolds in 1981. Expanding tourism enabled them to increase the size of the hotel to 46 rooms and a conference room. The Greens were a good operational team: Frank's organizational skills were useful in planning the development and dealing with specialists and suppliers, while Tatiana's dark Croatian good looks and strong character made her a hit with customers. Tatiana had maintained strong links with her family in Croatia and, after the troubles of the early 1990s, recognized that the region was ripe for development. Verdant invested in a run-down, 75-bedroom hotel on Croatia's Adriatic coast, and, by 1996, the hotel had been refurbished and was trading profitably.

Meanwhile in the UK, Frank Green was aware that the hotel market seemed to be changing around him. Hotel customers wanted less formality and insisted that bedrooms should be clean, comfortable and have en-suite bathrooms. For most hotel customers, clean and comfortable facilities seemed to be more important than service and this may have accounted for the dramatic rise in budget hotels. Frank determined that he would build a new hotel in Bristol and, in 1997, the Avon Valley Hotel was opened. The hotel was located closed to the M4 and M5 motorways and had 56 en-suite bedrooms and a small cafeteria that operated from 7 a.m. to 10 p.m.

From the opening ceremony, the Avon Valley was busy with leisure and business travellers, not least because it undercut the multi-unit budget chains by 10% and offered a more personal service to travellers. Frank and Tatiana Green took some time and trouble over the appointment of a General Manager for the Avon Valley Hotel, interviewing over 43 candidates for the post. At the final interview, the choice was between Andrew Billen from London and Carole McSweeney from Liverpool. Andrew's experience was with large-scale hotel operations in cities, while Carole exhibited the qualities of hardworking strong-mindedness that the Greens recognized in themselves. Carole threw herself into the task of creating the systems necessary for the operation of a busy hotel, but there were often differences of opinion with the Greens about how this should be done. In particular, Tatiana and Carole often clashed and Frank's diplomatic skills were required to ensure that these internal disagreements did not affect the smooth running of the hotel. Frank's practical disposition recognized that the hotel was doing well and that he ought to back off. Besides, his mind was fully occupied with the fourth and most ambitious hotel in Verdant Holdings' portfolio: the Heartlands Hotel and Conference Centre.

From the moment he saw the site, with outline planning consent for a 90-bedroom hotel, Frank Green felt in his bones that he was on to a winner. The location, close to the M1 motorway and Luton Airport, yet in pretty countryside with a lake, was perfect – both convenient and attractive. Nearby, the local town had a ready supply of labour with a College of Further Education that offered courses in hospitality and catering. Although Verdant Holdings were doing well, the Croatia hotel was still only marginally profitable and there were signs of renewed political instability in the former Yugoslavia. The White Swan was turning in consistent, although limited, profits, and the Avon Valley was successful despite high development costs. The high interest rates of the time persuaded Frank and Tatiana to finance the new project from their own resources. Their supportive bank manager was prepared to re-mortgage all three properties to release £750 000 for the project budget, with other funds coming from profits and loans secured against the site.

Frank Green knew that his organizational skills could be put to good use in making the Heartlands Hotel a reality and minimizing the expense of specialists whose exorbitant fees could drag down the project. His experience of developing the other properties would stand him in good stead and his operation background was more important than a narrow specialism. Tom Harris of Harris Associates had designed all Verdant's properties since White Swan days and, although not hotel specialists, they had been established for many years. Thinking that this project would provide an opportunity to become nationally recognized, Tom had readily agreed to working for a minimal fee.

Frank and Tatiana Green had big ideas for the Heartlands; there would be 150 rooms of four-star standard and conference and banqueting facilities for up to 750 people. Yet there was a tension between their vision of four-star luxury and the budget that limited their ambitions.

When it came to briefing Tom Harris, the three spent considerable time discussing their individual vision. While Frank was conscious of the financial limitations at the outset, Tatiana and Tom concluded that the building design should set new standards in hotel design. Tom arranged to survey the site. Frank, having rejected the idea of paying a specialist consultancy to prepare a feasibility study for the project, contacted Andrew Billin and persuaded him to assist in the preparation of their own study, with a long-term view to Andrew being employed as the future General Manager of the hotel.

From the outset, Andrew was in conflict with Tom Harris and Tatiana. Andrew, having prepared a detailed brief for the accommodation schedule of the hotel based on his research of the local market and preliminary financial forecast, was stipulating that the

building should be a low rise development, economically and efficiently planned with extensive parking. Tom meanwhile had developed his initial design scheme featuring a 6-storey, square building with a central feature atrium. While Andrew argued knowledgeably that such a design would be operationally inefficient, his view that such a modern building would be inappropriate for the setting were quickly quashed by Tatiana. Similarly his concerns about building costs were set aside by the quantity surveyor friend of Tom employed to advise on the project. Having worked together as a team on the Bristol hotel, Tom and the quantity surveyor assured Frank that as Bristol had only cost £40 000 per room to develop, their scheme for Heartlands could be realized for slightly more than £6 million. Frank, conscious that the local planners might resist such a building design was also aware that Andrew's research highlighted the fact there was little demand for weekend accommodation in the area. He therefore felt the scheme using less build area would allow for some further leisure development on site later to attract such custom. Although Andrew still argued that his brief reflected the criteria identified in the feasibility study, the others decided Tom's concept was much more exciting and allowed for further development opportunities on the site as a whole.

Returning from a visit to Croatia three weeks later, Frank announced that the project would have to be completed in 14 months time, 6 months earlier than originally planned. To his surprise, although Tom and his quantity surveyor voiced some concerns the main objections came from Andrew, who loudly complained that the latest plans would be operationally impossible to manage, with, for example, their being no direct access from the kitchen to the main conference and banqueting room among a whole list of deficiencies he had drawn up. Equally, he had found no one able to explain what monies had been allocated in the budget for FF&E. Tatiana cut short any discussion on the latter point by saying she was dealing with the interior design direct with a decorator friend. Equally importantly she saw that the feature atrium in the plan could not be set aside to provide for direct kitchen service to the conference room, especially as she felt that banqueting and wedding receptions were not the right profile of custom for what would be a chic, design hotel. Anxious to progress matters, Frank agreed that the planning application had to be submitted immediately and that the time to worry about detail aspects was later.

A week later Frank and Tom decided to speed things up, and that, rather than seek competitive tenders for the construction, they would negotiate a contract with a mutual friend who was the director of a family building contractor firm, one of the largest regional house-builders in the region. Furthermore, although the final cost of the hotel was critical to ensure Frank would be able to finance the loan funding, he was persuaded by the builder and Tom that to allow Tom enough time to complete his detailed design drawings, a management form of contract should be used. This way they could proceed with the building as the detail design was still being developed.

The next two months were not the happiest for Frank. While Tatiana was either travelling to the Balkans to speak with potential suppliers or preoccupied with sorting out colour schemes for the hotel interiors, her absence from the White Swan was impacting on its profitability. The tourist market in Croatia had collapsed as the news coverage of the unstable Yugoslavian situation increased. At the same time the planning application for the Heartlands scheme was meeting opposition from the planning officers and, worst of all, having rushed into agreeing a contract with the builder, virtually every day seemed to bring more bad news about the overall costs and so far the works were no further advanced than site clearance.

Nevertheless, Frank, having focused on aggressively lobbying the local councillors and persuading them of the benefits for local employment and the desirability of having a prestigious grand hotel in the locality, was relieved when the plans were approved albeit against the planning officers' recommendation. Relieved on hearing the news, Frank rushed off to meet his bankers, without waiting for the final consent papers, to negotiate additional funding as the latest cost plan now indicated the likely final cost of the hotel would be £7.2 million. While his bank was reluctant to provide a larger loan, they agreed in principle to increase the facility if an independent review by specialist consultants substantiated Frank's own financial forecasts for the project. Pleased that his discussions with the bankers had not touched on Verdant's current trading figures, Frank was not at all happy to learn about the details of the planning conditions attached to the consent. First, the public road would have to be altered to provide an access slipway to the entrance of the site. Second, any further development would be prohibited, the total square metreage of the building being defined as the maximum allowable. The other extensive list of conditions, while not so onerous, still materially limited any deviation from the approved plans, especially the height of the building, and required further detailed approval of, for example, external finishes.

At the same time Tom and the builder tabled some further bad news. The nearest gas supply was five mile distant from the site and required access through the neighbouring land. The requirements under the Building Regulations Act 1991 and the Fire Precaution Act highlighted by the local inspector meant that the design of the atrium would require a series of design variations due to fire precautions, including sealed guestroom windows facing onto the atrium and smoke extraction at roof level, among a number of points. What was equally worrying for Frank was that the builder, Tom, Tatiana and the QS were now all at loggerheads with each other. Each was blaming the other for their lack of foresight, experience or failure to communicate what they were doing. Tom felt that his modern building design was being ruined by Tatiana's latest desire to achieve a Mediterranean look in the interiors. The builder was complaining he was not receiving drawings and information in time to plan and price his work. While the QS blamed everyone for the cost increases and the fact that his original budget had been based on Andrew's brief and not the building now being constructed. The latter statement causing everyone to halt their arguments, as Andrew had withdrawn from the project a few weeks earlier following a heated argument with Tom and the QS about the way the project was being managed in terms of design and cost. Frank, in turn, was unhappy that the builder was using traditional methods of construction that did not focus on a fast track construction programme, while Tatiana seemed to be totally oblivious to costs in any way, having exasperated him by commissioning a water sculpture artist to create a hanging water feature for the atrium at a planned cost of £280 000, which would entail strengthening the roof structure that had only recently been completed on site.

A few days before his next meeting with the bankers to discuss the results of their independent consultant's appraisal, Frank started to consider the possibility of another party becoming involved with the Heartlands Hotel project. Although such thoughts were not really attractive to him, the latest developments with the project seemed to leave him with little choice. First he was not sure whether the banks would extend their funding to £7.2 million, but, even worse, the owner of the adjacent land was holding him to ransom over access to his land for the laying of the gas supply to the hotel, plus the cost of altering the main road access was proving exorbitant which, together with the fire prevention requirements and the insistence of the planners to have the building clad with granite instead of aluminium panels, meant the projected out-turn cost was now estimated at £8.4 million. Equally, bad weather had meant the building work was nearly 2 months behind schedule, the structure still not being watertight and the site a quagmire of mud.

The following meeting with the bankers could not have been worse, as the feasibility appraisal identified a projected, maximum, room rate of £75 and an occupancy level of 68% to be achieved in year 3 of trading. The latter was projected as achievable on the basis of good weekend leisure occupancy, underpinned by taking advantage of a high demand in the area for a good hotel suitable for wedding receptions and banqueting business. Importantly, the appraisal had identified that as Luton Airport was predominantly used by budget airlines and tour operators, the related hotel business would likely be low value airline crew accommodation and short notice overnight accommodation. While the report stated that an acceptable level of conference and corporate business could be developed in the long term, this would only be achievable if the hotel had a strong brand profile, low staffing and operational costs. The bankers were therefore insisting that Frank consider a franchise agreement with one of the major industry brand names. This was still in the context of the project cost not exceeding £7.5 million, let alone the current £8.2 million that Frank had felt it imprudent to declare at the meeting.

It was a contrite Frank that phoned Andrew to ask for help in gaining some introductions to the major hotel groups that offered franchise agreements. Andrew, now a senior executive with a national hotel chain, quickly assessed that Frank's problem might be greater than he was prepared to admit to himself. So he suggested an industry colleague in the USA might also be of interest to Frank if he was prepared to forego sole ownership of the project. Meanwhile he provided details of Vacations International Hotels, a major international franchise hotel company.

Following Andrew's introduction, a major international group with a range of famous brand products sent two of their development executives to review the Heartlands project. Frank and his team were somewhat reassured that their primary interest was focused on life safety issues, means of escape and whether room sizes were compatible with their minimum requirements. Tatiana was disappointed that such little interest was expressed in her grand designs and colour schemes and miffed that it was suggested the ten different guestroom schemes she had developed should be reduced to two. Nor were she or Tom too enthusiastic about the standard external signage they identified would have to be accommodated. Having reviewed Frank's financial forecasts and requested more detailed breakdown of FF&E costs, and suggesting Frank might give some thought to air-conditioning the guestrooms, the two departed.

Verdant Holdings' recent performance, however, was of immediate concern, not only to Frank but also to Tatiana. Not only had the worsening situation in Croatia meant the hotel there was running at a serious loss, but the management of the White Swan Hotel, that had been placed under Carole's control to allow Frank and Tatiana more time to devote to the Heartlands project, had also resulted in a dramatic decline in profits. Frank was quick to identify that this was due to Carole applying the same style and methods used in the Bristol hotel at the White Swan. Yet Carole was adamant that her action to reduce staffing and costs in line with Bristol was not the cause of loss of trade, but sensible in hindsight to reduce costs in line with the reducing market demand. What Carole had failed to realize was that by cutting the menu at the White Swan to a few basic dishes and cancelling all marketing promotions, she had changed an individual quality restaurant into a hotel breakfast room.

After much argument, Frank managed to persuade Tatiana that she would have to devote most of her time to improving the performance of the White Swan, while he took complete control of the Heartlands project. While Tatiana was not happy about that situation, a disgruntled Carole handed in her notice and this left little option but for Tatiana to concentrate on managing the White Swan and Avon Valley Hotels.

The response from Vacation International Hotels was not helpful, their view was that the hotel as planned would not attract any leisure business and could not capitalize on the weekend wedding business. These issues and their view of the running and maintenance costs indicated insufficient gross operating profit (GOP) and therefore insufficient cashflow and income to service long-term loans. A list of items that would have to be addressed to achieve their minimum requirements was attached.

Very conscious of the re-mortgaging terms applied to their existing operating properties, Frank determined to use his authority to cut costs on the Heartlands project. Unfortunately, during the same period the family ownership of the Heartlands contractor was sold to a national contracting company.

While site meetings had been robust but cordial previously, it soon became apparent to Frank that though the meetings were now even more cordial, the paperwork was much more extensive and onerous. Equally, no matter how much he focused on cutting costs, the more changes he introduced to reduce the work content, the less savings he seemed to achieve and the more extended the programme seemed to become. Even worse, it became obvious that Tom's ability to administrate the contract was limited, and the lack of definition resulting from rushing into a building contract before the design had been fully developed, was causing constant disputes as to what was included in the contract or not. While the greatest arguments in this regard related to FF&E, Frank's biggest problem was that he was now told that the guestrooms facing onto the Atrium did not comply with the regulations, the fact that the windows could not be opened meant the rooms now had inadequate ventilation. Equally, the new contractors' team, experienced in hotel construction, were quick to point out that the atrium design did not provide for the windows to be cleaned in accordance with the Health & Safety requirements.

It was a very depressed Frank who accepted an international call from an Al Fortunatello, calling at the suggestion of Andrew Billin. Al said he had formed the impression from a recent discussion with Andrew that Frank might be interested in divesting some of his ownership. Suggesting that he might be interested, Al confirmed his VP, Karl Neilssen, would visit to discuss matters.

Anticipating a cordial and general discussion, Frank was taken aback by the singular, focused attitude of Karl Neilssen in their first meeting. After the briefest exchange of formalities, Karl tabled a list of information he would require as well as a sequential series of individual meetings with Tom, the QS and the contractual team. While polite, it was obvious that Karl had no intention of discussing any general matters until he was fully aware of Verdant Holdings' latest performance figures, management structure and the financial status of the Heartlands project.

To: Al Fortunatello CEO Fortuna (Al@fortuna.com)

From: Karl Neilssen VP European Development (Knelson@fortuna.com)

Subject: Initial review Verdant Holdings

a) Bristol Hotel – excellent financial prospect

b) White Swan – fully managed – good prospect, requires repositioning

c) Croatia – fully managed tourist property – high risk

d) Heartlands Development – problematic – high risk

Possible deal, low entry cost (a) and (b), (c) single property in unstable political area, no return on optimum trading when accounting for management time. (d) sound commercial opportunity made unviable by emotive decision process, detailed report to follow.

VH in financial difficulty sale of (a) & (b) potentially offers way out for F&T to retain (c) & (d) in short term. Will seek confidential valuations on (a) and (b) and contact you Thursday to discuss.

Karl

Case study review

This fictional case study has been written to highlight some of the issues addressed in the various chapters of this book. The following checklist used by Karl Neilssen, VP European Development, Fortuna Inc., in preparing his report on Verdant Holdings is intended to be utilized by the reader as a basis for writing a more detailed report on behalf of Karl.

1 *Introduction*: Background to the report and the reason it has been commissioned.

2 *Concept*: Comment on the design process and choice of target markets; development strategy adopted, locational decision-making; use of asset management principles in maximizing the asset, management style

3 *Planning*: Comment on feasibility approaches taken; capital investment appraisal approaches, comparative performance of each property; the impact of legal issues on the properties

4 *Building*: Contractors and site operations; issues of building costs; construction problems

5 *Operations*: Operational relationships, design and operational efficiency; accommodation: design of bedrooms; food and beverage offerings

6 *Maintenance issues of operating in two countries*: Maintenance strategy

7 *Conclusion*: Summary of the main points from the above analysis

8 *Recommendations*: Suggested action plans on purchase of properties and subsequent operational strategy for increased performance. Any further information needed.

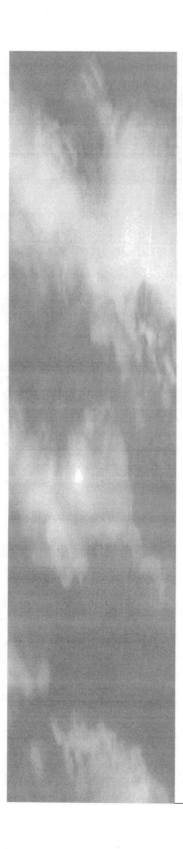

Glossary of terms, acronyms and abbreviations

ADRR Average daily room rate.

Architect The architect establishes the overall design and is often responsible for the detailed design of the fabric of a hotel. Architects are concerned with both the functional and aesthetic issues of building design. Typically, architects are appointed as lead consultants and will contribute to the project brief.

Area per room A useful guide to ensure the efficient use of space within the hotel. This is defined as the gross floor area of the whole building divided by the number of bedrooms.

ARR Accounting rate of return. The percentage rate of return earned by a capital investment project.

Asset Can represent a building or item of mechanical or electrical plant.

Asset management The process by which a property with money value is effectively controlled and managed as a business.

BoH Back of house.

BoQ Bill of quantities. A pricing document prepared by a quantity surveyor, which may include a detailed description of the type and quantity of the work involved.

Brands Brands are products, services or concepts that can be distinguished from other products, services or concepts in a way that it can be easily communicated and marketed. A 'brand name' is the distinctive name used to market the offer.

Brown field site Development land or site area that is contaminated or requires remedial works before new development or building can occur.

Brown goods   Describes household items of furniture such as television sets, chairs and tables.

Budget cost   The predicted cost as opposed to the actual cost.

Buildability   Judgement based on experience and practice as to the practicability of a construction method or form.

Building file   A requirement under the UK's Construction (Design Management) Regulations (1994) to keep a complete record of materials used in construction, all the construction drawings with maintenance procedures detailed and even how the building can be safely demolished at the end of its life.

CAGR   Compound average growth rate.

Casegoods   A term used widely in the industry for bedroom furniture.

CMBS   Commercial mortgage backed securities: bonds backed by mortgages on commercial property.

Commissioning   Establishing a building as a working operation.

Concept development   The process of identifying, defining and collecting ideas to create an image for a new business or product.

Condition survey   Inspection and report describing the current state of a building or item of plant.

Construction manager   The construction manager is a fee earning professional who is employed to programme and coordinate the construction works undertaken. The construction manager selects, supervises and manages the work of specialist trade contractors who are employed to undertake the work.

Cost of capital   The rate of return required by investors in the business.

DCR   Debt-coverage ratio.

Deal sheet   Summary of the major terms of the proposed loan.

Debentures   Fixed interest long-term loans.

Depreciation   The proportion of the cost of a fixed asset which is to be charged to the profit of the business.

Discount factor   The percentage rate of return which represents the opportunity cost of using the funds in different ways.

Discounted cash flow   The future monetary value of net cash flows expressed in present value terms.

Double loaded corridors   A corridor providing access to rooms on two sides.

Due diligence   A systematic process in which concerted attempts are made to unearth every fact that is relevant to the situation, and that might affect the decision to continue with the venture.

EBITDA   Earnings before interest, taxes, depreciation and amortization. Can be used to analyse the profitability between companies and industries, because it eliminates the effects of financing and accounting decisions.

EMV Expected monetary value. A weighted average of the values of the possible outcomes of some action, the weights being the respective possibilities.

Facilities management A contract to look after a property, which may cover not just building and plant maintenance and renewal, but also the provision of services such as security, laundry or computer facilities.

Feasibility study A written document prepared in the planning stage of a new development that represents research to justify the costs and benefits of undertaking the project.

FF&E Furniture, fittings and equipment. The components of a hotel bedroom which are 'loose', or not structural in origin.

Footprint A statement of the gross area of the building which covers the site at ground floor level, regardless of height or overhangs.

Franchise Under a franchise agreement the investor retains ownership of the asset and almost full control of the operating business, subject to meeting certain basic operating criteria and product standards established by the franchisor. In return the franchisee benefits from being able to use the company's brand name, reservation system and other forms of support (such as bulk purchasing agreements, employee training and development and financing advisory services).

FRI Fully repairing and insuring. A term applied to leasehold agreement in which the lessee or tenant has full responsibility to keep in good repair both the inside and outside of the leased building.

GAP General accounting principles: used in the USA.

GDP Gross domestic product.

GDS Global distribution system.

GOP Gross operating profit.

GOPPAR Gross operating profit per available room.

Green field site A parcel of land designated for the first time for new development.

Hold point A point beyond which work shall not proceed without the written authorization of a designated individual or organization.

Hurdle rate Target return on capital proposed for capital investment projects that exceeds the cost of capital.

HVAC Heating, ventilation and air-conditioning.

Interior designer The interior designer is responsible for the design of the finishes and furniture, fittings and equipment (q.v.) elements of a hotel. The interior designer may, if appointed at an early stage, be involved in the space planning of a hotel, but is often appointed at a later date.

IRI Internal repairing and insuring. A leasehold agreement in which the tenant agrees to undertake internal repairs.

IRR Internal rate of return. A method of assessment of capital projects in which future cash flows are discounted to equal the cost of the project. The rate of interest which is effective in achieving this is the internal rate of return. Where there are several projects being contemplated, the one showing the highest internal rate of return is usually chosen.

JCT Joint Contracts Tribunal. An independent body representing all parties and which produces and published standard forms of contract for use in the UK construction industry.

Joint venture An agreement by two parties with different expertise to jointly invest and/or manage a development or facility.

KPI Key performance indicator.

Lead time The time taken in planning or implementing an event until it actually occurs.

Lease contract A form of legal agreement to lease an asset that is owned by one party who receives rent from another party, the tenant. The tenant operates the business for a period of time in the expectation that the profits from the business will exceed the rent paid. The lease is normally long term (typically 15 to 20 years plus tenants' options to extend) with the property owner receiving a fixed rent.

LIBOR The London Interbank offer rate.

Life cycle The length of time a whole building or individual part may last, including maintenance required.

Life cycle costing A group of economic appraisal techniques which assess the sum of all relevant capital, operating and maintenance costs and incomes of an asset. All costs and incomes are brought together in a comparable form, allowing for the fact the cash flows occur at different times during an asset's life cycle.

LTV Loan-to-value ratio.

Maintenance Replacement or overhaul of a building component, for example windows or items of plant such as replacing the heating boiler to ensure that an agreed standard of service is economically achieved.

Management contract An agreement in which a hospitality management company not only offers a licence for the use of its brand name and reservation system but also takes full responsibility for the day-to-day management of the hotel as agent for the owner of the asset.

Massing The aggregation or volume of the components of the building(s), and their relationships to each other.

M&E Mechanical and electrical. Usually refers to building services.

Mechanical feasibility Mechanical studies are those which a client commissions in a feasibility study because it is required by a third party, for example in support of the application for funds, and this is the most common circumstance in which a mechanical study is prepared. Bankers, certainly, are less willing to lend on projects unless such appraisals have been well organized and have been carried out by independent professional organizations.

Mezzanine loan An additional loan which increases total debt financing from (say) 60 per cent of value to 80 per cent of value.

Negative feasibility study One which recommends that a project is not pursued.

NOI Net operating income

NPV Net present value. The current cash value of future discounted net cash flows arising from a project.

Opportunity cost An term in economics that means that the next best alternative that has been foregone. This may represent the time taken or money lost from not choosing a particular option.

OS&E Operating supplies and equipment.

Outturn cost The agreed final construction cost of a development project.

Payback method A method for discriminating between projects based on how quickly the original cash investment is repaid.

Planned preventative A phased schedule of regular property and equipment maintenance and repairs over time.

Principal contractor The appointment of a principal contractor is a statutory requirement under the Construction (Design & Management) Regulations 1994. The principal contractor must be involved in the management of the construction work, must be competent and able to allocate adequate resources to the task.

Pro-active feasibility One where the client who commissions it requires information to be provided in addition to projections of the return on investment.

Procurement Method of obtaining by care and effort the most suitable process of competitively priced element for construction or purchase.

Product building Where the building form is an integral part of a lifestyle product, such as a hotel.

QS Quantity Surveyor.

Rack stuffer Promotional material which fills hotel brochure shelves or racks.

REIT Real Estate Investment Trust. Started in the USA, a REIT is an investment vehicle that takes the form of real estate mutual fund permitting small investors to participate in large, professionally managed real estate projects.

RevPar Revenue per available room.

RFP Request for proposal, which seeks external support for services such as public relations or marketing.

Risk allowance A contingency sum that is set aside to fund the cost of construction variations.

Risk management A process used by project teams to reduce the impact of risks on the outcomes of a project, through the formal identification, appraisal and management of potential risk events throughout the life of the project.

Schedule of condition Details the state of the property at the start of a lease, as a standard by which the tenant must hand back the property at the end of lease period.

Sensitivity analysis An accounting technique that measures the relationship of cost and volume to profits. If small changes in factors such as volume, selling price, variable and fixed costs cause a large change in profit, it can be said that profit is sensitive to that factor, and that it is critical to the business.

Snag A building industry term which means incomplete work, or complete work not in accordance with the specification, identified prior to or at 'practical completion' or during the, 'defects liability period' or at 'making good defects' inspection.

Snagging list The joint identification of a list of faults or problems that need to be rectified before the final payment is made to the contractor(s).

Soffit The undersurface of an arch, balcony or ceiling.

Sous-vide A food production method in which cooked food is vacuum-packed in central production kitchens so that it can be easily reconstituted at the point of sale by comparatively less skilled staff.

Straight-line method This method charges an equal amount of depreciation to each accounting period that benefits from the use of the fixed asset.

Turn key projects A development project in which the sole contractor is responsible for construction, fitting out and commissioning the building, so that all the client has to do is turn the key and begin trading.

TWC Temporary works coordinator. One who is appointed on a temporary basis to supervise on-site construction works.

VM Value management. A process used by project teams to define the objectives of a project and to deliver these economically and quickly.

WACC Weighted average cost of capital. Represents the combined cost of the sources of finance ulilized by the business.

WTTC World Travel and Tourism Council.

Yield management A technique that aims to maximize revenue over a cycle of peaks and troughs by adjusting prices to suit market demand.

Zone split The physical division of a property to be refurbished between the parts that are open for business, and those that are to be closed for building work.

Index

Note: references in *italics* feature in the glossary of terms
Page numbers in **bold** denote a headed section